Betraying Teachers, Betraying Students

Betraying Teachers, Betraying Students

Higher Education's Malpractice in Teacher Preparation

Second Edition

Rich Waters

ROWMAN & LITTLEFIELD
Lanham • Boulder • New York • London

Published by Rowman & Littlefield
An imprint of The Rowman & Littlefield Publishing Group, Inc.
4501 Forbes Boulevard, Suite 200, Lanham, Maryland 20706
www.rowman.com

86-90 Paul Street, London EC2A 4NE, United Kingdom

Copyright © 2022 by Rich Waters

All rights reserved. No part of this book may be reproduced in any form or by any electronic or mechanical means, including information storage and retrieval systems, without written permission from the publisher, except by a reviewer who may quote passages in a review.

British Library Cataloguing in Publication Information Available

Library of Congress Cataloging-in-Publication Data

Names: Waters, Rich, author.
Title: Betraying teachers, betraying students : higher education's malpractice in teacher preparation / Rich Waters.
Other titles: Teachers at their best
Description: Second edition. | Lanham : Rowman & Littlefield, [2022] | Revised edition of: Teachers at their best, c2018. | Includes bibliographical references. | Summary: "The point of this book is to re-conceive schools as the primary places of teacher learning because, for better or worse, research tells us that is where teachers actually learn to teach"—Provided by publisher.
Identifiers: LCCN 2022020741 (print) | LCCN 2022020742 (ebook) | ISBN 9781475868500 (cloth) | ISBN 9781475868517 (paperback) | ISBN 9781475868524 (epub)
Subjects: LCSH: Teachers—Training of. | Teachers—In-service training. | Teachers—Professional relationships. | Professional learning communities. | Educational change.
Classification: LCC LB1707 .W38 2022 (print) | LCC LB1707 (ebook) | DDC 370.71/1—dc23
LC record available at https://lccn.loc.gov/2022020741
LC ebook record available at https://lccn.loc.gov/2022020742

Contents

Preface	vii
Introduction	xv
PART I: CONFRONTING THE FAILURE OF HIGHER EDUCATION IN TEACHER PREPARATION	**1**
1 Not Higher Education, a New School Model	7
2 The Emergence of Teacher as Learner-Collaborator-Leader	23
3 Toward an Intentionally Developmental School	41
4 School Culture, Human Development, Teacher Development	71
5 The Primacy of Culture and the Promise of Professional Learning Communities	91
PART II: THE PROMISE OF PROFESSIONAL DEVELOPMENT SCHOOLS	**109**
6 Professional Development Schools Interrupted	111
7 Professional Development Schools Foreshadow a New School Model	121
8 The Path to a New School Model: Teacher Development through School Development	131
9 Tina's Story: Aspiring Teachers Shop for Professional Learning at Local Schools	141

PART III: TINA BETRAYED: HIGHER EDUCATION'S REFUSAL TO CHANGE — **155**

10 Understanding Higher Education's Betrayal as Revealed in Low Student Achievement — 157

11 Understanding the Betrayal as Revealed in Higher Education's Fraud — 167

12 Understanding the Betrayal in Higher Education's Willful Blindness — 173

13 Understanding Higher Education's Betrayal in Poor Teacher Development — 179

14 The Future Darkens for Tina: Higher Education's Plan for the Future — 187

References — 193

Who Is Rich Waters? — 211

Preface

Consider this: Since the publication of *Nation at Risk* in 1983, educators in the United States have initiated a long line of reforms in an attempt to improve student achievement in our schools. These reforms have, in particular, targeted teachers in hopes of reforming what was broadly believed to be the cause of poor student achievement, ineffective teaching.

Efforts to raise the quality of teaching have included raising admissions standards to schools of education, making coursework more demanding during teacher preparation, providing novice teachers more clinical practice, heightening teacher licensing requirements, making teacher evaluation more frequent and more stringent, providing more teacher professional development, instituting more teacher-specific accountability testing of students, firing weak teachers, incentivizing teachers who successfully raise test scores, increasing the number of subjects tested, and extending the probationary period before tenor is granted.

Many probably think it all sounds like a reasonable effort. Most people do. But in these efforts the first layer of teacher betrayal may be seen. The effects of all of these efforts have been researched, and not one of these initiatives correlates with improved student learning. That is, when these changes were instituted, they didn't change student learning outcomes. The dismal learning outcomes for America's students will be reviewed shortly, but here's the kicker. Those who claim to prepare our nation's teachers have known for years about the ineffectiveness these efforts. They have known for a long time that higher education teacher preparation, with all of its "improvements," has had no correlation with improved student learning. That is part of the reason why the nation's report card has not indicated meaningful improvement in student achievement over the last forty to fifty years.

In spite of knowing this, teacher education in the United States has not changed in any substantial way, not since Sputnik, not since *A Nation at Risk*, not since *No Child Left Behind*, not since *Race to the Top*, not since the *Common Core*, not since the *Every Student Succeeds Act*, not ever. And again, that's the point. Higher education is to blame. The source of ineffective teaching in our nation is poor teacher preparation by higher education. And year after year, institutions of teacher preparation continue to do what they have done before, and they continue to get the same results. And the reader knows what Einstein said about such behavior.

Now consider this: Research has shown that schools structured around professional learning communities consistently have better student learning outcomes than schools without them. This book will detail how higher education teacher preparation has ignored the learning community research in favor of preserving its obsolete but financially lucrative on-campus classroom approach to teacher education. It is an approach that leaves the vast majority of our public schools to function in antiquated ways where teachers work in isolation and are deprived of a full career of personal and professional development as an outcome of working together.

The point of this book is to act as a whistleblower. Teacher education in this nation is being purposely misguided because that misguidance suits the business model of most schools of education and their affiliated colleges or universities. But, as will be detailed, the business model of most schools of education does not suit the welfare of our teachers and prospective teachers, and it certainly does not suit the welfare of our nation's kids.

The purpose of this book, then, is to change the conversation about teacher induction, preparation, and development and how we create effective teachers. Our national discussion about how to create effective teachers needs to move away from how higher education can do a better job preparing our teachers and move toward how our local schools can do a better job inducting, preparing, and developing our teachers over a full career.

There are two interconnected and irrefutable reasons for this. First, school culture supersedes all rational strategies for teacher development, and, second, teachers learn to teach in the schools where they work, not in higher education classrooms or any of the alternative routes which the ineffectiveness of higher education teacher preparation has caused to emerge.

With the affirmation of these postulates, this book clarifies that teachers are at their best when they are working together in collaborative cultures where teacher thinking and decision-making lead schools in continuous improvement and change. Elaborating on the importance of these best conditions for optimal teacher development, this book will insist that *it is the entirety of a school culture that produces effective teachers, and schools with authentic learning communities produce the cultures that produce effective teachers.*

This book develops a logic derived of research. That logic begins with the aforementioned premise that teachers learn to teach in the schools where they work, not in higher education teacher preparation programs or by way of other rational, professional development efforts to teach teachers how to teach. The logic is extended by a large and growing body of research on the powerful influence of organizational culture on the attitudes, beliefs, and the performance of the members of a given culture. In effect, it is by virtue of school culture that teachers learn how to teach. As one teacher candidate has put it, "In college you learn some nice theories about how to teach. Then, when you get a job, you learn what teachers really do."

Research shows over and over again that it is by way of this powerful, on-the-job force called *culture* that teachers come to develop and/or limit the various tools, outlooks, habits of mind and practice that make up the way an individual teacher or an entire faculty perform what we call teaching. One of the primary themes of this book is that this failure to employ the power of culture in teacher development has been grossly overlooked on a number accounts by higher education and other policy advocates. What is unfortunate is that it eventually becomes apparent that higher education has ignored this body of research because it stood to undermine and/or disrupt its current model of teacher preparation and its money-making capacity.

If educators face squarely this reality about the powerful force of culture and where teachers actually learn to teach, they should logically be moved to ask some questions about how we currently prepare and develop teachers. Specifically, they should be moved to question the role of higher education in teacher preparation because so much of what passes for teacher preparation takes place outside of actual schools.

Questioning higher education in this way, however, is highly problematic for our society. Making the best decision for our society is largely in the hands of higher education academics. Unfortunately, these academics bring a huge bias to the question of how we create effective teachers. Their bias is this: How our society creates effective teachers is all about how we prepare teachers in higher education. Getting members of the teacher preparation community in higher education to face this bias and its utter falseness has proven to be a nearly impossible task.

Raising this issue at conferences has proven to cause audience disbelief, insult, and outrage that anyone should challenge higher education's role and leadership in teacher education. That higher education campuses are the right domain for teacher education is such a deeply held assumption that some will not even consider a challenge to that assumption.

Add to this what must be an unconscious fear of disruption: If the traditional role of higher education in teacher preparation was shown to be ineffective, what would happen to the enormous teacher preparation industry and its terrific cash flow for higher education? This fear is likely very fundamental to the resistance higher education has to facing its own irrelevance.

What is true is that the creation of effective teachers is about the cultural influence on novice teachers in local schools. If the cultural influence is what it should be, teachers in a given school will steadily improve over the course of their careers. If the cultural influence is less than it should be, teachers in a given school may be invited into careers of stasis, withdrawal, or even toxicity.

The bottom line is that it is the culture of the local school that is the primary variable in the development of effective teachers. It absolutely is not what happens in the generic, decontextualized teacher preparation programs in higher education. Thus, what our society needs to be talking about is not how to improve teacher preparation in higher education. It needs to be talking about how our traditional schools can be changed so they become sites of teacher development that grow effective teachers. As the readers consider this, they must also keep in mind that regardless of the research, higher education will do what it can to thwart this challenge.

The logical endpoint of this book is this: If the schools where they work are the places where teachers actually learn to teach, then we need to develop a new school model that has been deliberately designed for *teacher* learning. Said another way, to create effective teachers, local schools should be explicitly designed for the induction, preparation, and development of its teachers for a full career. And another way, local schools should be designed to serve two learner populations, students *and* teachers.

What this book calls for then is a new school model that provides for both student and teacher learning. That means we are going to consciously reject the current traditional school model with all of its nineteenth-century baggage and its sideshow approach to teacher development and replace it with a model that is expressly designed to develop cultures that develop teachers and make them into effective teachers. Implicit in this new school model, of course, is a new conceptualization of "teacher" as what we may call a learner-collaborator-leader.

Thus, this book is about clarifying that new school model and the new teacher concept. Every effort will be made to paint a clear picture of what this new school model will look like and how it will operate. To this end, existing examples of such schools will be employed along with a narrative that attempts to apply the maxim in good writing of "Don't say it, show it." The narrative will be about Tina, a hypothetical teacher candidate, and how her induction takes a new path as she begins her teacher preparation, away from a higher education campus, and in a school that was explicitly designed for teacher learning and a full career of teacher development.

This effort to give concrete examples and paint clear pictures should be helpful in keeping at bay the reader's inclination to dismiss this work as too theoretical or unrealistic. This work shares the aim of the American Educational Research Association whose report, *Studying Teacher Education: The Report of the AERA Panel on Research and Teacher Education*, expressed the desire

> to identify and explain what the active ingredients are in teacher preparation programs whose graduates have a positive impact on pupil's learning and other important educational outcomes. Research that identifies these active ingredients and the conditions and contexts in which they are most likely to be present is the kind of research that can guide policy and practice in the 21st century. (Levine, The Education Schools Project, 2006)

What will be different in this case, however, is that this book will show that the active ingredients are in actual local schools, not in teacher preparation programs in higher education.

Clarifying how a new school model will have a positive impact on teacher learning and student learning will advance the cause of understanding how we create effective teachers. The fact is that identifying the active ingredients that create teacher effectiveness is not so elusive. What is proposed here for creating a new school model has already started to happen. There are existing schools that exemplify and demonstrate the new school model. And it is significant that it is public school teachers who are leading the way in this innovation. What is troublesome is that higher education has done little to contribute to such innovation no less identifying or advancing the active ingredients.

This brings us to some theoretical issues that need some discussion. Clearly, if educators were to accept the proposition of this book, it would stand to be very disruptive, particularly to the teacher preparation industry in higher education and the various alternative routes. Thus, explaining why our current approach to teacher induction, preparation, and development constitutes conscious malpractice will get some attention.

Discussion of higher education's failures in teacher preparation should not have the effect, however, of suggesting it is only opinions and preferences that are at stake here. Let's be clear. Teacher preparation in higher education does not work. It has failed. The discussion that follows is just an attempt to be very clear. It does not anticipate a rational response from higher education. Although there are surely those in higher education who have not yet faced it, we are past the point of discussion. Higher education teacher preparation does not work.

THE ILL-EFFECTS OF HIGHER EDUCATION TEACHER PREPARATION

There are two ill-effects of higher education teacher preparation that are the most serious. The first is the old complaint that too much of teacher preparation takes place outside of actual schools. Both teacher educators and aspiring teachers make this complaint routinely. Educators close to the teacher preparation process know the incessant complaint of teachers in training that what they learn on higher education campuses is too theoretical. And, study after study of teacher preparation practices by teacher educators has agreed with this observation and called for making teacher preparation more practical and less theoretical (Holmes Group, 2010).

This recommendation has resulted in many schools of education excitedly requiring increased field experience for aspiring teachers as if this were the ultimate silver bullet. While it seems like a reasonable approach, it misses the point. Extended field experiences do not cause teachers to become effective teachers. This dose of "field experience" is just another rational approach to teacher learning.

Yes, the idea is going in the right direction. But, inserting it into standard higher education teacher preparation is fundamentally deceptive. It gives the impression that the teacher preparation protocol is getting serious about field experience. In reality, this is nothing more than a head fake to the policy community and aspiring teachers who are shopping for teacher education programs. It gives the impression of seriousness in the field of learning.

The point here is that field experience is not one of the active ingredients. It's not even a placebo. It is as utterly fake in the creation of an effective teacher as power windows would be to the power train of an automobile. The active ingredient in creating effective teachers is actual participation over a period of years in an actual school culture that is derived of learning communities. There is no substitute, not stiff entry requirements, not portfolios, not coaching, not mentoring. Nothing.

Of course, higher education loves to broadcast to the policy community and program shoppers all of the adornments that they put on their teacher education programs. All of these adornments help all involved avoid the bigger issue: Involvement in a higher education teacher preparation program delays a novice teacher's entry into an actual community of practice. That entry is the active ingredient.

Higher education's requirement for more field experience and student teaching does not contribute to teachers becoming effective teachers. It is short term and not authentic participation in a school. It is also an orientation to old-school culture. Most significantly, it delays novice teachers' entry into the communities of practice that may ultimately shape them into effective teachers. Try as higher education might to think of new program adornments or hurdles for aspiring teachers, there is only one thing that will facilitate their development into effective teachers, being situated in a school culture that has the explicit purpose of creating effective teachers.

This brings us to the related second important ill-effect of higher education teacher preparation. Most local schools where novice teachers are placed do not have cultures that have the explicit purpose of creating effective teachers. Most are traditional schools where teacher learning is a sideshow of occasional, discreet "professional development" sessions. In the face of this reality, one would think that higher education would call on these schools where they place their teacher for field experience to change. But they do not.

In spite of the mountain of literature in education that calls for school reform, school transformation, and complete replacement of the traditional school, higher education has done little to nothing to expose the profound deficiencies of traditional schools for the twenty-first century. The end result is that our teachers get their field experience in such schools and go on to learn to teach, when employed, from the cultures of obsolete traditional schools.

THE ENABLING OF OBSOLETE SCHOOLS

Add to this that higher education teacher preparation not only condones but actually enables the reign of the traditional school by preparing teacher candidates for teaching in them. They do not prepare teachers to be change agents that understand the obsolescence of traditional schools and a teacher's role in changing them. Ignoring the deficiencies of traditional schools, higher education teacher preparation has continued to prepare teachers for their low-status and antiquated roles as isolated classroom teachers who have little influence in their schools. What we get at the end of higher education teacher preparation is a person prepared to extend the legacy of traditional schools, not change them.

For a moment consider the depth of this traditional preparation: Most teachers go to traditional elementary and secondary schools. Then they go to traditional colleges where, like the elementary and secondary schools they attended, "learning" is classroom based and consists largely of compliance work in completing readings, listening to lectures, taking tests, and writing papers. This emersion in traditional education is then capped off with a teacher preparation program that, remarkably, provides more of the same and ignores all that has been written about the profound deficiencies of the traditional school for the twenty-first century and, thus, prepares its teacher candidates for success in these obsolete schools.

By the end of this process, one can reasonably observe that these teacher candidates have the traditional school in their blood. Novice teachers come out of these institutions clueless about the need for and possibilities of innovation particularly with respect to their own professional growth over a full career. And it is this lack of teacher professional growth that is at the heart of this book's argument that higher education teacher preparation has betrayed teachers and why we need a new school model that is focused on a full career of teacher development.

Traditional schools were not designed for teacher development. They were designed to serve youth in very basic learning during the industrial age. Schools were intended for this basic student learning, not teacher learning. This book will demonstrate how the persistence of this notion about teacher learning continues to be true and continues to diminish the teaching profession and student learning. It is a betrayal of our teachers and their students.

Introduction

DEVELOPING A NEW SCHOOL MODEL AND A NEW TEACHER CONCEPT

In response to the failure of higher education teacher preparation, this book is primarily about the envisioning of a new school model and, as a consequence, a new teacher concept. The point is to reconceive of schools as the primary places of teacher learning because, for better or worse, research tells us that is where teachers actually learn to teach. Higher education's refusal to acknowledge the research and the logic of this perspective has been a betrayal of teachers because it has perpetuated teacher isolation and powerlessness in influencing its own development and the evolution of its schools. This is not an exceptional or radical idea. In nearly every other profession, communities of practice are where novice practitioners learn to become full practitioners. Amazingly and remarkably, this is not true in the teaching profession. But, it needs to be.

LOCAL SCHOOLS THAT FOCUS ON TEACHER LEARNING

Thus, this book looks to change the conversation about teacher induction, preparation, and development and how to create effective teachers. We do not need to be discussing how to achieve better teacher preparation in higher education. What we need to be discussing is a new school model. Why? Again, because it is in local schools that teachers actually learn to teach, not in higher education teacher preparation programs or any place else.

The discussion needs to be this: How do we get rid of the traditional school model? How do we replace it with a school model that explicitly serves teacher learning? Without rehashing all of the evidence of poor student learning in traditional schools, the most eminent reason for making local schools education centers for teachers is that student learning and teacher learning are not only correlated but have a causal relationship (Darling-Hammond, 2000). Improvement in teacher learning reliably translates into improvement in student learning. It all means that the way forward has to be about improving the places where teachers actually learn to teach, not higher education programs.

Discussing how to improve that one additional year in teacher preparation, as in the vaunted five-year program, in higher education teacher preparation pales in importance to discussing how we create a new school model that provides teachers with a full career of professional growth and makes every teacher an effective teacher.

When you think about it, this conclusion is not much different from deciding that swimming instruction is best done in water or that sport instruction is most effective when on the field. Yet, higher education still sees fit to have significant components of its teacher preparation take place in campus classrooms with instructors who have minimal public school teaching experience. It is a strategy that begs for revision. Synthesizing an array of research, this book will take a stab at how we can begin change.

A CLASSROOM TEACHER WROTE THIS BOOK

The entrance of this work into the national discussion on teacher education also needs some explanation. Most importantly, this book was *not* written by a member of higher education. Rather, it was written by a career high school teacher of thirty-three years who also earned a Ph.D. It is supported by a significant background as a professional development school coordinator and extensive experience with teacher induction, preparation, and development programs beginning in secondary school and extending to career-long teacher development. This was supplemented with doctoral research with high school students who aspired to be teachers.

Underlying this book's perspective is work for the State of New Jersey as the chairperson of a local Professional Development Board and the authoring of three books on teacher development. Much of the thinking and work was done in connection with and involvement with the professional development school movement going back to the 1990s. One outcome of this background has been to perceive the professional development school movement as the future of American schooling.

In deciding to advance this work into the national discussion, the text is directed to an audience of teachers and the writing comes in large measure from what has been learned from a whole career, the long view, not any particular strand of research. That long view has translated into these lessons: schools should invest more in the personal and professional development of teachers; as a matter of culture, teachers should learn more from each other, and teachers long for more growth as a person and for more professional stature.

Thus, in developing the case for changing the situation of teacher induction, preparation, and development, this book will address the current social clamor to improve student achievement by insisting that teacher development in local schools will ultimately prove to be the most significant factor in improving student achievement.

But there is a motive beyond the improvement of teacher learning for student learning. An important theme in this work is that teachers can't be happy unless they are in a career that grows them for a full career. Research on this need will be presented at length. The failure of higher education and local school leaders to acknowledge and serve this teacher need is a clear example of how teachers have been betrayed. More than any material benefits or altruistic satisfaction that might come from being a teacher, teachers want personal and professional growth.

Like other professionals, they like the idea of advancement. The research that points to this conclusion is substantial. There must be for teachers a sense of going somewhere professionally and of rising to new professional and personal levels as an outcome of learning at their workplace.

With acknowledgment of this perspective, it is hoped that this book will provide for teachers a frank, insider discussion about teacher preparation and development and how it relates to teachers' sense of thriving and well-being in their work throughout a full career. This frank discussion is provided out of a certain concern that teachers have lost perspective and don't see the mess that has engulfed them. And because of their traditional school mindset, most teachers have accepted this mess as just part of teaching in this era. Hopefully this work will allow some to see beyond the mess that has become a cave of sorts and to see some new possibilities beyond that cave that portend a brighter future for teachers.

TEACHERS LEADING

Not Policy People, Not Administrators, Not Higher Education, Not Unions

The reality of teaching can be different. Teaching does not have to be the frustrating enterprise that so many teachers currently experience. This book will invite teachers to think about themselves in a new way. It is a way that will elucidate the need for a new teacher concept and a new school model both of which will lead to greater job satisfaction and better student learning.

Some readers have asked, why address this book to just teachers? The idea is that teachers must take charge of their own destinies, and the remake of the teaching profession must come from teachers communicating with each other about the condition of student learning and its connection to teacher learning in our schools.

The author believes and research confirms that it is communication among teachers that will lead to the remake of the profession because bringing teachers together in this way will ultimately address the central obstruction to teacher learning and development: their exclusion from important decision-making in our schools. When teachers are excluded from important decision-making in their schools, they are denied the most important learning opportunities of all.

To reverse this condition, teachers can no longer rely on outside forces to help them, whether these forces be their local school leaders, their own unions, their central office leaders, policy makers, government leaders, or higher education. All of these entities have demonstrated an ardent commitment to the status quo while at the same time finding cover by parading the idea of teacher empowerment and teacher leadership. Watching this has been painful. It has given new meaning to the old idea of tokenism. To respond to this duplicity, this book will suggest to teachers some of the realities about which teachers need to talk frankly among themselves.

Teachers want real careers that involve real professional growth. To achieve that, they need to look inward, among themselves for ways to improve both themselves and their schools. They need to ask, "If it was up to us, how would we change things?" They will need to consider very new assumptions and school structures in order to restore the relevance of teachers. Relying on others to see the wisdom in this has decidedly not worked. The outside forces have a deep allegiance to the rational control of schools. They want to continue to issue standards and mandates and tell teachers how to do what most of them have never done, teach.

These outside forces have shown little appreciation for the wisdom of making schools generators of thinking and learning as an outcome of teacher collaboration. It is hoped that this book will assist teachers in finding the reason and the will to talk to one another, formally and informally, with the purpose of remaking and retaking the schools that should be theirs.

It is also a good idea that the people who inhabit the outside forces that purport to guide schools and support teachers know that we teachers are talking about them, that we are talking about how shallow and ineffective their guidance and support have been, that we are observing that the miseducation of new teachers by higher education has been nothing less than remarkable. It is important that these outside forces know that we are becoming increasingly aware of the bind they have put teachers and their schools in as they have claimed ever more and more authority and control over schools and have diminished the role of teacher thinking and decision-making.

A POSITIVE OUTLOOK GROUNDED IN TEACHER EXPERIENCE

It is from this perspective that a synthesis of experience and research may lead to insights about teacher preparation and development that yield more grounded conclusions about what is best for teachers. They are conclusions that have had no or scant application in the national discussion so far about teacher preparation and development. It is believed that these conclusions will ring more true to his teachers who, themselves, are increasingly reflecting on the grind of teaching and their frustration with being excluded from important decision-making in their schools.

Thus, a different perspective on teacher learning and development will be presented. In doing this, it is acknowledged that the analysis and outlook presented challenges to some eminent thinkers, interest groups, and policy makers in the field of teacher education. Working as others have, trying to unravel the mystery of teacher learning and development, there has been a careful review of the literature around teacher induction, preparation, and development.

This review reaches back to the 1970s and 1980s and the apparent discovery of a problem with our schools and our teachers that came to be voiced in the work *A Nation at Risk* (1983) and the ensuing controversy about schooling and teacher education that has lasted to this day. It considers some of the responding literature that looked to define and remediate the problems in our schools, works such as *A Nation Prepared* (1986) and the reports of The Holmes Group, *Tomorrows Teachers* (1986) and *Tomorrow's Schools of Education* (1995), and the 1996 report from the National Commission on Teaching and America's Future, *What Matters Most: Teaching for America's Future*.

Also considered are more recent reports that have come from a variety of advocacy groups and scholars. These included the recommendations of the American Educational Research Council as presented in *Studying Teacher Education: The Report of the AERA Panel on Research and Teacher Education*; those of the National Council for Accreditation of Teacher Education's 2010 Blue Ribbon Panel; the standards put forth by the Council for Accreditation of Teacher Education, *Better Teachers, Better Schools* (1999); a report from the Fordham Foundation; *The Mirage*, a report from The New Teacher project; *Teacher Preparation Review 2014*, a report from the Center for Teacher Quality; *Educating School Teachers*, a report from the American Educational Research Association (2006); the ACT testing group's report entitled *The Condition of Future Educators 2015*; and *Finding a New Way*, a report from the Aspen Institute. The National Board for Professional Teaching Standards has also contributed an array of standards, the effects of which have been considered.

The review also gave consideration to a number of scholars and writers who have submitted high-profile works about the state of teacher education and learning. These include the works of Arthur Levine, Linda Darling-Hammond, Marilyn Cochran-Smith, Susan M. Lytle, Kenneth M. Zeichner, and Ron Thorpe of the National Board for Professional Teaching Standards.

This book's insistence that higher education has gotten it wrong comes down to a common scholarly issue, the notion that something is missing. Our understanding of teacher development has a gap. Our national conversation about teacher education as it has been developed by many of our leading thinkers has left out important concepts and research. It is not totally clear why what is missing has been left out, but it is clear that things are missing. The subject of this book is that which is missing, or, better said, suspiciously missing. One might even go so far as to say that the ideas and research left out are the proverbial elephant in the room—the reality that, for whatever reason, people have chosen *not* to talk about.

What is missing, however, is not mysterious or obscure, a condition which makes its being overlooked all the more curious. What is missing is thinking and research in and outside the field of education that focuses, not on teacher deficiencies, what "teachers need to know and be able to do," but rather on teacher capacities and the building of those capacities. These are powerfully different perspectives.

As the current conditions of teacher preparation and development are sorted out, this book will clarify how the current focus of teacher preparation by higher education on teacher deficiencies is pushing out other considerations on teacher development and in so doing hurting teacher and student learning.

Specifically, important among what is missing from our discussion of teacher preparation is research in organizational theory as typically captured in the idea of "organizational learning," works about cultural learning within societies but, especially, within organizations and institutions, developmental theory and positive psychology as it might be applied to teacher development and building teacher capacity, and, finally, works that explore different conceptualization of teachers.

This includes authors that think of teachers as leaders and those that conceive of teachers as perennial students and researchers and, thus, creators of local knowledge and not dependent on the guidance of distant, outside entities that presume to know more than teachers about how teachers' work should be done.

It also involved works that reject the condition of teachers as isolated, standardized, compliant, lock-step workers who are moved by the carrots and sticks of distant authorities. It embraces new conceptualizations of teachers as creative, entrepreneurial risk takers who, communicating with each other and working together, are dedicated to change and innovation in learning and schooling.

One of the things that should stand out for the reader in reviewing the areas of research left out of the teacher education conversation is that they all involve study of what happens when people work together. Each of these areas of study sees human interaction as a phenomenon conducive to capacity development. From a variety of vantage points they drive to the conclusion that people working together achieve better results than people working alone.

Concepts like culture, organizational learning do this more explicitly, but the readers will see that developmental psychology and positive psychology, in focusing on high functioning and high achievement, not deficiencies, provide important new perspectives on the value of teachers working together and how we might reconceive of teacher preparation as one that focused on the capacity of teachers working together.

As this book unfolds, it will demonstrate how all of these areas of research and thinking not only point us to a greater and more accurate estimation of teacher capacity but also clarify how this capacity is best developed, *when teachers work together*, and where it is best developed, *in the schoolhouse itself and the local school cultures that are the real situations of teacher learning*.

THE INEFFECTIVENESS OF STRATEGY

In the last thirty years, policy advocates have gone to great lengths to get control of teacher learning by relying heavily on a strategy that focused on the creation of new standards and guidelines, new tests for teacher recruitment, new preparation curricula, and new certification and licensing requirements. As this book questions the value of teacher learning on remote higher education campuses, it will also question the value of all of these various standards, guidelines, and tests that come from higher education, remote policy groups, or government agencies. They have had little real impact on teacher learning or student learning.

In their place, this work will suggest the value of schools, themselves, as demonstration sites and how our energy would be better spent investing in such demonstration sites. The idea is that it is experience, itself, at a demonstration site by many types of visitors that will provide the learning that stands to influence and lead other aspiring schools to their own achievement in creating effective teachers and improving student learning.

From a frame of reference that respects the power of organizational culture, such an approach stands to be much more effective than issuing yet another list of standards, guidelines, or mandates to local schools. As organizational guru Peter Drucker has famously put it, "Culture eats strategy for breakfast."

Such a focus on these lists, in fact, shows a deep misunderstanding of how teachers learn to teach. While investing heavily in these lists, policy advocates and higher education have done little to get control of what is the strongest influence on teacher learning by far, the cultures of local schools where teachers are employed and do their daily work and where handbooks filled with standards and guidelines occupy the back of the lowest drawer of a teacher's desk.

This book will develop the importance of school culture as the primary influence on how teachers learn to teach. In this context it will further show how bringing to bear areas of research that focus on teacher capacity and teachers working together stand to better inform teacher education and development than those that focus on teachers' rational deficiencies, "what teachers need to know and be able to do."

Exploring these neglected areas of research will likely affirm the capacity of teachers in ways most teachers have never considered. Then they will begin to see the extent to which they have been betrayed. It will confront teachers with their own worth and expertise in ways they likely do not expect. Doing this, it will advance the idea that teacher preparation as we currently know it to happen in higher education or variety of alternative programs is ill-conceived and ripe for replacement. From a classroom teacher's perspective, that replacement is the subject of this book.

ORGANIZATION OF THE ARGUMENT

This book attempts to change the conversation about how to improve teacher education. It looks to move the conversation away from how we can improve teacher education programs on the campuses of higher education to how we can situate teacher education where it really happens, in local schools. In making the case for this relocation, there will be an extensive review of the academic literature that bears on school culture as the "active ingredient" in the creation of effective teachers and a discussion of how higher education has ignored this literature in favor of its current antiquated and obsolete teacher preparation programs.

In doing this, this book will blow the whistle on what must be seen as a national scandal, higher education's persistence in offering our prospective teachers an obsolete model of teacher preparation. The reader will be faced with the fact that this support for an obsolete model of teacher preparation is much more than a disagreement among academics. Rather, it is an example of malpractice with unsavory motives. Higher education has supported current teacher education programs all the while knowing they have shown no correlation with improved student learning over the course of decades and that higher education has gone to great lengths to disguise this.

This argument is made in response to our national quandary about how to create effective teachers. It will review the extensive efforts of many private and governmental entities to improve what is believed to be the most important variable in students learning at school, the teaching. It will also show that none of what has been done so far to improve teaching has, in fact, done so. To date, there is no evidence of a correlation between efforts to improve teaching and student learning outcomes.

In the context of these efforts to improve teaching, this book will cite various strands of research that show that student learning is correlated with teacher learning. It will further show that teacher learning and development is primarily dependent on its cultural situation, not on on-campus classes in higher education or incidental "professional development." It will expand on how the best cultural situation for teacher learning is one where teachers work together in learning communities and participate as meaningful decision makers in their schools.

Most importantly this book will aid teachers in envisioning how it all would work and turn out much better for them if teachers worked together as learning communities. This will include suggestions for a step-by-step, year-by-year approach to change. To support the envisioning process, the book will invoke a descriptive narrative about a fictitious character, Tina, and how her journey unfolds as she experiences the new approach to teacher preparation and development.

In assisting the reader to think through this book's argument and the narrative that shows how change would look and feel, it will be developed in four parts. Part I of this book is entitled "Confronting the Failure of Higher Education in Teacher Preparation." There will be a review of the literature that has pointed to new concepts of teaching and schooling. This section of the book will further detail how higher education has ignored important research because it did not support a continuation of their on-campus teacher preparation programs. In effect, the reader will see that over the latter part of the twentieth century and the early part of the twenty-first century, research and thinking emerged that suggested a new model for schools and a new role for teachers, but that this new research and thinking was deliberately ignored by higher education as it defended, often with sleight of hand, its obsolete model of teacher preparation.

An important component of the research ignored by higher education has had to do with literature that explains not only the power of organizational cultures but also their promise in developing new kinds of organizations. Important among these is the idea of an "Intentionally Developmental Organizations." It is a field of research that explores the potential of school culture to assist in both teacher development and overall human development. Pursuant to this line of research comes another field of research focused on how organizations, especially schools may learn and develop capacity as a whole.

Given Part I's review of new options in school structures and culture, Part II will focus on educational developments that anticipated a new school model. One such development has been the advent of the professional development school. Professional development schools have rightly attempted to make the school house a bigger part of teacher preparation. Unfortunately, this effort was interrupted by higher education which ultimately kept on-campus courses as the central component of teacher preparation, and the idea of professional learning communities was completely ignored. Still, from a historical perspective, the idea of bringing higher education and the local school together did suggest the development of a new school model. To make this argument more concrete than theoretical, Part II then will introduce Tina, a student who aspires to become a teacher under the new school model but who is ultimately frustrated by higher education's refusal to change.

Part III then details exactly how and why higher education refused to change and thereby betrayed Tina, all teachers, and the children they serve. This betrayal is developed in terms of poor student learning outcomes, higher education's fraudulent behavior, higher education's blindness to recent research, and its misconception of teacher development over a full career.

An important part of this section will be the presentation of conclusions from a variety of academic and private coalitions that have studied teacher education and, in fact, forwarded the same premise of this book, that schools must be reorganized so teachers work in learning communities. Then the reader will see the unprofessional duplicity of higher education as it endorses the conclusions of these various studies while at the same time the American Association of Colleges for Teachers Education undertook actions that, instead, protected their antiquated model of teacher preparation.

Part IV brings us back to the thesis of this book but at a deeper level. Having established that the creation of effective teachers would come best from placing them in a new school model where teachers work in collaborative communities of practice, this section will give further examples and rationale for making this change in American schooling.

As fakery has played such a prominent role in the thwarting of change for our schools, this section will also deal with the issue of authenticity. In education, change always leads to issues of authenticity (Supowitz & Weinbaum, 2008). When change is at hand, the research tells us that some choose to change, and some choose to pretend change (Supovitz & Weinbaum, 2008; Kelly et al., 2009).

Authenticity is a challenge that is faced by all groups from couples, to families, to small communities, to large organizations. If there is not a concerted effort to be authentic, to know and talk about what is really going on within the group, it will never be able to make itself better. Teachers will not be able to develop; schools will not be able to continuously change and improve.

Part I

CONFRONTING THE FAILURE OF HIGHER EDUCATION IN TEACHER PREPARATION

As this book urges a reconsideration of teacher learning as the most fundamental contributor to student learning, it looks to clarify the specific conditions that create effective teachers and ultimately calls for a new school model, one that is expressly designed for teacher learning and development. For clarity's sake, let it be restated: Teacher learning is the most fundamental contributor to student learning. As this book pursues this theme, it must face an obstruction: higher education teacher preparation destines our nation's teachers to ineffectiveness.

This book will tell the story behind that ineffectiveness. As in all such stories, many of the players at fault have gone to great lengths to obscure the truth. Thus, the necessity of this book. The issue comes to the fore as our nation's report card, the National Assessment of Educational Progress, and the media have again positioned student learning in our nation to be faced with such descriptions as "stagnant, flat-lined, static, and intractable."

A brief review of the data: According to our nation's report card, the National Assessment of Educational Progress, student achievement in core subjects has remained basically flat since the beginning of testing in the 1970s. This is particularly true of senior year results, the final assessment. The flatness has persisted in spite of billions invested by government and the creation of countless educational programs, including the U.S. Department of Education. Despite this investment, in recent comparison to other members of the Organization for Economic Co-operation and Development (OECD), the thirty-six richest and most developed countries, American students rank 25th in science, 24th in reading, and 35th in math.

Okay, there is room for discussion and argument about this slice of data and the many other slices that have been presented in countless other publications decrying the achievement failures of American schools. Although coming from different perspectives, many other authors have tried to bring together data that would constitute some kind of wakeup call for the American public. That wakeup call says, "What we are doing in our schools is not working."

The point is that a lot more negative data could be rehashed here but also the claims of actual progress, claims which stand alongside other claims of lowered testing standards, grade inflation, and routine social promotion and graduation. There is no question that making comparisons among all the various test results is very complicated, often unfair and that such comparisons are made even more complicated because they are often laden with the political agendas of multiple power players in the field of education.

But if we can step back from this bickering, the bigger point is that there is, in fact, a national consensus, although perhaps a quiet consensus. It is a consensus that says regardless of quirks in measurement or the efforts of some to put a positive spin on this score or that score, our schools could and should be doing a lot better. This consensus has been built by looking not only at big data but also by looking up-close at what goes on in schools. As a onetime student, the reader may find it quite understandable that some of the biggest critics of quality in our schools are teachers and students, both of whom, as reported in research, have indicated disturbingly low levels of teacher and student engagement along with low levels of real learning. From personal experience the reader probably knows some of the straining and twisting of standards and the falsification of achievement that was perpetrated right in front of you.

This book will explain why our schools are not achieving their mission and squarely point a finger of blame in a new direction, higher education teacher preparation. So, yes, the problem is the teaching, but more precisely, it is how teachers are prepared to teach and later developed, or not developed, into effective teachers.

Higher education has been steering the preparation and development of teachers for a century, and while its stewardship of teaching has been strenuously challenged in recent years, it continues, tellingly, to prepare teachers pretty much as it did at the beginning of the twentieth century.

Yes, there are other factors. But this story blames higher education because it is and has been the designer of teacher preparation. As circumstances to be explained will clarify, this story must be rightly considered a story of scandal because higher education has engaged in trickery and gone to great lengths to enforce its design and its antiquated ways in preparing teachers. All the while it has obscured its role in perpetuating how those ways have led to ineffective teaching and poor student achievement.

And yes, it is understood that calling higher education teacher preparation a scandal does sound like a stretch, but the closer look to follow should make it clear that higher education has been an active and deliberate perpetrator in thwarting change and improvement in how teachers teach. Meanwhile it has known what it was doing and continues to do it. For all the financial and human waste it has caused (affecting millions and wasting billions), higher education's actions should qualify as a national disgrace for the academic malfeasance it has involved. Its work has filled our schools with poorly prepared teachers most of whom, as research tells us, are unaware of their deficiencies and are destined to professional lives of averageness.

For the most part, these are the teachers you remember with fondness and/or disdain. The author must count himself as among them. Few of these teachers, most very decent, caring people, had or have any sense of what effective teaching is or how it is achieved. Since the inception of the National Assessment of Educational Progress, the national report card, this condition has been aggravated when our nation looks to very publicly hold these same poorly prepared teachers to account for our nation's ever lagging student achievement. It is a ritual that persists in spite of decades of research that beckons a new direction for teacher learning and development.

But, again, this story reaches scandal status for one reason above all others. It is about how higher education has consciously worked to protect its obsolete teacher preparation programs while knowing of their ineffectiveness and of better alternatives. It is a story of well-disguised, self-serving institutional recalcitrance that has had a very direct and hurtful impact on our kids, our teachers, and our society.

Now it is understood that the reader and most people do not walk around with a sense of outrage about teacher preparation. Most people think of teachers almost as victims, underpaid public servants whose quality variability is a lot like life. Some of it is good; some of it is bad. Changing that quality variability of teachers would be impossible. It is too much to expect. A school cannot have all effective teachers. It's not realistic.

But as this story is told, one of the most important lessons should be that this notion of quality variability is wrong. That you think in this way is, in fact, a product of the ineffective teaching from which the reader learned throughout your youth. But this book will help you correct that duped condition. Our teachers need not have the same quality variability as life. Schools can have all effective teachers. That's right, ALL. If you have learned otherwise, you have been misinformed.

Those in higher education teacher preparation are going to be angered by this article. It is going to expose the proverbial dirty laundry. Deans of education schools will be moved to migraines and obscenities, probably even worse. What's more, the entire teacher education community will, as they customarily do, rally a defense. They will say, in effect, "Honey, I can explain." Then will come forth the standard lie. They will tell of the extraordinary measures they have taken to make teacher education more comprehensive and more demanding. Tellingly, in their guilty but zealous rebuke, they will deliberately leave out what they have not done.

Let's begin by reviewing the old story. Educational achievement and engagement in our nation's schools continues to lag, and ineffective teaching has been and is still the problem. It is a story revived by news outlets every couple of years when the nation's report card, the National Assessment of Educational Progress, is issued by the U.S. Department of Education. This is followed by experts telling us, repeatedly, that the problem is ineffective teaching.

It's true. A great deal of often-cited research tells us conclusively that the single most important variable in students learning at school is the quality of the teaching. If students are not learning at school as they should, then the problem is the teaching. The data are clear. That's an old and tired story, and you probably already knew it. You probably knew it on some level as a student in elementary school.

You probably also know that dating back to 1983 and the publication of *A Nation at Risk*, the nation's efforts to solve the problem of ineffective teaching have included several major pieces of national legislation, *No Child Left Behind*, *Race to the Top*, the *Common Core Curriculum Standards*, and the *Every Student Succeeds Act*, all of which have focused on the quality of teaching and teacher accountability in our schools.

Efforts to raise the quality of teaching have included raising admissions standards to schools of education, making coursework more demanding during teacher preparation, providing novice teachers more clinical practice, heightening teacher licensing requirements, making teacher evaluation more frequent and more stringent, providing more teacher professional development, instituting more teacher-specific accountability testing of students, firing weak teachers, incentivizing teachers who successfully raise test scores, increasing the number of subjects tested, and extending the probationary period before tenor is granted.

You probably think it all sounds like a reasonable effort. Most people do. But in these efforts we may see the first layer of scandal. The effects of all of these efforts have been researched, and not one of these initiatives correlates with improved student learning. That is, when these changes were instituted, it didn't change student learning outcomes. And here's the kicker. Those who claim to prepare our nation's teachers have known for years about the ineffectiveness of these efforts. They have known for a long time that higher education teacher preparation, with all of its "improvements," has had no correlation with improved student learning. That is part of the reason why the nation's report card has not indicated meaningful improvement in student achievement over the last forty to fifty years.

To that end, the first section of this book, chapters 1, 2, 3, 4, and 5, provides some historical background about the concept of teacher learning, particularly developments in the past few decades that have advanced the idea that, more than instructors, teachers are best defined as a learners-collaborators-leaders who develop best in intentionally developmental, collaborative cultures.

Briefly stated, this advancement has moved away from thinking of teacher learning as coming from discreet, rational training sessions or workshops that were presented to teachers as "professional development" by experts. It has moved to thinking of teacher learning as a cultural phenomenon derived of teachers' collective effort to develop themselves as thinkers, leaders, and decision makers in the creation of local knowledge for the continuous improvement of local schools.

Chapter 1

Not Higher Education, a New School Model

The core idea of this book is that local schools are the best places for teachers to learn how to teach. Thus, what our national discussion on teacher quality needs to be about is how we can create model schools that have been explicitly designed for teacher learning and do, in fact, create effective teachers. This will be done recognizing that the only places that teachers really learn to teach are in the cultures of local schools, nowhere else.

What we do not need to continue discussing is how to improve teacher preparation in higher education. Like many old models, that one needs to be replaced with a better one. This book invites its readers to consider the better one, a new school model which implies a new teacher concept. History is rich with how better models replace older ones. Now is that time in teacher preparation.

The rightness of this outlook is supported by a growing body of research, although much of that research is not what would be called "educational research." These varied strands of research will confirm this book's thesis on the power of cultural learning in teacher development. They will confirm that, for better or for worse, the power of cultural learning makes local schools the only places where teachers actually do learn to teach.

Teachers do not learn to teach in the decontextualized classrooms of higher education or the short-term alternative programs which the ineffective programs of higher education have caused to emerge. Most importantly, these strands of research will also introduce how thinking of teacher preparation as cultural learning, rather than rational learning, opens the door to a renaissance in teacher development.

For clarity about how a new teacher would experience preparation in a model school instead of higher education, this book will offer examples of actual existing schools and organizations along with a narrative that details the experience of Tina, a hypothetical aspiring teacher. All of this will point to how teacher development is about school culture, not the creation of new standards and guidelines, new tests for teacher recruitment, new preparation curricula, new evaluation protocols, or new certification requirements.

CULTURAL LEARNING

Let's consider the idea of cultural learning a little bit further. The proposition is this: For good or bad, cultural learning is the strongest force in teacher development. Its presence as a force in teacher development is, however, usually overlooked in favor of rational approaches to teacher learning which research shows have far less power to improve teaching.

What are rational approaches to teacher learning? Rational approaches are what we usually think of as "learning at school." Rational learning comes when we assert conscious or critical thinking. Most often it comes from examination, manipulation, and figuring out. What is most characteristic of such learning is that it is deliberately thoughtful and intellectual. We can all think of thousands of things we have learned by applying our intellects and achieving understanding or competence. From the Rubik's Cube to the cause of the American Civil War, we have all seen ourselves acquire knowledge and know-how through rational learning.

Cultural learning is different. It is not rational. Under most circumstances, you don't consciously think about what you are learning from culture. Unless you are an anthropologist, you are unlikely to be aware of such learning. In most cases we are all occupied with rational learning to do our jobs, while in the same moments cultural learning is quietly having its way influencing our ways of being and behaving in a given organization.

In cultural learning, one does not assert intellect. There is no connecting the dots or drawing logical conclusions. There is no learning of facts or assembling evidence for a certain argument. As Deal and Kennedy have famously put it, in a given culture, people learn "the way we do things around here" (Deal & Kennedy, 1982, p. 4).

In contrast to rational learning, cultural learning is largely unconscious. It doesn't happen as an outcome of paying attention and figuring things out. It happens, in large measure, as an outcome of people coming together in groups such as families, neighborhoods, and various kinds of organizations. Anthropology and psychology tell us that in these communities, there is an inclination to fit in and to become a member, a member who respects the norms of the community. This inclination to fit in is the foundation of cultural learning.

Take a moment to ask yourself about powerful things that you have learned that came with no instruction, no paying attention, no guidelines, no oaths, no commandments, no laws, and no speaking at all. These are things we all likely learned as children in our homes, in our neighborhoods, and in our communities. Without any direct instruction we all came to know certain norms: in this family we do this and we don't do that. In this neighborhood we always do this. We never do that.

This knowledge of norms may be best understood in terms of our attitudes toward sex, personal relationships, and community experiences. Cultural learning is about how people manage their togetherness. It may involve attitudes toward strangers, toward money and status, toward one's place in the world, toward education, or toward the future.

The proposition offered to the reader is that research to be presented shows us that the quiet influence of cultural learning in schools is a much more powerful influence on teacher development than rational and intellectual learning. That is especially true if the content of this rational and intellectual approach to teacher learning has come from distant authorities in policy circles, government, or higher education.

CULTURAL LEARNING IS DEEPER LEARNING

One of the most important characteristics of cultural learning is that it is more deeply seated learning. Think of all of your rational learning. Think of how much of it you have forgotten, all the facts and procedures you once learned but you can no longer recall. Now think of your cultural learning. Most of it is still with you. What you learned in your family, in your spiritual institution, in your neighborhood, and in your local community is still there, maybe even some things you may not like but find it hard to get rid of.

What we learn from community and culture tends to find a deeper place inside of us. It is not information, per se, but attitudes, norms, habits, habits of mind, habits of practice, and the ways we live with each other. When we recognize that cultural learning finds this deeper place in ourselves, we should want to know how such learning can be facilitated, particularly, in this case, in teacher preparation and development where we would want to establish effective habits of practice.

THE DYSFUNCTION OF HIGHER EDUCATION TEACHER PREPARATION

If we objectively examine this fundamental reality of cultural learning, it allows us to see that higher education teacher preparation programs are not only ineffective but also actually dysfunctional. That is, they work against the development of teachers. Appreciating this harsh assessment will require, however, that the reader step away from some common assumptions. Let's look at some of the most crucial of these assumptions.

1. One assumption is that it is a reasonable practice for higher education to focus on the generic development of individual teachers for placement in disparate schools, all with very different conditions. But is this generic preparation a good idea or would aspiring teachers be better served if they were prepared for a particular school by that school?

    Local schools, after all, are unique in a lot of ways. Would teacher preparation be more effective if a teacher's preparation took into account a school's uniqueness? What's more, when a teacher's preparation is generic, what is the likelihood that it will have application at a unique school? The educational frame of reference of any particular school, if there is one, will be very likely different from that of an institution of higher education.

    Because it is very unlikely that there will be a good match in the first place, the value of taking a year or two for generic teacher preparation and the inherent expense is very questionable.
2. Higher education tends to prepare teachers in generic ways as individual actors. It does this when what aspiring teachers really need is an individualized induction into a local school where teachers work together in a collaborative school culture derived of learning communities. The experience of this collaborative condition where teachers generate their own knowledge about unique circumstances of the populations they serve cannot be provided in higher education where the focus is on the teacher as an individual actor in a particular classroom.
3. In focusing on generic teacher development, higher education also fails to recognize that the best personal and professional support for teacher development happens in the context of a culture of learning communities, not in the classrooms of higher education where busy students have little time or inclination to form cohesive communities of practice, no less give personal or professional support.

    This happens in the face of conclusive research that teachers learn to become most effective when they work together in collaborative learning communities. Higher education intrudes on and interrupts this process when it delays entry into the culture of a local school by requiring a year or more of campus-based work.
4. Overlooking the capacity of teachers working together, higher education encourages teachers to misunderstand their relationship to knowledge and learning. Higher education encourages them to see knowledge as coming from outside the schoolhouse as opposed to teachers creating their own knowledge as they work together inside the schoolhouse.

In effect, higher education misguides teachers into thinking that those that have the "essential knowledge" about teaching and schooling are people outside of schools, people like those from central offices, those from the halls of higher education, or those in the offices of state or federal authorities. This influence has had a very diminishing effect on the teaching profession.
5. In all of this, higher education affirms the structures, practices, and cultures of the traditional school where most teachers have worked in isolation for more than a century. In so doing, it discourages teacher entrepreneurship and diversity in educational thinking.

It is important to reemphasize that what was presented above are not complaints about the ineffectiveness of higher education teacher preparation. It is evidence of their dysfunction. They hurt the process of teacher development, and the remote, on-campus approach to teacher education needs to be ended. The narrative will illustrate more fully how this might happen.

When considered in light of the detail this book will put on these observations, teachers will be faced with a choice. That choice is to keep the current concept of what it means to be a teacher and a traditional school or to evolve and change our concept of both by affirming teachers' capacities and making local schools for both student and teacher learning.

TEACHERS IN THE CROSSHAIRS

This choice for teachers must be seen in the context of contemporary circumstances. Teachers are certainly aware that they are at the center of a national controversy about education in America. They are very conscious of this because they are so frequently blamed for so many of the failings of our nation's schools.

It has been observed over and over again that when schools are presented by the media as failing, teachers are first to be blamed. Then a process unfolds that plays out over and over again. It starts with some authoritative pronouncement or legislation that teachers read about in newspapers or see on television. It then filters down to teachers at faculty meetings when they are advised of new mandates, guidelines, curricular changes (more lists), and/or more high-stakes testing.

All of these directives have had an underlying assumption. It was a belief that by explicitly telling teachers what they should be doing and by providing some targeted "professional development," teachers could be made into the effective teachers our schools need. Embracing this assumption, at all levels of the teacher induction and preparation pipeline, a litany of standards and directives have outlined what many educational leaders came to believe would change teachers' personal qualifications and behavior and make them effective teachers. But it didn't happen.

When teachers didn't change and student learning didn't improve, what happened? There were more studies, more blue ribbon panels, and more reports which resulted in more lists of qualifications, standards, guidelines, and directives. The cycle continues to this day. The idea that policy makers could change the nation's schools by fiat continues to be strong, but like higher education, it is so self-involved that it overlooks a much more powerful force in teacher learning and behavior, local school culture.

It is this overlooking of the power of school culture that makes both teacher preparation in higher education and teacher development by policy fiat profoundly ill-conceived. It confirms for teachers in actual schools how removed from reality are higher education and the policy makers that they would think change could be so easy. How could they not know that teachers learn to teach in and as a result of the culture of the schools where they work? As the famous students of organizational culture, Terrence Deal and Kent Peterson explain,

> Although policy makers and reformers are still pressing for tight structures and rational assessments, it is important to remember that these changes cannot succeed without deeply engrained cultural support at the local level. (Deal & Peterson, 2016, loc. 292)

This book will show that for lack of engaging the culture of local schools in teacher induction, preparation, and development, both higher education and policy advocates have failed to provide teachers the professional growth that they deeply desire. Moreover, it is also a time for teachers to consider that had they been included sooner in developing strategies to improve student learning, their school cultures might have been enriched and better results might have been achieved. That bar is not high!

HOW DO WE CREATE EFFECTIVE TEACHERS?

This book hopes to make a contribution to our understanding of how culture can be the basis for positive teacher development. Its review of how and why higher education and policy makers have failed to provide teachers the learning they need necessarily leads to the following question: How do we actually create effective teachers? In recent years, the question has dominated the work of politicians, policy circles, and teacher preparation programs in higher education.

In the face of the national clamor about lagging student achievement in our nation's schools (real or perceived), research from a variety of quarters has clarified the paramount role that effective teachers play in advancing student learning. It has also clarified that there are too few effective teachers.

Into the national quandary over this question, this book advances a divergent but definitive answer, an answer derived from research: *It is the entirety of a school culture that produces effective teachers, and schools with authentic learning communities produce the cultures that produce effective teachers.*

For clarity, it is not teacher preparation programs on the campuses of higher education and it is not incidental "professional development" that respond to the dictates of policy leaders. It is not lists of guidelines or standards. Rather, it is school culture. All of the argument and research to be presented in this book will revolve around this idea as it clarifies the need for a new school model and a new teacher concept.

If we acknowledge the importance of school culture on teacher learning, a logical extension emerges. The creation of effective teachers depends on moving the location of teacher preparation out of higher education and into the cultures of actual local schools, schools which have the explicit purpose of developing teachers and which operate as learning communities, all in the service of student learning.

REAL OBSTACLES IN REAL SCHOOLS

In spite of the logic that supports this idea, the proposition faces two primary challenges. First, those in the schooling biz for a long time, including teachers, know that they have talked about and heard about the ineffectiveness of higher education teacher preparation programs for decades. Regrettably, teachers take this ineffectiveness as kind of a given—life is full of disappointments and meaningless hurdles.

At the same time, most leaders in education also know that the idea of making local schools places of teacher preparation has been quietly rejected before. To this day, many eminent scholars in the field of teacher preparation continue to insist that higher education teacher preparation programs are the only way to go. They persistently press the idea that local schools really can't do, or even attempt to do, what higher education attempts to do in teacher preparation.

Linda Darling-Hammond's famous essay "The Case for University-based Teacher Education" stands as a pillar among the many arguments for this point of view. Her argument, however, is flawed on a number of levels. One, it presents a faulty dilemma. The choice is not between preparing teachers in a traditional school setting or at a university (or a combination of the two).

Two, as is the case with most who argue for university-based teacher education, Darling-Hammond ignores the power of local school culture in the mix of influences on our novice teachers. Her essay barely makes reference to school culture.

A third flaw is that making local schools centers of teacher education and development may be perceived as demanding radical change. That schools are for kids is the traditional assumption. They are not for teacher learning. These assumptions/perceptions inaccurately make the whole notion of local schools having the purpose of teacher education seem a radical departure from the way we have done things in the past.

The closer look this book will offer, however, shows these perspectives to be unfounded. The fact is that for decades, there have been school leaders who have embraced the reality of cultural learning and attempted to engineer school cultures that are developmental. These are places where teacher learning is more deliberate and most often embedded in their daily work. And, it is learning which is uniquely suited to the circumstances of their schools.

In effect, these schools have abandoned the traditional school model of treating teachers as individual actors and developed collaborative school cultures where teachers feel the pull of their professional work in learning communities and exercise high levels of decision-making and innovation in creating a new school model. It is a model that provides teachers professional development for a full career.

A REFUTATION OF DARLING-HAMMOND'S

"The Case for University-Based Teacher Education"

The most significant flaw in Darling-Hammond's case (Cochran-Smith et al., 2008) is that it draws a faulty dilemma. It encourages the reader to think that the choice is between a traditional school's capacity to provide teacher preparation and that of a university. But, there is another choice: that is, to replace the traditional school with a new model school that does, inherently, prepare and develop its teachers.

What, on the surface, makes Darling-Hammond's case seem reasonable is that she puts forward many studies that show that when it was tried in the 1960s and 1970s, the on-the-job training of teachers did not have the hoped-for outcomes. She also advances research that demonstrates that teachers who have had higher education teacher preparation tend to outperform those who have not had it or had some shortened form of it. All of this may be accepted as true, but it misses the point. That is, we need a new school model that focuses on teacher learning and does effectively prepare and develop teachers.

Said in another way, the fact that teachers prepared in higher education tend to outperform those who have had less training does not necessarily lead us to the conclusion that higher education is the optimal site for teacher preparation. It is just better than preparation that is weaker (and we won't get into all of the uncontrolled variables). The contention here is that neither higher education nor the shortened alternatives do a good job at teacher preparation. And there is plenty of research to support that observation. Point: there is another choice.

IGNORING THE CHOICE OF A NEW SCHOOL MODEL

What is most interesting about Darling-Hammond's "Case" is that it never really considers the idea of a new school model. Yes, there is some glancing discussion of professional development schools (PDSs), but even in that discussion she fails to seize on the prospect of how PDSs might foreshadow a new school model. Instead she continues her insistence that only the university can serve teacher preparation as it needs to be served.

Let's focus there for a moment. In effect, Darling-Hammond is saying that teachers cannot learn to teach in our society's centers for teaching, our local schools. They must go to universities to learn how to teach. Consider what that means for the quality of our local schools. If you go there as an apprentice, you cannot learn how to teach there. Really?

Regrettably, on this point, Darling-Hammond is probably right, but for a reason she does not mention or adequately appreciate. Because most of our local schools are traditional schools, they are not well disposed to teacher development, and they certainly are not good places for teacher preparation. In these schools, novice teachers would just learn how to be traditional teachers who work in the isolating conditions of a traditional school and have little decision-making influence in their schools.

Think, also, for a moment, think about what other professions would have practicing professionals say that it would be better for apprentices to learn their profession away from where it is actually practiced. This is what Darling-Hammond is saying in her "Case." That point should tell us that there is something wrong with our schools if they are not good places to learn how to teach.

In light of this, everyone involved in a school should ask themselves if their school would be a good place for a novice teacher to learn to teach. If the answer is no or even equivocal, that should tell us that the school needs to change. If one's school would not be a good place for a novice teacher to learn to teach, then it probably isn't that good for a veteran teacher either.

And the implications for student learning are equally troublesome. Teacher development is probably not an inherent part of the culture. It is probably a traditional school culture that focuses on student instruction and makes teacher "professional development" an occasional, fad-based event. Knowing this to be true, is there any other option but change?

Equally problematic, however, is the alternative that Darling-Hammond proposes, university teacher preparation. The reality is that they are both bad choices. We need a new school model that focuses on teacher development as an essential purpose of every local school. If a school is functioning properly as a community of practice, it should inherently be an ideal place for the development of novice teachers.

The reality is that schools could develop the capacity to prepare and develop teachers. They could, in effect, change their model. Why would they do this? They would do this because it acknowledges an old reality that is newly realized and supported by recent research: *It is the entirety of a school culture that produces effective teachers, and schools with authentic learning communities produce the cultures that produce effective teachers.* Knowing this, school leaders would have to do what all organizational leaders must do, make change within the organization to deal with change outside of the organization.

Again, the reality is that the research is now conclusive. Teachers who work collaboratively produce better student outcomes than teachers who do not. As teachers work collaborative in schools studying the effects of their teaching, they are effectively creating cultures that develop teachers for a full career. They are providing the conditions whereby teachers learn the habits of mind and practice that result in effective teaching. This reality demands that we change the school model so it has a strong focus on teacher learning. This is the choice that Darling-Hammond leaves out as she justifies the continued requirement to prepare teachers in higher education.

MODELS: THEY DO NEED TO CHANGE

As we consider the need for a new school model, let's consider the concept of a model itself. Perhaps the most accessible idea of a model is a new car model. Why do car models change from year to year? They change to accommodate car buyers. New models make changes that provide greater ease and service in the driving experience. A new model represents a better configuration of old components along with new technology and accessories that provide greater comfort, functionality, or luxury.

Would it be a good idea for schools to also think about a model change? Could such a model change provide students with better learning experiences?

Consider another area where model change has had more universal benefits for society, energy. The human race has a history of changing energy models. Those energy models have advanced from human labor and human-propelled machines to beast-driven models, to steam-driven models, to internal combustion–driven models, to now a variety of renewable and inexhaustible energy-driven types like wind and solar. Each new model was an advance because it promised unique benefits to both users and society as a whole.

One has to wonder why this need to change models as circumstances in the world change has not had the same influence on the thinking of educators as it has had on other organizational leaders. As has been well documented, the model of our traditional schools has pretty much stayed the same for more than a hundred years. While there is change currently happening on the margins of the educational world, little of that can be attributed to the influence of higher education, which, itself, has resisted model change as it continues to prepare teachers to teach in traditional schools.

If we know that it is by virtue of school culture that teachers learn to teach, then we too need to create a model whereby teacher preparation can happen in a positive school culture. It must be a model that is deliberately developmental and by its very nature creates effective teachers. The necessity of this is, in fact, confirmed by the testimony of many in higher education teacher preparation who complain, as Lee Teitel has explained, that concepts and practices taught in higher education usually "wash off" when teachers settle into actual schools (Teitel, 2003, p. 1). This "wash off" reality is that what we must face. What really sticks is what happens at the schools where teachers work!

If we accept this reality, wouldn't it be a better idea, and more realistic, to choose a new school model and create the conditions that create effective teachers? That is, we could take all of the money and energy that goes into university-based teacher preparation and put it into creating the conditions within local schools where we know the forces of culture will have their relentless impact and ensure that that impact is, in fact, positive.

The choice is not university teacher preparation or traditional school teacher preparation. The choice is university teacher education or teacher preparation in a new school model, a model explicitly designed for teacher development. It is a model that is within our grasp because it has already been achieved if only on the margins of the schooling world.

A final consideration is that those advocating for university-based teacher education imply that making local schools centers of teacher education and development demands radical change. That schools are for kids is the traditional assumption. They are not for teacher learning.

These assumptions/perceptions inaccurately make the whole notion of local schools having the purpose of teacher education seem a radical departure from the way we have done things in the past. This book will show, however, that as shown by the PDS movement, which Darling-Hammond favors, making schools into sites for teacher education does not demand radical change.

As the reader considers this idea, it must be reemphasized that it is based on research. This book will review research that tells us clearly that teachers are most effective when they work in cultures derived from collaborative work and learning. And remember, these are circumstances that cannot be authentically created in a university-based program. Add that a new school model could offer both rich practical and conceptual guidance because the new model should include a robust partnership with one or more institutions of higher education and bring the practice of scholars and teacher development to the campuses of local schools.

Is this author dreaming? No. Even Linda Darling-Hammond knows that what has been described above has already been achieved by some schools and is taking shape in many others. As this book unfolds it will present recent research on the creation of such schools and organizations that Kegan and Laskow Lahey (2016) have called "deliberately developmental organizations," entrance into which necessarily leads to personal and professional development. Why wouldn't we want to have schools that follow the same model for creating effective teachers?

Deal and Peterson see the challenge of taking a cultural view of teacher learning in poetic terms, terms that bring new light to the force of culture.

> The challenge is daunting because many of the pressure for focusing education on a constricted view of learning are external. The vital task ahead is not one of adding more structure and standardization to schools or ramping up an already over-hyped testing agenda, it is more a matter of reviving the spirit, bringing back the joy and love of learning, and celebrating the majesty of teaching that once held sway before the constant top-down batter snuffed out the story and soul of what it means on a deeper level to teach and to learn. There is something magical or enchanting about the warm rapture of learning and gift of teaching that touch places in us where little else can reach. Now is the time to snatch it back from the coolness of rigor and rationality that seems to rule the day. (Deal & Peterson, 2016, loc. 699)

NO CHANGE IS A DARK CHOICE FOR TEACHER DEVELOPMENT

The author is keenly aware of the challenges in attempting to change current thinking on teacher education. Imagine the upheaval in higher education and in our local schools, themselves. But also imagine continuing to do what we know does not work. The research is very clear; teachers are most effective when they work collaboratively, and the most powerful force for teacher development is school culture.

But the vast majority of our schools do not have collaborative cultures. These schools are basically structured the same as they were a hundred years ago. The outcome of this is that most of our novice teachers are now becoming acculturated in communities of practice that have an industrial-age orientation wherein innovation, teacher collaboration, and teacher learning, itself, are low priorities.

If this indictment seems too extreme, consider this. Educators are now more than two decades into exercising two concepts that truly promised to push the evolution of teaching, professional learning communities (PLCs) and PDSs. These concepts promised that teachers would participate in important school decision-making and give teachers broad participation and leadership in guiding the learning of students, their own learning, and the learning of novice teachers.

PLCs and PDSs stipulated this promise because it was the wisdom of our finest organizational thinkers (Senge, 1991; Garvin, 2000; Gruenert & Whitaker, 2015, Gruenert & Whitaker, 2017; Teitel, 2003; Goodlad, 1984), all of whom called for, and still call for, the broad participation of all organizational members in the effort to continuously improve an organization. This thinking has had a much-heralded application to schools supported by many publications and has led to the concepts of PLCs and PDSs becoming widespread.

Now, some thirty years later we learn that these programs did not even come close to fulfilling their promise. A 2013 Gallup poll of teachers indicated that among all occupations tracked in their survey, teachers were the least likely to say that their opinions counted at work (Busteed, 2014).

And, our teachers are right. Their opinions count for very little. Most of them are now situated in a school that is not focused on teacher learning, thinking, or decision-making. Our teachers do not follow routines rich in lesson study, reflective practice, or collaborative application of teacher thinking. Instead, their schools are focused on compliance with the mandates of central authorities.

These are the central authorities who are now doing the important thinking with respect to standards, goals, curricula, and standardized assessment. Teachers even find themselves marginalized with respect to lesson design and what teachers should say in delivering lessons as publishers attempt to "teacher proof" their textbooks. It is clear evidence that these schools were not designed for collaboration or teacher learning. When you take away teacher participation and decision-making, you take away the most important learning opportunities for teachers.

Apart from the logic of doing what research tells us is right, one of the most compelling reasons for change is that teachers themselves are professionally frustrated. Out of this professional frustration, they have expressed a clear desire for a school model that involves them in more consequential thinking and decision-making about not only their classrooms but the overall operation of their schools (Farris-Berg et al., 2012; Senge et al., 2000, 2012; Will, 2016).

Unfortunately teachers' expressed desire for more consequential roles in their schools has been met with token "leadership" programs which have become a recent fad. Evidence that these teacher leadership programs are hollow is evident in the fact that they never result in significant change in the structure or cultures of our traditional schools. Except in some marginal instances that will be highlighted, our traditional schools, even with teacher leadership programs, have steadfastly maintained their top-down authority structures.

As this trend has unfolded, what many in government and policy circles have continued to overlook is research that suggests that really giving teachers greater influence in their schools may be the answer to improving our schools. There is significant evidence that student learning increases as teacher influence and the resulting teacher learning increases.

This book is about providing teacher preparation that creates effective teachers. It is a message that expresses what teachers want for themselves, a full career of professional development as a foundation for effective teaching. In developing this message, this book will offer an argument derived from research that connects professional learning that makes teachers consequential thinkers and decision makers in their schools with improved student achievement.

It will show that creating effective teachers is not about standards, curriculum, essential knowledge, or field experience or any of the other particulars that are often the focus of policy makers. It is about how teachers work together, learn together, and act together and the cultures derived from those efforts.

TWO IDEAS ARE FUNDAMENTAL

Please consider this quick review of core concepts. The reasoning behind the idea of moving teacher education out of higher education, or some of the alternative routes that have recently emerged, is founded on two ideas. The first is an irrevocable reality. Like it or not, for better or for worse, teachers learn how to teach in the schools where they work. They do not learn how to teach in remote programs outside the cultures of local schools.

The second is the idea that teachers, themselves, are capable of creating the knowledge and the circumstances necessary to develop novice teachers, create effective teachers, and configure effective schools that advance student learning and teacher learning. It should be observed that it is, in fact, counterproductive to teach teachers that it is not them but higher education or the policy makers in state capitals or Washington, DC, that have the sources of what many have come to call the "essential knowledge" for making teachers or their schools better.

The teaching profession itself would be more vibrant and rewarding if teachers were educated to believe in their own capacities—that they can configure, reconfigure, and run schools. Schools, in fact, would be better by virtue of being grounded in teacher knowledge derived from a particular school, its population, and its community and not the fads that come from those who believe they know more than the people in the schools.

In this regard, it would be helpful to recall an observation made by John Dewey in his work "The Relationship of Theory to Practice in Education" (1904). Dewey observed that teachers were increasingly being unduly influenced by fads and trends from outside of their schools. This condition is probably doubly true for teachers teaching in our era of accountability. They have been inundated with policy directives, standards, and other compliance demands.

In response to this apparent self-deprecating-other-directedness of teachers in his time, Dewey responded by saying that teachers needed to be more "adequately moved by their own ideas and intelligence" (Dewey, 1904, retrieved at https://people.ucsc.edu/~ktellez/dewey_relation.pdf. Pages not numbered).

This book makes the value of teachers relying on their own ideas and intelligence a central premise of its argument. It thinks of teacher development as a bringing-out process, not an input process. It further asserts that this notion of teachers attending to their own ideas and intelligence should be at the core of teacher preparation, induction, and education.

Teachers should be prepared to become decision makers and encouraged to see that because of their grounded and special expertise and by virtue of developing their knowledge in the communities of practice in local schools, they are better poised to think wisely about what schools do than purveyors of "outside" knowledge that purport to guide the development of teachers and their schools in generic ways.

CONCLUSION

Emphatic Review: The thesis of this book is that the national discussion about teacher induction, preparation, and development needs to change from how higher education can do a better job to how induction, preparation, and development should be resituated to local schools. This thesis is underpinned by two fundamental concepts. One, teachers do their real learning about teaching in the local schools where they work, nowhere else.

Two, teacher learning will be optimal when schools are expressly designed for teacher learning over a full career. That is, schools need to be configured as places for the development and application of teacher expertise as they are encouraged to develop their own capacities through a social learning growth mechanism called learning communities and encouraged to trust in themselves and their processes as creators of knowledge and effective decision makers.

Chapter 2

The Emergence of Teacher as Learner-Collaborator-Leader

The central focus of this chapter is to clarify the concept of teacher as a learner-collaborator-leader, its historical emergence, and how the concept contrasts with the traditional notion of a teacher who works alone in a traditional school classroom. Yes, as part of this new concept, a teacher may still be seen as an instructor, but that part of a teacher's work would be better seen as subordinate to the larger mission of teacher learning, leaning that improves instruction but also many other aspects of schooling.

Perceived in this way, the teacher is a consequential actor who, working with other teachers, is in a constant process of solving problems in schooling and continuously improving the school. This chapter's development of this concept of a teacher as learner-collaborator-leader when seen in contrast to the current traditional role will assist the reader in understanding why we need a new school model and why current approaches to teacher induction, preparation, and development, via higher education or alternative routes, are ill-conceived and ineffective.

As this book is addressed to teachers, it will attempt to clarify for them how this failure of traditional schools and higher education to focus on teacher learning has diminished the teaching profession. Adherence to traditional school assumptions and practices has perpetuated a way of life in schools that has neglected providing teachers what they most want, a career of professional growth and achievement. It has perpetuated this failure partly by using teacher preparation in higher education to get teachers to discount their own capacities in favor of following the dictates of distant authorities in government, policy circles, and higher education.

To understand how the teaching profession has gotten to this point, teachers are asked to review Table 2.1. It is intended to show the contrast

Table 2.1 A Choice for Teachers

A Career of Frustration Today	A Satisfying Career in the Future
Lack of Self-determination	Self-determination
You lack a sense of control over your work. For the most part, the nature and design of student work, its implementation, and its evaluation are dictated by legacy practices of federal, state, or local officials or publishers with whom you have little contact and who do not ask your opinion.	You have a sense of purpose and feel control over your work. You make important choices and play a key role in the design, execution, and evaluation of your work.
Sortive Evaluation	Supportive Evaluation
You feel little power over your own evaluation. You believe there are criteria included which should not be there and other important factors left out. You see the process as a way of sorting teachers and not very helpful in supporting your improvement as a professional.	You inform how you are evaluated. You have helped design the evaluation process. You play a critical role in how the process is applied. You believe the others involved in your evaluation care about you and are supporting your growth as a professional.
Teacher Technician	Teacher Professional
You see yourself as a worker/technician tasked with implementing standards, goals, curricula, lesson design, and even scripts dictating what you should say in delivering lessons to students. You are never asked to reflect on or give judgment about what is being taught, how it is taught, or the overall assumptions underlying this instructional approach.	You are a Member/Stakeholder: You feel like a respected member of a professional team. You helped the team create a vision for optimal functioning and you work collectively with it to learn and to take action to apply that learning. As part of this, you are often called upon to bring your judgment and imagination to important decision-making.
Lack of Community	Caring Community
The school you work in is large. There are many hundreds, maybe more than a thousand students and over a hundred staff. Many people don't know or care about each other. The friendships that form are part of cliques that are unrelated to the school's goals and culture. There is often animosity between groups. Student and adult behavior often shows disconnection and disregard for others. There is a lot of negative gossiping and complaining. Students' achievement is usually the outcome of compliance or competition not high engagement.	The school you work in is a deliberately designed small community with the stated purpose of creating a culture of caring where both adults and students are committed to a high level of kindness and respect for all members. Members feel connected. They believe that such a caring community is the foundation for human engagement in life and learning. Caring and engagement are seen as the basis for high academic expectations and high student achievement. Members of this community work harder but happier.

(Continued)

Table 2.1 A Choice for Teachers (Continued)

A Career of Frustration Today	A Satisfying Career in the Future
Technical Learning	Professional Learning
Your professional learning is focused on the implementation of standards created by others and preparing students for success on an array of standardized proficiency assessments and year-end standardized tests created by others. Neither you nor other teachers are asked to reflect on the value of these standardized tools nor many of the other assumptions and practices of your school. If you disagree with their use, you are regarded with suspicion. A lot of research, including research suggesting the ill-effects of standardized testing is ignored. You experience a high level of frustration and find your thoughts turning to self-protection, not aspirations for personal and professional growth.	You are aware that your school community is heavily invested in your professional learning. There is ongoing reflection on the effectiveness of a broad array of learning and schooling strategies for both students and teachers. Professional learning is embedded in your everyday routines. Research is happening everywhere. There is a collective eagerness to consider imaginative and entrepreneurial ideas for instructional change and overall school improvement. You see and feel your continuous growth as a person and a professional within this culture as you move up the stages and take on new challenges and ever greater responsibilities. You feel respect as a professional.

between where the profession is as of now, per the influence of higher education and the accountability movement, and where it might be if teachers were conceived of themselves as learner-collaborator-leader and this became their frame of reference as they worked to create a new school model.

A CHANGE IN THINKING ABOUT TEACHER LEARNING

With this set of contrasts in mind, teachers should understand that the idea of teacher development as derived of collaborative learning has been a theme in education's professional and academic literature for many decades. This book is not proposing something unheard of. The concept became especially popular in the late 1980s and early 1990s. And even in these earliest days it was presented as a contrast to thinking of teacher development as discrete, decontextualized professional development presentations in higher education or local schools.

Let's begin with two important developments in the late 1980s and early 1990s that foreshadowed big change in the professional lives of teachers and teacher education: professional learning communities, PLCs, and professional development schools, PDSs.

Scores of books and articles have been published that have explored and explained the value of an organizational approach to learning as it was manifest in and provided by "learning communities," "communities of practice," and "professional learning communities." PLCs and PDSs are largely derived of this line of research, theory, and writing. In both movements, increasing educator collaboration was a primary goal.

It is notable that much of the rationale for both movements which developed then was captured in the 1997 publication *A New Vision for Staff Development* (Sparks & Hirsh, 1997). As this book attempts to do now, *A New Vision for Staff Development* brought together many strands of research that bore on both organizational development and teacher professional development. *A New Vision for Staff Development* pointed to the need for profound cultural changes in schools and sounded a new day of sorts for teachers and teacher learning as it outlined and explained how teacher learning is correlated with student learning and why it needed to become more collaborative.

Such teacher learning was presented as intended to continuously transform schools as teachers learn more and more about the impact of their teaching on student learning and share perspectives with each other, with members of higher education, and with a broad range of community and school stakeholders, especially their students. The intended outcome was continuous change, continuous school improvement.

It was from this perspective of organizational learning that one could begin to see the commonsense reasons why teacher preparation in higher education was ineffective and is now. Higher education simply does not have the capacity to instill in teachers the most critical aspect of teaching, working as a member of a learning community. This most essential of educational experiences can only be provided by situating a novice teacher in a real community of practice for a sustained period in an actual school.

THE FAILURE OF HIGHER EDUCATION AND THE ALTERNATIVE CERTIFICATION PROCEDURES

As we consider why it would be better to move teacher preparation out of higher education, it is important to note that higher education, itself, has admitted its ineffectiveness in the preparation of teachers. Over the past few decades, there have been a remarkable number of commissions, studies, reports, blue ribbon panels, and so on, that have tried to address the issue of teacher ineffectiveness and its relationship to teacher preparation. Most of these will be referenced in due course. Each of these has, in effect, acknowledged our nation's complaint that students aren't learning what they should and that our teachers seem ineffective.

It has, in fact, come to agree with its critics in questioning why teacher preparation programs cannot take quality candidates and reliably turn them into effective teachers who actually improve students' learning (Levine, 2006). These admissions were the basis for the many recommendations that emanated from these various groups.

Regrettably, the coming of the alternative programs in teacher preparation may be seen as a symptom of the problem with teacher preparation in higher education. Few have real confidence in the work of higher education which has made the idea of an alternative all the more acceptable or appealing. Many observe that it couldn't be any worse than what higher education is doing. It should be noted, however, that in the view of this work, the alternative programs probably are worse, certainly no better.

From the standpoint of research, it should, in any case, be clear by now that these alternative routes in teacher preparation are no more effective than what happens in higher education. There have been no reports of how they have resulted in improved student learning. The fact is that these alternative routes are founded on the same mistaken notion as higher education. They attempt to prepare teachers outside the culture of a local school. They ignore the extensive research that tells us that teachers do not learn to teach outside the cultures of local schools.

In the overall, higher education's continued fumbling of teacher preparation has led Arthur Levine, former dean of Columbia University's Teachers College, to observe in his 2006 report for the American Educational Research Association, "There is a real danger that if we do not clean up our own house, America's university-based teacher education programs will disappear" (Levine, 113).

It is the contention here that the reason higher education has repeatedly failed to fix teacher preparation is because it has not recognized that it is the situating of teacher preparation in higher education that is the problem. The campuses of higher education are the wrong places for teacher preparation. It is one of the main points of this book to explain why.

In the meantime, consider this: Schools of medicine do not teach doctors *how* to provide care, hospitals do. Physicians learn about medicine in higher education. They learn the application of medicine in hospitals. Thus, we see that hospitals deliver their service in a variety of different ways. Each has different protocols and procedures. Each community of practice is different depending on its circumstances.

In schools of law, lawyers learn about the law. Lawyers learn to apply the law in law firms or other institutions of practice. Each law firms is different in the ways it serves its clients. Each has different protocols and procedures whereby novice attorneys learn the application of law and to engage courts and serve their clients. In both the cases of hospitals and law firms, the ways they do their work is an outcome of thinking done within the hospital or law firm about what works best for their circumstances and the populations they serve. Physicians and lawyers learn to practice outside their respective schools of study.

THE LEARNING OF PRACTICE MUST BE A COLLECTIVE ENTERPRISE

The same should be true for teachers and schools, but higher education interferes with this process. In higher education, students rightly learn about the subject of their interest. But then, once prospective teachers have achieved a degree in that field, it should be the local schools themselves that help them learn about how to teach students about their field of interest.

Just as with hospitals and law firms, the practical aspects of the application of expert knowledge are defined in significant measure by the unique circumstances of a hospital or law firm and the people they serve. Similarly with teachers, teachers are best prepared to apply their expert subject knowledge when they learn to practice in the context of a real community of practice that serves a real population of students with their unique strengths and needs.

A proper reconciling of this condition is to reconceive of local schools as places of teacher learning where school leaders and fellow teachers take collective responsibility for the development of teachers and help them become effective teachers. When individual teachers show weaknesses, it should cause the collective school to question itself as much as it may question the teacher.

This notion should further cause educators to question whether our teacher retention problem would be so severe if individual teachers felt secure in the knowledge that they were in a culture that assured their success and they saw that success unfolding in themselves.

When a school takes a collective responsibility for creating effective teachers, a new dynamic is introduced. Although evaluation of individual teachers would still have value, evaluating individual teachers would be of less importance than evaluating the overall culture of learning within a school. The effect of this would be to keep the eyes of all members on what really drives teacher effectiveness, culture. Members would always be asking, "Is the culture of our school inherently conducive to the creation of effective teachers?" and "How can we do a better job?"

Seen from this perspective, the current focus on evaluating individual teachers may be seen as the failure that it is. Teaching is hard work. Mastering it is hard work. If that hard work is attempted in a school culture that is not cohesive in its support of teacher learning, failure or profound discouragement is a very understandable outcome.

Consider how teacher morale would be different in a school that took collective responsibility for teacher development and focused on evaluating school culture for its effectiveness in creating effective teachers. Consider how it would be different if teachers were empowered and having conversations about the conditions of their own learning, their own personal growth, and how that was supported by the school culture.

Consider further that those who lead law firms and hospitals are constantly thinking about the practices and protocols of their institutions with respect to how they will inform and influence the development of their intern members. Local schools should have the same perspective. Like it or not, when novice teachers enter a local school culture, it is that culture that will begin to define their development. With this understanding, school leaders must then begin to consider how that culture needs to be "rewired" (Gruenert & Whitaker, 2015, 2017) to provide for the optimum development of novice teachers.

TEACHER ISOLATION FAILS TEACHERS

Traditional schools do not see themselves as having such a mission for teacher learning. Yes, there are some induction programs and, perhaps, novice teacher mentor programs, but in the overall, these are mostly incidental add-ons that are not part of an overall, systematic approach to teacher development. After a year of this fledgling support, most second-year teachers, if they have lasted that long, will settle into their isolation and resort to doing what they incidentally see others doing in their school. And like the teachers they see around them, they activate the mental models of what they have seen in classroom throughout their own education, individual teachers teaching in closed-door classrooms.

The deeper problem is that this notion of the individual, isolated teacher teaching in a closed-door room is reinforced by their teacher preparation. Higher education teacher preparation is, as will be documented, all about preparing the individual teacher as a singular soldier and how to function as such in a traditional school in their customary isolated situations. Little to nothing is done to alert teachers to the need for schools to become more collaborative and for teachers to become change agents in obsolete schools.

What is especially counterproductive in teacher learning is requiring teachers to go to a teacher preparation program for a year or so before they enter a school. This is, as attested to by most teachers, because what is learned in teacher education programs is so out of context that it ultimately has little application to the challenges a teacher faces in actual classrooms and schools. This, of course, is an old story. Going to a preparation program in higher education actually interferes with and delays what novice teachers really need, membership in a community of practice where a stated purpose is the development of teachers as they work together to improve the practices and protocols of their schools.

WHAT TEACHERS DO TOGETHER

Thus, it is at this juncture that the thesis of this book needs restating. *It is the entirety of a school culture that produces effective teachers, and schools with authentic learning communities produce the cultures that produce effective teachers.* This reminder is made to further the observation about the failure of higher education to effectively prepare teachers *because of its focuses on individual teachers.* Proper teacher preparation should focus on novice teachers learning about the learning community process and how to work effectively with other teachers.

One of the ways we can see why it is a mistake to focus on individual teachers is by looking at the research. As this book will present over and over again, research on teachers working collaboratively shows that it reliably results in improvement in student learning compared to control groups where teachers do not work collaboratively and have poorer outcomes. Such research should move us to infer that what we need to do is focus on how teachers work together for the best possible results.

In the course of this work, we will see that over and over again, policy people and, then, higher education focus on rational and quantitative standards and guidelines for individual teachers. We will see that very few of the recommendations that have emerged from these policy reports focus on how teachers work together or the unquantifiable benefits of bringing people together in a process of solving local problems but also developing capacity.

Evidence of overlooking the power of teachers working together and its capacity-building effects may be seen in Arthur Levine's report for the American Educational Research Association (2006), *Educating School Teachers*, which provided five recommendations:

1. Transform education schools from ivory towers to professional schools focused on classroom practice.

2. Focus on student achievement as the primary measure of teacher education program success.
3. Rebuild teacher education programs around the skills and knowledge that promote classroom learning; make five-year teacher education programs the norm.
4. Establish effective mechanisms for teacher education quality control.
5. Close failing teacher education programs and expand excellent programs by creating incentives for outstanding students and career changers to enter teacher education programs at doctoral universities.

The first observation that must be made about these recommendations is they that they do not question the validity of higher education teacher preparation. This is curious. Reading the full report, one sees that Levine does come close to questioning higher education's role, but ultimately, when recommendations are made, he does not challenge it. One wonders if Dr. Levine, who was the former dean of Columbia University's Teachers College, just couldn't bring himself face the reality.

Rather, his recommendations focus on improving higher education's approach to preparing teachers (Levine, 2006, pp. 102–111). There is no reference in these recommendations to how teachers work together, no reference to collaboration, learning communities, teacher teams, or anything similar. When one considers that the research on teachers working collaboratively consistently shows improvement in student achievement, how is such an oversight rationalized?

In this important report for one of the leading educational organizations in the world, there is no focus on the most important factor in teacher learning, the culture of the schools where teachers work. It ignores the reality that all professionals learn their work in communities of practice, not in remote locations where practice is talked about.

In the report, Levine, himself, observed what has previously been suggested here, "In major professions, like law and medicine, induction is considered the responsibility of the hiring organization, not the school that prepared the new professional" (Levine, 2006, p. 44). Yet, Dr. Levine's recommendations are silent on what happens in the cultures of local schools where teachers actually get jobs.

Unfortunately, this perspective is not isolated. Consider the National Board for Professional Teaching Standards. It provides certificates to individual teachers for their efforts at individual development. Yes, this is good on one level. But the overall emphasis on the individual teacher exposes the same flaw that is in Levine's report and others: It focuses on individual practice.

In emphasizing individual practice, it misleads all involved into thinking that the success of schools is mostly about the practice of individual teachers.

While effective individual teachers are certainly important, research shows that the something else is much more important. Reams of research show that the schools most successful in advancing student learning are schools with high levels of teacher collaboration. It's the collaboration, not individual performance that makes the big difference.

A similar example comes not from a report but from one of the most popular works on teacher education in recent years. This work is Linda Darling-Hammond's *Powerful Teacher Education: Lessons from Exemplary Programs* (2006). Again, like Levine's report, this work is fundamentally flawed because it affirms the important role of higher education in teacher preparation. In the course of developing that affirmation, it clarifies what Darling-Hammond believes are the "Common Components of Powerful Teacher Education."

- A common, clear vision of good teaching permeates all course work and clinical experiences.
- Well-defined standards of practice and performance are used to guide and evaluate coursework and clinical work.
- Curriculum is grounded in knowledge of child and adolescent development, learning, social contexts, and subject matter pedagogy, taught in the context of practice.
- Extended clinical experiences are carefully developed to support the ideas and practices presented in simultaneous, closely interwoven coursework.
- Explicit strategies help students (1) confront their own deep-seated beliefs and assumptions about learning and students and (2) learn about people different from themselves.
- Strong relationships, common knowledge, and shared beliefs link school- and university-based faculty.
- Case study methods, teacher research, performance assessments, and portfolio evaluation apply learning to real problems of practice (p. 41).

What is regrettable about this list of guidelines for good teaching and good teacher education is, again, that it affirms higher education's role in teacher education and, in so doing, sees it happening on higher education campuses and focusing on the preparation of individual teachers as individual actors.

It would be hard to argue with the value of any one point, but as with Levine's report, something huge is missing. There is no mention of what teachers do together, no acknowledgment of the socio-cultural impact of work in a local school culture. Most significantly there is no reference to concepts like collaboration, learning communities, teacher teams, or the like.

While it is certain that Darling-Hammond and others would likely say they agree that collaboration in schools is important, it is notable that it is not important enough to be a point of focus in her list. One can only infer that for

Darling-Hammond, teacher preparation is conceived of as higher education getting individual new teachers to have the right visions, frames of reference, standards, and strategies.

While it is quite understandable that they would want this, higher education fails to see that these objectives are wrapped around an enormous oversight. Teachers will ultimately learn to teach, for better or worse, in the local schools where they work, not from the polished visions, guidelines, essential knowledge, or standards they were exposed to in higher education.

This focus on the individual teacher's performance may be found in many other prominent reports on how to improve teacher education. They will be referenced in due course. But, this focus on individual practice is not universally true. To clarify that the standard of checking for references to collaboration is not an unfair standard may be seen by a review of another set of recommendations.

Those of the Consortium for Policy Research in Education clearly show a different perspective. If the reader notices the word choice below, it becomes apparent that the Center does recognize the importance of teachers working together. The Center recommends school cultures

- Where teachers worked together, sharing ideas and responsibilities and enjoying exchanges of information that included joint discussions of their practice.
- Where teacher networks provided access to a "professional community" in which their expertise and experiences were respected and where they could be active participants in a professional discourse about improving their practice.
- Where schools and colleges collaborated effectively to create and implement teacher training and professional development programs.
- Where professional development schools, based on the model of teaching hospital, brought novice and experienced teachers together with college faculty to improve professional practice through observation, experimentation, reflection, and coaching.
- Where teachers themselves, in cooperation with colleagues and college faculty, are engaged in education research that informs their practice
- Where teachers meet the standards of certification proposed by the National Board for Professional Teaching Standards (NBPTS), a process which in itself would provide a considerable amount of professional development. (Consortium for Policy Research in Education, 1995)

This different perspective from the Consortium for Policy Research in Education (Corcoran, 1995) helps us see two things: (1) the ideas in this book are not out of the mainstream and (2) the observations of The Consortium for

Policy Research are part of a growing recognition in some circles that what teachers do together is at the core of successful schools. The conversation should not be about improving higher education. It should be about a school model where teacher collaboration is the basis of school culture and teacher development is an explicit purpose of the school.

RESEARCH CALLED FOR A COLLABORATIVE APPROACH

This tendency to focus on the conduct and frames of reference of individual teachers is the core flaw in higher education's attempt to prepare teachers. What makes it even more troublesome is that higher education has persisted in this focus during a period when research in and outside of education indicated a need to reconsider how we organize our institutions from corporations to schools.

The central message of this research was the value of distributed power and leadership in organization. It concluded that all members of an organization must have a sense of ownership, must think of themselves as agents of continuous change and improvement (Deming, 1983; Schlechty, 2011; Senge, 1991; Senge et al., 2000, 2012).

One has to wonder how all of this research and writing did not find its way into the thinking of policy makers and schools of education. Why there was no effort to incorporate this thinking into teacher preparation? Why it was not seen as more powerful than lists of standards and guidelines? Why did it never occurred to any, "Maybe we need to rely more on the thinking of teachers."

The fact is that there were any number of researchers and scholars that attempted to explain the application of this new organization thinking to schools and called for schools to be made into learning organizations (Schlechtey, 2011; Senge, 1991; Senge et al., 2000, 2012). But for policy makers and higher education none of it ever took on the power that developed around the accountability movement.

This failure to embrace the merits of bringing teachers together in the learning organization model became evident in many research projects. What was observed in our schools was that from classroom to classroom, from school to school, teaching and learning was uneven. Some teachers were strong, some were weaker. Some students were learning. Some were learning a lot less (Morris & Hiebert, 2011, p. 6).

Most significantly, teachers didn't know what was happening in other classrooms. Teachers worked in isolation from one another. This condition inspired both laymen and scholars to ask, how can teachers have such varied frames of reference about the nature of effective instruction? How can so many credentialed teachers not be able to impart effective instruction? Is there no universal agreement on what constitutes effective instruction?

What is worst about these conditions is that this approach is what teachers were taught in higher education about how teachers do their jobs. It reflects the focus of higher education on preparing individual teachers as traditional teachers. It reflects higher education affirmation of the traditional school model. These are teachers who do not look to influence school-wide change but who are accustomed to working in isolation doing what teachers have done for nearly a century.

This focus on the practice of the individual teacher then reinforces what these aspiring teachers saw and learned about teaching in their own primary and secondary schooling, individual teachers doing their own thing, not working together. This is exactly what our aspiring teachers do not need, and higher education does little to nothing to change this perspective. By focusing on individual teacher qualification, characteristics, and professional performance, higher education has ignored research that tells us that it is not individual performance but what teachers do together that matters most for student learning.

As will be detailed, this book's thesis contradicts the current efforts of nearly every approach suggested by teacher training programs in higher education, by private teacher training programs, or by policy advocates. In the overall, all of these entities have looked to improve teacher education by intensifying the focus on a number of particulars: Improving candidate quality, raising academic standards, providing essential knowledge, and increasing clinical experience are among the most commonly cited. Notice the focus on the characteristics and performance of individual teachers.

CULTURES AND SYSTEMS ARE IN CONTROL

While all of these particulars have a striking commonsense quality, what has emerged from their application is an irony. Schools have gotten better quality novice teachers. They have not gotten more effective teaching. Why we haven't gotten better teaching can be best understood if we look at how higher education has overlooked the cultures of schools and/or failed to recognize the power that systems and cultures have over teacher learning. We can get a better understanding of the impact of this oversight by considering a brief review of systems theory and how it bears on cultural effects.

Systems theory tells us that it is not the individual parts of a system, in this case the teacher, that control outcomes. Rather, it is the system itself—how the parts come together and relate to one another. This view of nature and organizations has a complicated history, but, briefly put, it became popular in the United States in the 1970s when the systems theorist W. Edwards Deming

(1983) used systems theory to revolutionize automobile manufacturing in Japan. In large measure his contribution accounts for the success of Japanese cars, especially Toyotas, in the United States.

Since Deming's success, a number of other systems theorists have made important contributions on the idea that outcomes are controlled not so much by individual parts but by the relationship of those parts, by the overall system and/or culture, itself. An important implication of this view is that all members of an organization or culture need to be considered, involved in, and take responsibility for the success of the system or organization.

One of Deming's most important admonitions was that "everyone must be involved." Thus from the board room to the assembly line, organizational members are pulled together in teams to think about the improvement of their work. The implication for schools and the contribution of teachers is clear.

An example that illustrates the application of systems theory to an educational culture would be helpful. One such commonly cited example comes from the study of the effects of teachers working in teams by Gallimore et al. (2009). They studied the effects of teachers working in teams on the improvement of teaching techniques and student achievement. In presenting their results they cited similar work by Grossman and McDonald (2008) who emphasized the importance of "the organizational contexts in which work takes shape" (Gallimore et al., 2009, p. 538).

Gallimore et al. (2009) reported the positive effects of an organizational structure where teachers, working in teams, make interacting with each other a standard part of their working lives as they inquire into their impact on student learning. In this study, the researchers detailed the school-wide improvements in teaching techniques and student achievement. It was also reported that, working in teams, teachers were able to know what each other was doing. Their teaching techniques and goals were shared, and unevenness in learning was reduced.

More examples of research that focuses on how teachers work together will be presented in due course. The main point here is that it is research such at this that highlights the importance of teachers working together. It is research that puts into question the strategy of higher education and others to focus on the characteristics and performance of individual teachers. It suggests an inadequate focus on a much more powerful factor, the systems and cultures in which individuals perform their duties, interact with peers, and develop professionally.

Ross C. Anderson (Anderson in Zhao, 2016), at the Educational Policy Improvement Center, confirms this emphasis on the social component of learning and creativity in a recent essay. He explained, "Research shows that creativity grows out of interactions between an individual and the world he or she works and plays in. It also grows from relationships between the individual and other human beings" (p. 107). He goes on to cite Fischer,

Giacacardi, Eden, Sugimoto, and Ye who insist, "creativity does not happen inside a person's head, but in the interaction between a person's thoughts and a socio-cultural context" (2005, p. 485).

The importance of this socio-cultural-systems context emerges in another way. By focusing on the individual characteristics and performance of individual teachers in teacher preparation, higher education preparation programs likely engender in novice teachers a greater sense of being on their own in the early days of their careers. These novice teachers do not learn to see their own development as a social process of interacting within a community of learners. Nor do they see their development as an effect of culture.

Rather, they come to see their development as highly individualistic, as a result of being on one's own behind the door of their classroom. One has to wonder how those early days of teaching would be different for novice teachers if they saw themselves as part of a teaching team or learning community that was explicitly devoted to their development.

This view of the teacher as an individual actor has been compounded by popular works such as Brill's *Class Warfare: Inside the Fight to Fix America's Schools* (2011) or Elizabeth Green's *To Make a Better Teacher* (2012) both of which give lengthy considerations of what is at stake in the creation of effective teachers but give scant consideration to the value of professional learning communities, a condition that provides teachers what they want, long-term professional growth, and students what they need, increased focus on leaning. The effect of these works has been to contribute to a controversy that considers teacher development as an extraordinary mystery. But it is not.

There is increasing evidence that this controversy may be over something that is more apparent than real. Over and over again, research shows that the failure of teachers to be or become effective may be attributed in large measure to their *not* working together. The contention of this book and the research it will present is that much of the variability in student learning can be explained by the fact that most teachers work in traditional schools where there is *not* a high level of teacher collaboration and teacher learning is not an explicit purpose of the school.

Moreover, there is evidence that teacher learning has little to do with guidelines and standards for individual teachers. What teacher preparation programs try to do in the application of all of these standards and guidelines for individual teachers simply does not translate into novice teachers who actually become effective teachers. Famed economist Eric Hanushek long ago declared the lack of correlation.

> Extensive research shows that commonly measured attributes of teachers, such as more than three or four years of experience, master's degrees, and even state certification, are not related to effectiveness. In fact, all of the regulations that

go into defining what is needed to be a fully credentialed teacher neither screen out bad teachers nor ensure that credentialed teacher are any more effective than uncredentialed teachers. (*EducationNext*, "An Effective Teacher in Every Classroom," Summer, 2010. Vol. 10, No. 3)

IT ALL LEADS US TO A NEW SCHOOL MODEL

As this book develops the superiority of the learning community model in teacher preparation and development, it will clarify a choice. Our society can continue to employ the current model of educating our teachers in decontextualized situations in either higher education or alternative models, or we can undertake a new school model which would replace the traditional school and have the explicit purpose of educating two groups, students *and* teachers. A careful look at this issue will ultimately show that for a number of reasons the logical choice is to educate and prepare our teachers in local schools.

Again, underlying the logic of choosing to educate our teachers in local schools is a stubborn reality: For better or worse, it is in local schools where our teachers actually acquire their habits of practice and learn to teach, not on the campuses of higher education or in other remote alternative programs that look to prepare teachers outside the context of an actual school.

And, if our schools fail to make teacher learning a primary and intrinsic purpose of schools, then teachers will learn to disassociate personal and professional growth from what they do with students. They will continue to do their best in traditional ways, mark their time in isolation, and try to get through their days without incident.

Trying to understand how teachers learn from this systems/cultural perspective is not really an intellectual reach. Long strands of research in anthropology, sociology, and organizational theory tell us that, over time, it is that context in a community or a community of practice that will become the primary source of a teacher's learning about the work of teaching (Lave & Wenger, 1991).

Consistent with this systems-socio-cultural theory of learning, anthropologist William F. Hanks advises leaders of organizations, "Rather than asking what kinds of cognitive processes and conceptual structures are involved, they [should] ask what kinds of social engagements provide the proper context for learning to take place" (Lave & Wenger, 1991, p. 14). Leaders in higher education teacher preparation programs would be well disposed to steer their thinking away from the cognitive processes and conceptual structure they try to influence through standards and focus on the systems-socio-cultures of schools, the real places where teachers are formed.

There is no getting around the reality that when new members enter a culture, they will be exposed to some explicit teaching about cultural norms to help them behave correctly. We see this in manuals and handbooks. But even more, they will be influenced by implicit messages that are more forceful but unrecognized as directives. Organizational theorist Edgar Schein explains

> Perhaps the most intriguing aspect of culture as a concept is that it points us to phenomena that are below the surface, that are powerful in their impact but invisible and to a considerable degree unconscious. Culture creates within us mindsets and frames of reference . . . culture is to a group what personality or character is to an individual. (p. 14)

The reality of this condition is underscored by years of research on culture. When individuals enter a new culture, they adapt based on the implicit signals they receive.

New members to a culture begin doing things the way they see them being done around them. Thus, in every school they enter, teachers will learn and begin to abide by "the way we do things around here" (Deal & Kennedy, p. 4). Hanks underscores this perspective explaining,

> Even in cases where a fixed doctrine is transmitted [standards and guidelines], the ability of a community to reproduce itself through the training process derives not from the doctrine but from the maintenance of certain modes of co-participation in which it is embedded. (Hanks in Lave & Wenger, 1991, p. 16)

A CHOICE

Traditional School Isolation or Developing Learner-Collaborators-Leaders

If teacher educators respect the overwhelming power of socio-cultural learning in schools, we should then ask about where and how it can be best provided. Would it be better to educate our teachers in school cultures where teachers are actively collaborating, creating their own knowledge, and making critical decision on how to improve student learning?

Or should we continue to employ the old, traditional school model where teachers are prepared on remote campuses disconnected from the context of a local school only to then enter a local schools where they work in insolation behind closed doors and receive only reactive and episodic "professional development" which is more often than not disconnected from the challenges of classroom instruction and has little effect (TNTP, 2015)?

CONCLUSION

This book advocates two outcomes: One, a reconception of teacher as a learner-collaborator-leader, and two, a new school model that is explicitly designed for teacher learning. *Teacher learning is not about individuals. It is about school cultures. The true source of teacher effectiveness is participation in an authentic collaborative community of practice in a local school teaching among teachers teaching.*

There is some question about whether Peter Drucker really did say this although he is commonly reputed to have done so. www.quora.com/Did-Peter-Drucker-actually-say-culture-eats-strategy-for-breakfast-and-if-so-where-when?

Chapter 3

Toward an Intentionally Developmental School

Chapter 1 was about the advent of thinking of teachers as learners-collaborators-leaders and how this frequently written about concept never came to prevail in most schools. Instead, the accountability movement and higher education worked together to maintain the status quo which restricted teachers' working together and teacher leadership in their schools.

Chapter 2 moved the focus toward how we might conceive of a school that reverses these conditions, schools that are predicated on teachers working together in communities of learning with all of the capacity building and professional development that makes for an intentionally developmental culture.

The idea of having local schools provide teachers not only a professional-grade induction into teaching but also a full career of professional development presents another occasion where research largely outside the field of education must be applied. Such is the case in introducing the idea of an "intentionally developmental organization." This term is borrowed from the famous psychologists and organizational theorists Robert Kegan and Lisa Laskow Lahey (2016) as developed in their work, *An Everyone Culture: Becoming a Deliberately Developmental Organization*. This book is a report on an academic study of organizations that were explicitly designed to develop their members.

The gist of Kegan and Laskow Lahey's study is that organizational leaders have discovered that organizations function better, produce more, and earn more, when growth and development for all members is built into the culture of the organization. One might say that by virtue of any person joining such an organization, that person will then be drawn into a growth process that is at once organizational in breadth but also very individual. Growth is a fundamental force of the organization's culture. It is a condition of membership, and it is a condition into which all members are immersed.

Of course, this condition stands in contrast to organizations that become harbors of stasis as members do their work with a pro forma spirit that gets the job done but, at the same time, does little to advance the organization's productivity, innovation, or market edge. Like many other studies, Kegan and Laskow Lahey's study addresses the question of how organizations improve. Their answer is that organizations improve when cultures are constructed that grow all the members in the organization. It's not just about key stakeholders. It's about everyone (2016)!

In their research, all of the organizations studied are commercial businesses, but Kegan and Laskow Lahey's study of them automatically brings to mind the viability of such a concept for schools. The study leads us to ask whether schools could become deliberately developmental organizations where membership in the organization automatically demands and leads all members to growth and away from stasis.

Can schools become organizations where all the members are always pushing and helping each other toward higher levels of development? Most importantly, can educational leaders begin to recognize that the success of schools is so directly correlated with the development of teachers that such development must be an intrinsic function of the school, a function for which all members are responsible?

GOOD SCHOOLS GROW EFFECTIVE TEACHERS

As explained earlier, it has been observed that there is a gap in the national discussion about teacher education and preparation. That gap has to do with teachers' capacities and the development of those capacities. It was earlier observed that most in education seem to think that teachers have low capacity.

There is evidence of this in the behavior of central authorities and higher education where they communicate to teachers that they need to be told what to do. Teachers can't succeed by their own devices. There is the idea that in order to get teachers to be effective, outsiders have to institute all sorts of guidelines, standards, and tests to get teachers to do what these outsiders think needs to be done to improve schools.

There is, however, research, to be presented shortly, that suggests the opposite. Teachers function at their highest levels when they are part of collaborative cultures that are focused on overall school improvement. Like those organizations described by Kegan and Laskow Lahey, in these schools teachers see their work as part of an organizational effort to continuously get better. They do not see their work as that of an individual actor whose primary work is to focus on what happens in their classroom.

Such schools look to draw on teachers' capacity to think, analyze, and learn in order to make key decisions about what happens in classrooms and the school overall. In these schools teachers can, in effect, engage in an interactive social process within learning communities that grows them as they create knowledge and enable themselves to rise to any level necessary to effectively teach and run schools. Most importantly, they can do this without reliance on outsiders telling them what to do.

With respect to the gap in the national discussion about teacher preparation and effective teaching, one has to wonder why the research that focuses on teacher capacity and its great potential has not had a more prominent role in that discussion. Like that of a number of other organizational scholars, Kegan and Laskow Lahey's work studies organizations that focus on capacity development as an intrinsic feature of the organization. The concept of a deliberately developmental organization points the way to a more evolved concept of school.

HIGHER EDUCATION HAS FOCUSED ON TEACHER DEFICIENCY, NOT CAPACITY

The upcoming discussion of the conditions that stand to develop teacher capacity requires that we momentarily revisit our previous discussion of higher education's focus on teachers as individual actors who need higher education to teach them what they need to know and be able to do. It is fundamentally a strategy of remediation for passive recipients sitting in classroom desks. In an out-of-context setting, aspiring teachers are "taught" what they need to know and be able to do in order to be teachers. They are taught that only higher education can provide them this teaching.

But, of course, there is another perspective. Teachers could be taught that the development of teacher capacity is the central point of teacher preparation and that it comes from their interaction with other teachers in an active process called *learning communities*. We all know that work is usually more efficient and effective when people join together with focus on a common purpose.

It's called team work, and the benefits of team work around a common purpose are supported by not only common sense but also a long history of organizational research. More and more, those benefits are being recognized and configured for application in schools, especially in recent years (DuFour et al., 2006; Fullan & Hargreaves, 2012; Reeves, 2010; Schmoker, 2006, 2016).

Much of the research cited above finds little in teacher preparation, however. Why it plays little role becomes evident if we ask where are novice teachers most likely to learn *how* to work together and apply all of the positive effects to schooling? Will aspiring teachers learn it on a college campus taking generic classes where they talk about teaching? Or, will they learn it best in a local school where they get an individualized induction into learning community culture and the common purpose of solving the real, on-the-ground problems associated with instruction, schooling, and student learning?

The fact is that novice teachers cannot learn this *how* of working together or the habits of mind and practice that are inherent to a learning community in a higher education setting. They certainly cannot learn it in an alternative setting. There are three reasons for this lack of capacity. One, higher education students are a disparate group. They come to their higher education programs from various backgrounds and then go their separate ways when the program ends.

There is no time to develop the habits of an authentic community learning. Even if a higher education program were to contrive some group or "community learning" experiences for a short period, there is not enough time to develop a true cultural effect and to develop the habits of mind and practice that would come from long-term participation in a real community of learners.

To fully grasp the effect of this disparity, one has only to compare the year or so higher education preparation programs have with their students to the many years teachers will spend in a school where they work. Only one of these situations has the capacity to instill cultural learning, the local school. Higher education does not. One has to ask, then, why we would invest the time to prepare teachers in a remote higher education environment that does not have what it takes to mold teachers in ways that will be of value and sustained throughout their careers.

The second reason has to do with sustaining the learning of aspiring teachers. An aspiring teacher may intellectually encounter some very good values, concepts, and even practices in a higher education or alternative teacher preparation program, but the likelihood of those values, concepts, and practices being sustained and further developed in a teacher's place of employment is low.

The reason is the variability of programs. There is high variability in teacher education programs. There is also high variability in the cultures of local schools (Levine, 2006). The likelihood of a novice teacher being hired into a local school that emphasizes the same values, concepts, and practices that were emphasized in higher education is very low.

Even if a teacher enters a highly collaborative school to start their career, the likelihood of that school emphasizing the same values, concepts, or practices of a higher education program is still very low. Schools rightly have their own priorities and protocols that are the outcome of local thinking.

The idea that higher education teacher preparation programs can generically prepare teachers to fit into such schools is far-fetched. Why try to do it, when we could simply prepare teachers in schools where what they learn in the early years of their intern work will truly be in line with the values of the school and contribute to the latter years of their development?

A third reason goes back to Dewey. Teacher preparation in a higher education situation implicitly reinforces the idea that local schools should depend on knowledge that comes from outer sources, principally, the university or central government agencies. What worsens the matter is that when novice teachers come to realize the irrelevance of the theoretical learning they did in their teacher preparation program, they may become disposed to thinking that all such book learning is irrelevant to what they do day to day. In how many schools do we see teachers passing books about education around?

In our current custom of preparing teachers on the remote campuses of higher education or alternative programs, a novice teacher is then put in the position of having to relearn in order to adapt to her real working environment. Thus, the time and effort invested by an individual teacher in higher education stands to be nullified by entry into this real school culture. Time, effort, and money have been wasted, and the novice teacher is left to ask why all the money was spent to learn things that don't eventually get applied in the new environment.

It is this reality of cultural learning that ultimately must lead us to choosing to educate our teachers in local schools. If local schools are reconfigured to be intentionally developmental cultures explicitly designed for teacher preparation and development, this waste of time and money could be eliminated.

RESEARCH SUPPORTS RELOCATION

The fact is, however, that the common sense of situating teacher preparation and development in local schools is also underscored by research that reaches back decades. Again and again this research confirms that people are more effective when they work together. As far back as 1937, May and Doob (1937) published their research in *Cooperation and Competition* which demonstrated that people working in cooperation achieved better outcomes than people working alone.

Numerous works from anthropology, sociology, and psychology have come to support the same conclusion. Anticipating and influencing the birth of the PLC and PDS movements in the field of education, James Moffett's *Student-Centered Language Arts* (1968) program was published and became a popular adoption in many schools throughout the nation. Therein students and teachers worked in small groups.

This move in education was supported by the research of Johnson and Johnson which was published in *Working Together and Working Alone: Cooperative, Competitive, and Individualistic Learning* (1975) and gave further evidence of how students and teachers working in cooperative groups stood to learn more and achieve better outcomes.

Unfortunately, back in the 1970s and 1980s, such research was new to educators and not perceived as thoroughly validated. Moreover, it was presented to school leaders as one of many options for restructuring schools that emerged after the stir caused by *A Nation at Risk* (1983). Seeing teacher collaboration as just one option among many for restructuring schools, many schools did not choose it. Moreover, although numerous grants were provided to schools to initiate programs that involved high levels of teacher collaboration and, in some cases, have students do the same, they were not long lived.

In most cases, these grants, intended to spur change, were enacted with school leaders having minimal conceptual insight or understanding of the group or team process, and when the grant money ran out, schools went back to the traditional practices they had been doing before the grant (Supovitz & Weinbaum, 2008; Kelly et al., 2009). For many school leaders the collaboration movement was just another passing fad they had to deal with to keep federal money coming into their districts.

As the research for learning communities in schools achieved greater and greater clarity and increasing practice, higher education did little to recognize the implications of this nascent but growing trend. Aspiring teachers were not taught to anticipate their involvement in learning communities once they took employment in actual schools.

They continued to be prepared to be lone actors in the tradition of the isolated teacher behind the closed door of a classroom in a traditional school. Thus, when they got to their schools, novice teachers did not look for such involvement. They looked to teach as they were taught in the traditional schools they went to.

While higher education continues to prepare its teachers as lone actors, the professional learning community movement and the professional development school movement have changed how these innovations should be perceived. Yes, school leaders may still be sensitive to compliance issues that keep federal money coming to their districts, but their perception that greater teacher collaboration or learning communities are just another fad is no longer tenable. *We have reached a period where we can say the research on the effectiveness of teachers working collaboratively is conclusive. It is clearly the best way to structure a school for improving student achievement.*

TEACHER COLLABORATION
PRODUCES BETTER RESULTS

The number of more recent studies which have come to attribute improved student learning to the collaboration of teachers is ever growing. While a full review of this literature is beyond the scope of this book, some highlights are in order. It is noteworthy that as the examples to be given are relatively recent (last twenty years), it makes one wonder why this research did not have more influence on higher education teacher preparation and the many panels which have studied teacher preparation in the last two decades. It all suggests the need for a new school model comprising learning-collaborator-leaders.

An assortment of smaller studies of individual schools or districts has reported student achievement improvement. Frequently cited examples include that of Wheelan and Tilin (1999) who studied a high-risk school and found "faculty groups functioning at higher levels of development have students who perform better on standardized achievement measures" (p. 59).

Morris and Hiebert (2012), who attempted to confront large variation in classroom instruction, studied teachers using "shared instructional products" that were "jointly constructed" which translated their cooperative approach into better, and especially more even, outcomes from classroom to classroom. Trimble et al. (2000), who also studied a school with at-risk students reported "changed classroom practices" and "increased student performance" as a result of teachers working in team structures (p. 1).

Larger studies looked at student achievement results for a greater numbers of schools to determine if there were correlations between teachers working in professional groups and rising student achievement. Gruenert (2005) who studied the relationship of testing outcomes and collaborative cultures in eighty-one schools in Indiana found a significant correlation between faculties that worked collaboratively and rising student achievement.

Even larger studies have reviewed a range of individual studies. Vescio et al. (2008) completed a review of eight other studies which focused on the impact of PLCs on teaching practices and student learning. They reported "all eight studies . . . that examined the relationship between teachers' participation in PLCs and student achievement found that student learning improved" (86). More such studies will be reviewed in due course.

Significant with regard to this book's thesis is that a second aspect of many of these studies which report improved student learning also reported improved teacher learning. Like, but even before the Trimble et al.'s (2000) study, Hord (1991) reported extensive learning benefits for teachers. She explained,

For staff being part of a professional learning community reduces teacher isolation, increases commitment to the mission and goals of the school, creates shared responsibility for the total development of the students, creates professional learning that defines good teaching and classroom practice, and enhances understanding of course content and teacher roles.

While doing this, it also, tellingly, increased teacher satisfaction and morale while reducing absenteeism (p. 1).

This sampling of studies only begins to make the point that schools where teachers work in collaborative communities provide both teachers and students the best conditions for learning. Yet, the number of schools that continue to operate as traditional schools where teacher collaboration is marginal and episodic or just pretend far outnumber schools derived of collaborative learning cultures.

This slowness in the proliferation of a practice supported by research may be attributed in large measure to higher education. These institutions of higher education that claim to convey the "essential knowledge" do little to convey to their students that research tells us that learning communities are the real foundation to teacher development and school success, not teachers as lone actors.

Higher education teacher preparation programs fail to introduce their students to the idea that teachers can grow their own capacity and create their own knowledge through the learning community process, knowledge that will have much greater relevance to the conditions their local schools confront. In effect, they steer teachers away from recognizing their own deepest and most important capacities. The idea of reinventing the traditional school is rarely considered.

REAL LEARNING IS ABOUT PARTICIPATION IN COMMUNITIES OF PRACTICE

The idea that we need a new school model brings us to a fine point about the nature of learning. The "doing-learning" is quite different from the "information learning" of most teacher preparation programs. When a teacher candidate does her preparation learning on the job among teachers teaching and learning as a community, there is no issue of transfer because what is learned is less about information and more about habits of mind and practice.

It has behind it the force of culture and, in the best circumstances, an intentionally developmental culture. And while information is a component of habits of practice, it is a different kind of learning. It is a product of doing, among others who are doing. It is not about listening or short-term field observations.

The abundance of data supporting the value of schools operating as collaborative cultures actually suggests a revision of the common concept of learning not only for students but also for teachers. That common concept of learning that pervades our schools (and our society) and higher education teacher preparation defines learning as the acquisition of new information and practices. Thus, in traditional schools, professional development presents teachers new information about learning and how to teach. The emphasis is put on individuals acquiring informational knowledge and skills.

There is a contrasting view. There are many strands of research which tells us that real learning has less to do with knowing and more to do with participating. That is, the very act of participating in a community of practice, a culture, instills a knowledge that is not informational and in many respects may not even be conscious. This notion is foundational to the concept of an intentionally developmental culture.

It is what Polanyi (1969) referred to as "tacit knowledge." This is a knowledge that is better explained not as some information unit that can be recalled but rather as perspectives, inclinations, mindsets, dispositions, and habits of mind and practice that are quietly acquired by the act of participating and all of the complex give-and-take and socialization implicit in the concept.

Tacit knowledge is a knowledge that is clarified by noting the difference between "knowing" and "know-how," between "remembering," and "instinctive practice." The act of participating is at the same time the act of learning even though it is not explicitly instructional. Tacit knowledge is "what we do around here" that is learned via participation. Learning and participation cannot be separated as higher education attempts to do in teacher preparation. Higher education has low capacity for providing authentic participation.

Convergent with this notion of tacit knowledge is a long-standing agreement among organizational theorists that professionals do their real learning about professional practice in communities of practice, not in institutions that teach *about* professional practice. Of course, the most commonly cited example of such professional learning is that of intern physicians in hospitals. But when one thinks about it, it applies to nearly every profession. Again, as Levine explained, "In major professions, like law and medicine, induction is the responsibility of the hiring organization, not the school that prepared the new professional" (Levine, 2006, p. 44).

A review of the literature which explains the value of participation as providing the essential knowledge for practice would make for extensive reading. A good start on that reading might include *Situated Learning: Legitimate Peripheral Participation* (Lave & Wenger, 1991) or *Cultivating Communities of Practice: A Guide to Managing Knowledge* (Wenger et al., 2002).

There is also an excellent essay entitled "Fires in the Mind: Open Education, the Long Tail, and Learning 2.0" (Brown & Adler, 2008) which clarifies the fundamental social nature of authentic learning. The organizational theory perspective is also well developed in Senge's *The Fifth Discipline: The Art & Science of The Learning Organization* (1991) and later Senge et al's application of learning organization theory to schools in *Schools that Learn* (2000, 2012).

These works point in one direction. That direction is the local school. Teachers learn to teach in local schools. What education leaders need to do is reconceive of schools so they become the intentionally developmental organizations we need in order to develop teachers into effective teachers. What is more and more clear is that development cannot take place in higher education teacher preparation programs. We need to look to institutions of practice, schools derived of learning communities, for the development of our teachers.

THE TEACHER AS LEARNER AND RESEARCHER

This discussion about how participation is at the core of teacher learning moves us to seeing teachers from a different perspective. Their role in schools should be much broader than just instruction. Full participation requires that they are involved in not only instruction but the evaluation of the effects of that instruction and, then, improvement initiatives for both classrooms and whole schools as an outcome of the evaluation. And, such participation would, clearly, be very developmental. It is that participation that points to a new school model, one that moves away from teacher isolation.

As learning leaders, teachers are not just facilitators of student learning, but necessarily evaluators of the impact of their facilitation on individual students and the school as a whole. This self-evaluation function implies, then, that teachers must analyze, study, and research the effects of their instruction and schooling, overall. In effect, teachers have a responsibility to insure their own learning and knowledge creation in the process of supporting student learning.

This is not a new idea. Years of scholarship have suggested the value of teachers working collaboratively to study instructional problems, instructional techniques, and the effects of their work. One more example of such a perspective, and the effectiveness of teacher collaboration in general, is found in the work of Gallimore et al. (2009) where they discuss the value of teachers as researchers and present the positive results of an investigative research project that "demonstrated that grade level teams in nine Title 1 schools using an inquiry based protocol to solve instructional problems significantly increased achievement" (Emerling et al., 2009, p. 537).

Placing their work in historical context, Emerling et al. (2009) explained that "early empirical support for this thesis was provided by Little's (1982) case study of six schools where 'Teachers in successful schools more often jointly planned, designed, and evaluated instructional materials and taught each other the practice of teaching'" (Emerling et al., 2009, p. 538).

While building a substantial research base for school-based teacher learning over the years has been difficult, that research base has now become substantial. It has been built in spite of traditional schools being unwilling to put greater focus on teacher learning as fundamental to student learning, and, of course, the recent focus on outer controls on schools as part of the accountability movement has made school leaders ever more fearful of losing focus on standardized test success.

In this scenario, most educators put the focus on compliance with central authorities. The idea of supporting the development of teacher via teacher research is never raised or never seriously considered. Nevertheless, in the midst of this resistance from the inner source of tradition and the outer source of state and federal governments, the idea of teachers as students and researchers has progressed, although on the margins of schooling.

Notable for this book's audience is that Emerling et al. (2009) found that teachers expressed a significant preference for working in teams for planning and instructional problem solving (p. 549). This teacher preference has also been noted by Farris-Berg and Dirkswager (2010) in their book *Trusting Teachers with School Success: What Happens When Teachers Call the Shots*.

Although many teachers may feel wary of taking on this level of responsibility, it should be noted that both of these works speak to how teachers came to prefer their increased responsibility over time. It proved to be an acquired taste. That slow development in preference is something that should be kept in mind as this book's case is further developed.

Cochran-Smith and Lytle (2008) have also noted this preference by teachers in their work *Inquiry as Stance: Practitioner Research for the Next Generation*. The book explains that in spite of the countertrends arising around the accountability movement, the idea of teachers as researchers and creators of local knowledge has actually continued to thrive because of voluntary teacher participation since its beginnings in the 1970s and early 1980s.

As Emerling et al. (2009) explained about teacher preferences for teamwork that emerged in their study, Cochran-Smith and Lytle (2008) found evidence of this preference in the fact that many initiatives have developed from the 1970s forward outside of the realm of the compliance environment brought on by the accountability movement, NCLB, and Race to the Top.

The initiatives detailed by Cochran-Smith and Lytle (2008) in their work, *Teaching as Stance*, have both interrogated the work of teachers and inspired teacher research to examine issues of equity, engagement, and teacher agency, itself. They further stressed the value of teachers creating knowledge that arises out of and addresses local conditions affecting schools and learning. Conceived of in this way teachers have greater importance and greater agency. They create the foundations for important school decisions and become important decision makers themselves (Cochran-Smith & Lytle, 2008).

Cochran-Smith and Lytle (2008) further cite a substantial list of other works that have acted to support the development of a conceptual framework for teacher research along with the many communities of inquiry that have also emerged. These communities include programs of national reach like the Bread Loaf Teacher Network, the National Writing Project, the Carnegie Foundation's CASTL Program for K-12, and the Teacher Leaders Network. More local groups include the Philadelphia Teachers Learning Collaborative and the North Dakota Study Group (Cochran-Smith & Lytle, 2008).

What is notable about these groups and the many not mentioned is that large numbers of teachers probably engaged in many of these projects without fully realizing that they represented a significant departure from how they have conceptualized the work of teachers in their own everyday work. Nor did they probably fully comprehend how the cited initiatives affirm teacher capacities in contrast to much of their classroom work that has been derived of compliance with authorities from outside of their school.

It is noteworthy that Cochran-Smith and Lytle make a point of distinguishing between PLCs and practitioner inquiry. They do this acknowledging that the concepts have significant overlap. They also acknowledge that no two groups of practitioner inquirers or PLCs are the same or necessarily the same. A range of conditions influence the respective groups to take on a variety of unique characteristics.

This book holds these movements as complementary without disparaging their historical, philosophical, or theoretical underpinnings. The overriding point is that teachers collaborating in the interrogation of what they do along with continuous reflection and opportunities to lead are the ingredients for better teacher performance and the creation of intentionally developmental schools. They point the way to a new school model that focuses on teacher learning.

If we are honest, educators will admit that this notion of teacher as researcher and builder of new knowledge about teaching is not a definition that most aspiring novice, or even veteran teachers, would recognize or use. This idea of the teacher as learner-collaborator, of studying the act of teaching while doing it and then reporting back to a group where every member is doing the same study, is not a concept familiar to most teachers, no less new teachers.

Add that to the idea that as part of their research, teachers would voluntarily seek out peers to view and critique their instruction and study their performance looking for problems would not seem credible. The idea of the teachers working in teams to solve problems and develop knowledge is truly a reconceptualization of teaching. Most regrettably, it is rarely a point of emphasis in most higher education teacher programs.

EDUCATORS HAVE BEEN HEADED IN THIS DIRECTION FOR A WHILE

Even though the importance of communities of practice in professional development has not been thoroughly acted upon in our traditional schools, over the last few decades its importance has been acknowledged in the literature by many leading educators and policy groups (Holmes Group, 1986, 1990; National Commission on Teaching and America's Future, 1996; NCATE, 2010). These groups and many more researchers have produced recommendations that call for more teacher collaboration and for more teacher preparation to take place in actual schools.

This perspective has been most recently attested to in the book *Professional Capital: Transforming Teaching in Every School*, by Hargreaves and Fullan (2012), two of the foremost researchers and education writers in the world. Their book, like this book, addresses the problem of how we create effective teachers. As their work details the benefits of professional learning communities, they insist, "Teaching, like any other profession, doesn't come down to individual skill or will. It's also profoundly affected by the environment—by the culture of the workplace where the job is carried out" (20).

It is this proper focus on the culture of the workplace that best explains why higher education teacher preparation programs cannot predictably produce effective teachers. Higher education has ignored this powerful influence on new teachers to focus on specific factors like candidate quality, academic standards, curriculum quality, or clinical experience.

While all of these considerations have merit, they do not compare to the overwhelming influence of context, the culture of the workplace. As maintained by Kegan and Laskow Lahey, it is an intentionally developmental culture that drives individual and organizational growth. It is such a culture that should be the centerpiece of teacher induction, preparation, and development.

THE GOOD AND THE BAD OF CULTURAL LEARNING

Another way to fully appreciate the impact of school culture on the development of teachers would be to reflect on how people learn from cultures generally. We will do this to better understand how it comes to have such significant bearing on teacher education and the creation of effective teachers. The research and theory to be discussed will be from both educational and non-educational research. This will include works from anthropology, organizational theory, organizational learning, and the application of such thinking by educators to how schools might get better at what they do.

Many management and organizational theorists attribute to the organizational guru, Peter Drucker, the often-cited idea that "culture eats strategy for breakfast." As this statement implies, cultural learning is more powerful than strategy even though it is not learning that comes from commands, laws, direct instruction, directive memos, or a documented strategy.

Instead, culture is a kind of silent, almost ghostly influence. It does its work without notice. Like a fish is unaware of water, it can be difficult for people to be aware of the influence of culture in their everyday activities and choices.

Cultural learning comes from emersion. We know that foreign language learners usually achieve their best learning if they enter the culture where the language they are trying to learn is spoken and become immersed in it. One effect of this emersion is that an individual begins to do things the way he or she sees them being done by native members of the society.

Such students experience thousands of events, many of which are either unnoticed or are imperceptible but which, nevertheless, quietly guide behavior and language acquisition. As a result of being in the location of a culture, not just reading about it, people learn from this complex ocean of events in unconscious ways. They learn and do the ways of the culture. While people feel they make conscious choices, culture guides them not only in how they perceive and think of the conditions they face but also in how they respond.

How a child acquires language in its family may also be a helpful analogy. The child learns its spoken language at home not from instruction but from being there, in the everyday mix of family life. Yet, the child's acquisition of the language is extremely nuanced. It takes on the accents of family members, their intonations, their common expressions, and the values (authoritarian, egalitarian, angry, or civil) implicit in the language. They even learn when not to speak.

Cultural learning in schools has much of the same nuance and subtlety. Novice teachers, who are by their nature eager to get approval and fit in, look around them and unconsciously begin to learn the culture, the language, of their school. Embedded in that language, which is the ebb and flow of life at the school, are the norms and values of that culture. People, by their nature, mimic behaviors they see around them. Because of their newness, novice teachers are especially prone to imitating what is around them. They begin to internalize the culture and do as others are doing.

Again, this learning can be extremely nuanced. While certainly including the explicit classroom work of teachers (and the stuff in the Handbook), it most certainly also involves the whispering outside the main office, looks and gestures in the faculty lounge, the jokes that people tell in the hallway, the gossip heard at the water cooler, the cake Mary brought to the meeting, or who talks to whom in the parking lot after school. It will involve shared memories and frequently repeated stories.

The combination of the multitude of things that make up culture teach the people in the culture what the norms are, what is acceptable and unacceptable, who is who and what is important, why we should do this and not do that. It does all of this without direct instruction or ever having these norms being posted, discussed, or documented. Thus as with children in families, new teachers learn the cultures in the schools where they begin their careers.

As will be discussed shortly, these norms could be positive or negative. They could be productive or unproductive. What is most difficult to reckon with about such cultural influences is that they most often trump strategy. Thus, Peter Drucker tells us that "culture eats strategy for breakfast."

And, like Drucker, scores of organizational theorist have warned policy makers, legislators, and school leaders that they can document all sorts of visions, mission statements, standards, and goals, but if those documents are not supported by a school's culture, they will ultimately be ineffective (Demings, 1983; Deal & Peterson, 2016; Schein, 2010; Senge, 1991).

As a result of this understanding of culture, there has been in the last sixty years the development of an enormous literature on the influence of organizational culture, how it can be changed and how hard that change process is. In all of this, however, it is important to be clear: Cultures can be changed. Cultures can be created that convey to members the most idealistic and productive messages that result in high-functioning organizations that achieve their missions and evolve into ever better organizations.

Where organizational theory has led us is to understand the power of culture over our stated intentions. It should allow us to see that in spite of our efforts with teacher candidate quality, standards, curriculum quality, or clinical experience, none of it will matter if it is not sustained by a reinforcing culture. If we don't provide teachers a positive, sustaining culture, the teachers will learn what the traditional culture teaches—good or bad—whether we want them to or not. Teachers learn to teach in and from the local schools where they work.

Let's remember that when teachers leave their teacher preparation programs, they will enter cultures that vary greatly. Even if these novice teachers learned wonderful techniques and values in their preparation programs, the likelihood of those techniques and cultural values being the same as the schools where they are hired are very small. Teacher preparation programs have great variability and local school cultures have great variability (Levine, 2006).

School cultures may range from highly professional and collaborative to downright negative, even toxic. Regardless, the new teacher will learn from the new culture. Hofstede (2004) reminds us, "When people are moved as individuals [as novice teacher will enter their new schools], they will adapt to the culture of their new environment" (201).

In the face of this reality, this book has a particular vantage point on culture. It stipulates that research points us in one direction, the culture derived of learning communities. These are the cultures that create effective teachers. Schools where teachers work together as learning communities should be the base model for a new school model and a new approach to teacher education that takes place within a local school culture.

Perhaps more than any other research, that of John Hattie is significant in this regard. Dr. Hattie's research reviewed over 800 studies that examined the work of teachers in collaboration. In explaining his research he emphasizes that it showed that more than any other influence, teachers have the greatest influence over student learning at school. In his elaboration, he clarified, moreover, that teachers are an influence on student learning over which schools have control. Schools can develop their teachers and help them get better and better. Most importantly, schools can help teachers improve by having them work together (Hattie, 2011).

This working together is critical because John Hattie's research found that when teachers work together as evaluators of their impact on student learning, it has a distinctly more powerful effect on student learning in comparison to all other school influences. (www.youtube.com/watch?v=rzwJXUieD0U).

This conclusion, explained in Dr. Hattie's recent, *Visible Learning* (Hattie, 2011) tells of an exhaustive study, one that should give everyone involved in schooling a pause. If this "working together" component is so powerful, why isn't it part of every school? Why do most schools continue to adhere to the traditional school model?

With this understanding, this book looks to explain how school culture, and not strategy documents, is how we can find our way to creating effective teachers. Understanding the power of cultural learning helps us understand that participation in the context, the context of an actual school, is what counts, not information, talk, or strategy about the context provided in disconnected professional development or remote teacher preparation programs.

Like most other professionals, teachers do not learn how to be effective at what they do from college lectures or textbooks which provide information about professional practice. They learn from practice among other practicing teachers.

If educators are willing to acknowledge this power of culture, then they must be able to anticipate that even those promising novice teachers who graduate from the most outstanding teacher preparation programs stand to lose what they have learned if and when they enter a local school.

It should further confirm for those in higher education that teacher preparation can only properly be done in the culture of an actual local school. Furthermore, to create effective teachers, teacher preparation should be done in a school culture that is derived of learning communities and has the explicit purpose of preparing and developing its teachers for a full career and as part of an intentionally developmental organization.

A NEW ROLE FOR HIGHER EDUCATION IN TEACHER PREPARATION

Before proceeding, it would be important to take another look at the argument made by many in higher education that local schools cannot provide the teacher preparation that higher education provides. This second look will further the argument that we need to take teacher preparation off the campuses of higher education. It will also, however, make an important clarification.

The role of higher education in teacher preparation should not be eliminated. It should be resituated to the communities of practice in local schools and then applied in new ways that assists schools in their cultural evolution as centers of teacher learning as dictated by the needs and strengths of the local community.

Yes, the content of many of the courses that prospective teachers are asked to take in higher education have real substance. Where this book rejects the value of higher education in teacher education programs is, again, a matter of context. By asking students to take such courses on a college campus, higher education fails to acknowledge or to take advantage of the positive power of a local school's culture. Ignoring that positive power is not good for our aspiring teachers.

In deciding which is more effective, learning on a higher education campus or learning in the context of a local school's culture, the following points show that learning in the context of a school's culture is clearly better for the teachers.

Consider these reasons why.

1. Deciding which courses of background, essential, and/or practical knowledge is best left to a school's local stakeholders who likely have a better idea about what knowledge will have the most meaningful application for the circumstance of their particular school. While it certainly would be a good idea to get input from higher education scholars about what content has value, the choice should be left to local practitioners who are close to the real circumstances of a school.
2. A related matter is this issue of control. People in general like having control over their lives. They like having choices. Local school stakeholders will have the same desire to see themselves as in control of how they develop teachers and provide for students. When they come to fully understand the positive potential of preparing their own teachers, school leaders and teachers will want to have control over their teacher preparation.

   When novice teachers are educated in the context of a local school's PLCs, they thereby gain control over teacher learning and student learning. If the development of teachers is left to higher education, it becomes generic, is out of the control of local stakeholders, and is necessarily diluted by program/school variability.
3. While teacher knowledge is important, teacher habits of mind and practice are more important. Local schools can establish in teachers habits of mind and practice. Higher education cannot. There is just not enough time. And, even if they could, who is to say those habits will be the habits desired by a hiring local school?
4. Learning of important background or practical knowledge is better done in context. Conceptualization is best done in the context of application opportunities. This is not possible on a university campus in a classroom of other aspiring teachers where everything must be theoretical.

   Yes, there is some possibility for this in "student teaching" or field experiences, but it will not lead to the same quality of conceptualization as an in-context learning situation. Moreover, what a novice teacher learns in student teaching may very well not apply in the school where the teacher is actually hired.
5. Learning in a local school is better because what is learned in higher education will likely not be sustained by practices at a school where novice teacher is hired. As explained earlier, there is great variability among teacher education programs and great variability among the cultures of local schools. Aspiring teachers cannot count on getting a perfect match after graduation. It would be better for them to get the important knowledge right from the start while working in a local school.

6. Learning in a local school will be better because the novice teacher will get to read and reflect with actual colleagues who are facing the same situation in real terms, not a disparate group from many different backgrounds whose learning is largely theoretical.

    Novice teachers will get more benefit from learning with the same people with whom they will later work to build programs, refine instruction, develop curriculum, and routinely solve problems in the schooling, teaching, and learning processes.
7. Schools with learning community cultures are about teacher leadership in continuous school improvement. These school cultures are about change, specific change, for continuous school improvement. Novice teachers develop a disposition to change as part of continuous school improvement. That is not possible in higher education because there is no school to improve and no possibility for authentic collective action.

    In higher education programs *most aspiring teachers are encouraged to expect to teach in a traditional school over which they will have little influence.* They are taught that their job is to teach, not change the school.
8. Learning in a local school is better because it favors a community approach. When aspiring teachers learn in higher education, they learn outside of a learning community. When they learn in a school, they stand to learn inside of a learning community. Their habits of mind and practice will be established and sustained over the course of many years of working in collaboration with colleagues.

These specific points should clarify for the reader why teacher learning on the job in a local school is superior to learning from a higher education teacher education programs on a remote campus. The reality is that whatever can be "learned" on a higher education campus, can be learned better and more authentically in the context of a local school culture.

That might include group readings, paper writing, and project completion similar to what happens in a higher education program. All of this should lead readers to ask, if we know that the real places that teachers learn to teach are the places where they work, why would we attempt to place that learning anywhere other than where it really happens?

STILL, LOCAL SCHOOLS NEED HIGHER EDUCATION

It is important to emphasize that this book does not contend that local schools should divorce themselves from higher education. Rather, the implication is that higher education needs to move into local schools. If this idea sounds radical to the readers, it should not. As will be detailed shortly, this moving of higher education personnel to local schools has been underway for many years as part of the professional development school movement. A discussion of the professional development school movement is upcoming.

Bottom line, it is very hard to argue against the value of learning in the context of a community of practice in a local school. It would be the place where novices stood to witness firsthand the intersection of theory and practice. It is should also be considered that in many organizations, leaders often seek bright people who have had no specific training for the work they may be hired to do. Such previous training is often seen as a possible interference with new training protocols. In the case of higher education's involvement in teacher preparation, it clearly is.

Following this line of thinking, when local schools get fresh hires without previous training in higher education, it allows schools to train its novice teachers in exactly the way the school needs them to develop. This perspective, in fact, calls on schools and their leaders to be much more thoughtful about how staff development furthers the mission and goals of a given school.

Further, it militates against business as usual and generic thinking where visions and mission are not genuine considerations in a school's operation. Organizations and schools should have their own home-grown theories and models for operation that are the outcome of study and reflection.

BRINGING THE CULTURE OF THE TRADITIONAL SCHOOL INTO QUESTION

This discussion of the superiority of a local school for teacher preparation naturally raises the issue of the quality of a local school's culture. While this book has qualified this idea by insisting that it is collaborative cultures that are best for teacher development, some additional observations about traditional schools are needed here.

What if the local school culture is not one beneficial to teacher development? What if it is just a traditional school culture, or a traditional school culture that only pretends to be collaborative? What if it is an orderly okay school but with a culture committed to business as usual, not student learning, and just getting through days without incidents? What if it is outright toxic?

The answer is that we wouldn't want these schools to be training sites. As has been made clear, the teachers in most traditional schools are denied a chance to think, reflect, reconsider, reconfigure, and lead schools in new directions. Why would we want to induct new teachers into such cultures?

But there is a greater point here. Just as a matter of general practice, we need to encourage teachers in teacher preparation to begin to question traditional school cultures. They should be encouraged to question it because it is unhealthy for them. It denies them the career-long development that they deeply want.

This is something that higher education teacher preparation programs clearly do not do. Most traditional school cultures are not places where teachers have thought deeply about the school's structures, assumptions, and practices. Most teachers have just accepted that the traditional school model is what school is, as if there were no alternatives. Higher education has done nothing to prepare teachers to enter these schools with the idea that these schools are obsolete, and they will need to change them.

When teachers who have graduated from higher education programs without a disposition to change the schools they enter, they are unprepared to confront the most degrading of conditions, teacher learning as a low priority. Most traditional schools do not have long-term, research-based, community-learning approaches to professional development that focus teachers on student achievement.

This reality of such poorly focused efforts to improve teaching has to be faced squarely. As such, professional development is thought of as an add-on that is short term and primarily reactive to fads or compliance issues. In this mindset, teachers are thought of as an audience. They have little sense of ownership over their own growth and development, and the data suggests that such traditional professional development does little to improve teachers (TNTP, 2015).

What makes this condition even darker is research that indicates that unless schools can achieve highly focused professional development *that are fundamentally collaborative*, the programs are thought of by many teachers as a waste of time (Schmoker, 2016; TNTP, 2015). These conditions beg for a new school model to replace that of the traditional school.

The poor effect of current approaches to teacher development can in significant measure be attributed to the design and structure of the traditional school which has a keep-the-status-quo-going relationship with higher education. The primary design flaw in traditional schools is that it was not designed for change and evolution. Rather, traditional schools were intended to function in the same way year after year after year.

As a result, what we see is that most public schools adhere to the same assumptions, structures, and procedures that they had at the beginning of the twentieth century. As part of this, schools simply do not think of themselves as places to develop teacher capacities as part of improving student learning. It is another part of the traditional school concepts which sees schools as primarily for student learning.

Another degrading condition faced by new teacher is that on top of antiquated notions of professional development, many new teachers stand to enter school cultures that are negative or even toxic. There are many shiny new school buildings that house cultures of professional unhappiness, teacher disengagement, and students who are just going through the motions of achievement.

Such schools are able to exist because like many of the isolated teachers in them, these schools also keep their doors closed. They focus on paper compliance with local, state, and national authorities. As long as a school is reasonably orderly and these arbiters are kept at bay, the school may be considered as doing okay. And, as one educational leader and PDS pioneer has put it, these schools develop a mindset of being okay with just being okay (Yergalonis, 2016). If new teachers have no disposition to change the schools they enter, they are doomed to acclimate to such negative conditions.

The result of this is that the learning a teacher does in such a school could, of course, be negative. Just because it is in a local school doesn't make it good place to prepare teachers. The culture of a particular school, like many, may be such that it encourages a low-effort, play-the-game, CYA approach to teaching which requires following the rules and norms of the school without making a genuine personal investment or becoming part of a school-wide investment in student learning.

Such a school may involve little collaborative effort to learn how to improve teaching or the school. More than anything else, what is at stake in such a culture is staying employed. Teachers close their classroom doors, work in isolation, and do what they believe must be done to satisfy authorities. The reality of this condition in many schools is something most educators are shy to admit.

Such a low-key culture has an unspoken focus on appearances (Waters, 2012) (going through the motions), on business as usual, on getting through the day, and on keeping "incidents" at a minimum. It is not focused on learning outcomes. Professional development is but occasional, episodic, pro forma, unfocused, and in reaction to fads and demands by central authorities. Therein, teachers over the years will acclimate to the many attitudes and assumptions that motivate this low drive, low achievement, business as usual culture.

It is very bad indeed that because traditional schools were not designed to change, year to year, such low-effort cultures can easily take hold and thrive. Even teachers with good attitudes and good intentions begin to feel stuck because they see that they have little influence over what other teachers do. The lack of communication makes such influence nearly impossible.

THE POSSIBILITIES FOR TEACHER LEARNING IN A NEW SCHOOL MODEL

Or, a school culture could be a highly professional, reflective environment with teachers collaborating in many different ways, always trying to understand their impact on student learning and how it might be improved. When teaching, teachers examine and reflect on their practice. When dealing with students or parents individually, they examine and reflect on their practice. When collaborating with each other, they examine and reflect on their practice. Everyone gets a lot of feedback on what they do.

In these cultures, professional development is embedded in the very work of being a teacher. Every act and assumption is examined. In everything they do, teachers find their perspectives and knowledge being deepened and expanded. They frequently assemble to read together, study their work, report research, reflect, and plan change.

Teachers monitor their own personal and professional growth. The school, itself, frequently changes as better ideas emerge over time. Teachers take the personal and professional growth they experience as the norm of the school. It doesn't feel like an add-on or exceptional. It's just the way the school is. In the spirit of Kegan and Laskow Lahey's work, such a school might be called an "Intentionally Developmental School."

The upcoming narrative, "Tina's Journey," will develop what happens in such a school in greater detail. No doubt, these details are important although they will be different, and should be different, for every school. The main point here is that the conditions of a traditional school present a contrast with a new school model that has as an explicit purpose the development of teachers. For their own benefit, teachers should want to move in the direction of that new school model.

THE RIGHT CULTURE MEANS ALL STRONG TEACHERS

Traditional schools most often have a self-defeating mindset about teacher quality. Leaders believe that in every school there are some strong teachers, some adequate teachers, and some that are weak and recalcitrantly so. By and large, this condition is accepted as "reality." No school can have all strong teachers, and all involved have to learn to live with this reality.

While this belief seems perfectly reasonable, it is not. It is part of the legacy of traditional schools that never thought of themselves as sites for the preparation and development of teachers. With the support of some occasional, decontextualized "professional development" teachers have been expected to mature and improve their own practice by virtue of being in the classroom for a period of years. Research shows us, however, that this was never a valid assumption. Experience by itself does not lead to expertise.

The advent of systems theory has led us to understand that poor organizational outcomes are better understood in terms of overall systems of operation rather than individual performance in that system. Thus, this book is suggesting that effective teachers can be created if we create systems and cultures in schools that are designed with the specific purpose of creating effective teachers. The research of Robert Kegan and Lisa Laskow Lahey (2016) affirms the reality that, overwhelmingly, it is the system or culture that guides the growth of teachers, and cultures can be developed that lead teachers to becoming effective teachers.

What is proposed here is that like the commercial organizations studied by Kegan and Laskow Lahey, schools could become deliberately developmental organizations. They could be designed so that by virtue of being on the staff, a teacher would continuously grow in effectiveness and schools would continuously change to become more effective.

THE VALUE-ADDED APPROACH

In the context of this discussion, it is important to note that as higher education teacher preparation programs have come under heavy criticism, some scholars and foundations have devised another approach to bring effective teaching into our schools.

Briefly put, the idea is to expand the number of effective teachers by careful measurement and evaluation of their performance and then eliminating teachers who perform poorly. That is, they do not improve student learning as measured by standardized testing. It is an approach founded on the idea that it is possible to develop a faculty of effective teachers just by getting rid of those that, when measured and evaluated, are found to be ineffective.

Implicit in the *No Child Left Behind*, *Race to the Top*, and now *Every Student Succeeds Act* legislation is a deep, skeptical concern over teacher effectiveness. In the view of many, the public is paying a lot for schools, and test scores and other measures suggest they are not getting the return they should reasonably expect. Supporting this skepticism has been a flood of statistics, which will not be rehashed here, but which suggest that American students are neither as engaged as they should be nor learning what they should.

Of course, the focal point of this concern has been teacher quality and effectiveness. With this thinking as a basis, the idea of more carefully evaluating teachers has seemed very persuasive to many. Presumably, the reader is aware of these developments. Regardless of the unfairness of many of the accusations made against teachers, a reality has emerged in our schools that place measurement and evaluation as the centerpiece of our nation's plan to create more effective teachers. These strategies are core components of *NCLB*, *Race to the Top*, and the *Every Student Succeeds Act*.

Making measurement and evaluation so important in our schools has already had dramatic effects on school cultures and teachers' cultural learning. And, because this approach has been in place for more than a decade, we are at a point where we can reasonably ask: Has this approach worked?

Has it had a positive effect on school culture, teacher learning, and student learning? While the data is certainly mixed and the author wishes to avoid partisanship, there is increasing evidence that the focus on testing students and using those tests to evaluate teachers has not resulted in the gains that were promised or hoped for.

HOW VALUE-ADDED THINKING GETS IT WRONG

At this juncture, it is important to remember that as the national conversation on the creation of effective teachers has unfolded, there have been some who do not see investing in teacher development as the way to go. Rather, many have come to think of good and great teachers as benefiting from inherent qualities they were born with. This is why, they would explain, we see teachers become good and great in unpredictable ways. For them, it is not about developing effective teachers. It is about finding them.

By this line of thinking, when school leaders hire teachers, what they then need to do is carefully assess them. They need to find out how good they are. They see the evaluation of teachers as the device that will spur teachers to better performance. Again, famed economist Eric Hanushek asserted the concept of "value added" as being found in the proper measurement of teacher performance. "We need to refine the evaluation of teacher effectiveness, and we need to introduce the serious use of evaluations into the schools, evaluations that guide tenure, retention, and pay decisions" (EducationNext, "An Effective Teacher in Every Classroom," Summer, 2010. Vol. 10, No. 3).

In effect, the strategy is for school leaders to keep searching for and finding naturally gifted teachers and keep firing those that get poor evaluations and show themselves to be ineffective. There is, of course, a compelling logic to this approach.

Anyone in education for very long knows that our schools have unacceptable numbers of ineffective and uncommitted teachers, teachers which schools are unable to fire because of tenure laws or other collective bargaining agreement stipulations. There is no argument here. If these teachers are not giving students good service, they should be removed from their positions. It's about giving our kids good service.

The fact that teacher unions often go to great length to protect ineffective teachers notwithstanding, the value-added strategy has, itself, been shown to be ineffective on two accounts. First, it has proven to be offensive. It violates certain conditions of trust and care in supervision, something that any professional novice should be able to count on as they enter the profession. The academic literature on the importance of trust in the workplace is extensive (Dovey, 2009; Song et al., 2009). Moreover, a recent survey by the Gallop organization found that teachers were last "in agreeing . . . that their supervisors create an open and trusting environment" (Busteed, 2014).

As novice teachers begin their careers, it is easy to understand how it is offensive to be confronted with suspicious testing and evaluation schemes before beginners have gotten their professional bearings in a classroom, something that can take years. Teacher reactions and resistance to this offensive scheme are proof enough of its ineffectiveness. It simply lacks basic human understanding. Ask any professional, would you like to be in an organization that is constantly measuring and assessing your performance or an institution that is constantly supporting you toward high performance?

The second point of ineffectiveness to the "value-added" approach is that it fails to account for other bodies of research that indicate that teachers, and other high-performing professionals, are not born but are created (Colvin, 2008). One body of research shows that organizations have for decades been training and developing employees to do what they need them to do with great success. This includes positions where discretion and decision-making are a core function of the work, not just rote activity (Colins, 2011).

The other body of research, which has received much attention in recent years, is that body which attests to what it takes to achieve mastery and expertise. The idea that it takes 10,000 hours to become an expert at a particular skill is now a well-accepted notion that is supported by considerable research and professional agreement (Colvin, 2008; Gladwell, 2011).

Also well accepted is the notion that it is not practice (years in the classroom) that leads to mastery, but reflective practice. Reflective practice requires the frequent observation by an expert, expert input, reflection, and mutual reflection and then more and more practice for years and years. And, as will be developed in the course of this book, this notion supports the view that teaching is a skill developed only with years of reflective practice, which is, of course, a staple of the learning community concept.

In light of this information, now years later, that we can reflect on how value-added thinking affected schools and teaching. We know as *No Child Left Behind* and *Race to the Top* unfolded on the ground, evaluation as the centerpiece of teacher improvement created a lot of controversy more than it left teachers feeling like they were getting vital feedback on their performance. By and large teachers felt the scheme put them on the defensive rather than left them feeling that they were truly being helped and supported by people who cared about them.

Yes, there is a considerable academic literature on both sides of the "value-added" controversy. In the context of this book's thesis, however, consider this choice: If we teachers want to help all teachers become effective teachers, would it be most helpful to make evaluation the centerpiece of that approach or guided, reflective practice in supportive learning communities? This isn't a leading question. The choice is real.

We can take novice teachers and put them in a culture that is intentionally developmental and guides the improvement of instructional practice in careful, methodical ways. Or, we can confront teachers with an evaluation system that many think is unfair, many do not understand, and many believe is not supported by research or common sense and expect them to get to work and measure up. To which of these systems are teachers likely to respond in a positive way?

Of course, teachers are going to be more responsive to a system that they perceive as helpful, trusting, and supportive. But this emotional response should not be seen as shallow or just sentimental. The fact is that the research on developing expertise in practitioners does not highlight the importance of high-stakes evaluations.

Rather it focuses on reflective practice where the performance of a practitioner is guided toward expertise by experts who give regular, nuanced feedback in ways that the teacher being critiqued will accept as caring, helpful, and supportive. Teachers are in this way like their students.

While evaluation is necessary, making it the centerpiece of a plan to identify and cultivate effective teachers has lacked balance. It conceived of teachers more as laborers to be made more productive than as adult learners. It signaled to teachers a message of "this is what we want to get from you." It did not send the message of an intentionally developmental school of "this is the skill level that we are going to help you achieve."

The fact is that, on the whole, the emphasis placed on teacher evaluation has substantially overlooked the importance of ongoing, career-long professional development in creating great schools. Given how we know teachers responded to it, the strategy of measure, measure, measure, is not going to be as effective as guided practice in a supportive, collaborative culture.

Moreover, in the context of a learning community, the evaluation of teacher performance will focus primarily on teachers' visible use of best practices in achieving higher levels of student learning. Yes, it will certainly include consideration of learning outcomes but will not be represented by one summary document at the end of the year. Rather, it will be represented by the accumulation of artifacts and demonstrations of good practice all of which suggest a developmental trajectory which is focused on the teacher understanding of her impact on student learning.

The desirability of guided practice over measure, measure, measure should be clear for another reason. If schools hire teacher candidates who have a personal history of achievement, then the likelihood of helping these novice teachers become effective teachers is not really an unrealistic projection. There is an extensive literature on training techniques that get practitioners to the levels local schools need.

It must be inserted here, however, that no harsh intentions are attributed here to the advocates of value-added approaches and better measurement of effective teaching. Rightly, these advocates want to upend school cultures where there is a ho hum, get-through-the-day attitude and weak teaching is condoned. They want to create cultures where teachers are focused on results and better student learning.

They are rightly concerned about school cultures that develop where teachers are not fully engaged or motivated. Those cultures do exist in many schools. These advocates rightly want to get rid of such cultures, and they are especially right to want to get rid of the low-end teachers who make a racket out of doing their job by the numbers so they can hit the parking lot at 3:00 with no books or papers in hand.

THE NEW SCHOOL MODEL

Now consider a different kind of school. In this school the teacher has two jobs that are equal and interdependent. One job is to advance student learning. The other job is to learn and develop as a teacher. Both jobs have equal priority. The job of developing as a teacher is not just coincidental with routine experience or occasional training. It is based on teachers working in learning communities where growth opportunities are embedded in their continuous evaluation of their effect on student achievement and their attempts to change and improve instruction and schooling practices. Their school is always evolving.

In doing this work teachers discuss their progress with colleagues, formally and informally, every day. It is at once the subject of gossip and laughter but also serious study and research. All teachers, including veterans, are conscious of their responsibility to develop and demonstrate that development year by year. As this unfolds, each teacher is conscious of his or her developmental stages from which he or she strives to achieve a higher stage over the course of decades.

As the reader considers this ideal scenario what matters most is the acknowledgment that it is this cultural influence that is at the root of creating effective teachers. To create effective teachers, we must get control of the cultural influence. More than candidate quality, academic standards, course offerings, or even clinical experience, what matters most is getting the culture right.

As Polanyi has put it, it is the "tacit learning" within a community of practice that constitutes the real acquisition of a practice. Teachers learn to teach when they are among teachers teaching. Teachers learn best when they teach in learning communities with an intentionally developmental culture. That is the irrefutable bottom line.

MAKING SCHOOLS FOR TEACHER LEARNING, TOO

There Really Is No Choice about Where Teachers Learn

There is no choice about this matter. Like it or not, teachers learn to teach in the schools where they work. We only get a choice when we consider what teachers will learn and where they will learn it. Thus, teachers can learn to teach in schools where there are no learning communities, where they work in isolation, and where teacher development is a low priority and episodic at best. Or, they can learn to teach in schools where there are learning communities and teacher development is an intentional and explicit purpose of the school. In either case, teachers will learn a way of teaching. They will acclimate to the existing culture and begin to do what they see happening around them.

CONCLUSION

Chapter 2 began our consideration of a new school model. It is a model that would comprise learning communities and be conducive to the career-long development of teachers as learners-collaborators-leaders. As part of describing a new school model, the chapter introduced the concept of the "deliberately developmental culture" as presented in the work of Kegan and Laskow Lahey (2016). In effect, a new school model would be dedicated to the development of its teachers as an intrinsic feature of its operation and service to student learning.

The introduction of this concept places responsibility for teacher development not only on the individual but also on the organization as a whole. It advances thinking of teacher learning as a collective activity and part of an organizational learning process intended to continuously transform the school and coming from teachers, themselves, as they study their teaching and share perspectives with each other, with members of higher education, and with a broad range of community and school stakeholders, especially their students.

Such an approach to teacher development has demonstrated it strategic superiority to the routines of traditional schools and to the "value-added" proposition primarily because teachers respond more positively to the proposition of career-long development as opposed to pretend professional development or to career-long measurement and evaluation.

It has been observed that the optimal development of teachers calls for the resituation of higher education teacher preparation from higher education campuses to local school cultures. In the context of the discussion about how to create effective teachers, research supports the idea of teachers learning best in schools that have the explicit purpose of developing teachers and that are cultures derived of professional learning communities.

Chapter 4

School Culture, Human Development, Teacher Development

Chapter 2 began our consideration of a new school model. It is a model that would comprise learning communities and be conducive to the career-long development of teachers as learners-collaborators-leaders. As part of describing a new school model, the chapter introduced the concept of the "deliberately developmental organization" as presented in the work of Kegan and Laskow Lahey (2016). In effect, a new school model would be dedicated to the development of its teachers as an intrinsic feature of its operation and service to student learning.

The introduction of this concept places responsibility for teacher development not only on the individual but also on the organization as a whole. It has advanced thinking of teacher learning as a collective or cultural activity and part of an organizational learning process intended to continuously transform the school and coming from teachers, themselves, as they study their teaching and share perspectives with each other, with members of higher education, and with a broad range of community and school stakeholders, especially their students.

Having introduced the concept of a deliberately developmental culture in describing a new school model, this chapter invites teachers to take a deeper look at teacher learning as a developmental process. As part of this process, readers will be asked to take a fresh look at their own professional development as well as those around them for what particular experiences have advanced development or what experiences have prompted stasis or withdrawal. As part of this exercise, this book joins a number of other works that have suggested that teacher development is best conceived of as happening in stages (Evans, 2002; Steffy et al., 2000; Troen & Boles, 2003).

In taking this perspective we will also draw on various developmental theories in human psychology and acknowledge that all aspects of human development happen in stages. Organizational historian and theorist Fredrick Laloux explains that the concept of stages has been applied by many of our most important psychological theorists.

He explains that Maslow (1961) saw human development as happening in stages that stretched from the basic physiological to existential aspirations for self-actualization. Gebser (1986) saw stages of human development in the unfolding of worldviews and cultural frames of reference. Piaget (2008) and Erickson (1994) observed stages in human cognitive development, and Graves (2004) observed them in the development of values. Kholberg (1981) observed stages in moral development. Loevinger (1976) reported stages in self-identity and Fowler (1981) in spirituality. Cook-Greuter (1985), Kegan (1983), and Torbert (2004) traced stages in organizational leadership (Laloux, 2014, loc. 480).

It is also important to note that while the concept of stages is intellectually helpful, there is another dimension of benefit. When we begin to think and talk about stages of development, those acts in and of themselves advance movement through the stages. Ken Wilber explains that research tells us that just knowing the stages that one must pass through helps the individual achieve the stages that are ahead of her (Wilber, 2016, p. 94).

Heeding Wilber's observation this discussion of the stages of teacher development will maintain that thinking of teacher development as happening in stages is actually critical to the improvement of teacher learning and performance. Without such a perspective we are left with the muddle that now dominates our mindset about teacher learning and development. If local schools are actually to become the central places of teacher development, there needs to be a way to conceptualize and track that development. Drawing on the work of a variety of seminal theorists, this chapter will focus on how conceiving of teacher development as happening in stages will assist the process.

SCHOOL CULTURE, HUMAN DEVELOPMENT, TEACHER DEVELOPMENT

This book is about the best way to develop effective teachers. To this point, it has been stipulated that the development of effective teachers depends on placing novice teachers in a school culture derived of learning communities where teachers collaborate with the common purpose of continuous school improvement. This commitment to continuous improvement necessarily applies in two areas.

The first of these is that teachers work to improve their own learning and performance. The second is that they work with students to improve student learning and achievement. One is irrevocably tied to the other. School cultures that are dedicated to improving student achievement must also be committed to understanding what it is that actually advances teachers' professional performance.

Before proceeding with a discussion of the stages of teacher development, however, let's consider the present condition—the muddle—in schools where the idea of teachers passing through stages as they develop throughout their careers is practically non-existent. Yes, we do think about teachers as being new or veterans or even older teachers. But we do not have descriptions of these stages that come from careful observation, documentation, or peer review.

Moreover, these "stages" are more associated with time on the job than they are with developed expertise in the job. They to do not attempt to describe teacher behaviors that demonstrate growth or being more developed. They do not describe what a teacher does that is better, more evolved, than what she used to do. Our current conception of the stages of teacher development does not attempt to describe or track the improvement process.

The developmental process is not part of a school leader consciousness, nor are the experiences that lead to higher performance. Neither is the school's role in developing teacher high performance or a teacher's withdrawal. Really, in most cases there isn't even acknowledgment that there is a process which involves stages and that teacher development is more than the luck of the draw.

What is most significant about seeing teacher development as passing through stages is that teachers like the idea. On the one hand, they like the idea of professional growth, of achieving new skills and deeper understanding throughout their careers. They also like the idea of others recognizing their professional growth and being given increased and broader responsibilities for the success of their schools.

When we make stages clear, then teachers have a frame of reference for understanding the quality of their performance and the long-term implications for their improvement and development. When teachers do not have this frame of reference, as is the case now in most schools, teachers have little frame of reference for determining the quality of their performance. Many lack the sense that their development as teachers is a long-term proposition that will unfold over their whole career.

This observation that teachers lack a frame of reference for assessing their own development came into clearer focus after an extensive academic study of teacher professional development by The New Teacher Project. The TNTP concluded

> School systems are not helping teachers understand how to improve—or even that they have room to improve at all. Teachers need clear information about

their strengths and weaknesses to improve instruction, but many don't seem to be getting that information. The vast majority of teachers in the districts we studied are rated Effective or Meeting Expectations or higher even as students outcomes in these districts fall far short of where they need to be. Perhaps it is no surprise, then, that less than half of teachers surveyed agreed they had weaknesses in their instruction. Even the few teachers who did earn low ratings seemed to reject them; more than 60 percent of low-rated teachers still gave themselves high performance ratings. Together, this suggests a pervasive culture of low expectations for teacher development and performance. These low expectations extend to teachers' satisfaction with the development they received. While two-thirds reported feeling relatively satisfied with their development experiences, only 40 percent reported that their professional development activities were a good use of their time. (TNTP, p. 2)

To help teacher develop a frame of reference for assessing their own growth, there needs to be a way of determining how we know a teacher or the school is actually getting better. We must have some idea of the stages the teacher will and need to go through.

Also consider what it means not to think about teacher or school development as happening in stages. Under the traditional school model, teachers are periodically observed to see that they are actually teaching and doing it with some success. Behind this exercise there is no overarching model that looks to develop teachers from one stage to the next over, say, a five-year period. Not only is there no such model, there is very little idea of how a teacher might be expected to develop over a five-year period or longer.

The teacher, who gets only occasional supervision or professional development, comes to believe that it is the experience of teaching over a period of years that provides the growth they need although that growth is nowhere described, and the teacher has very little frame of reference by which to measure growth or assert personal expectations for change.

By contrast, a key concept here is that under a new school model where schools have the explicit purpose of developing teachers, teachers would know that they must do more than just keep an orderly class and deliver the approved curriculum with some success. They must insure that students learn. They must constantly be evaluating their teaching and its relationship to student learning and how that is achieved via new behaviors and outlooks.

A DEVELOPMENTAL VIEW OF TEACHER DEVELOPMENT

Of course, the reader wants to know more about these stages. What is in them? To whom do they apply? In the context of these questions, we should again affirm the value of local thinking and imagination as the best avenue to developing our schools and their teachers. Remember that moments ago the readers were prompted to self-examination and asking: What experiences were pivotal in my own development or withdrawal as a teacher? Mindful of this self-examination, let's consider how teachers, themselves, would describe the stages teacher go through as they develop over their careers. This chapter will focus on developing a new school model which as a center of teacher education requires that we take a developmental view of teacher learning.

The word developmental as used here deserves special attention. Yes, it is a commonplace term in the education literature, but one that is often used when it should not be. The word development is used here because historically its use in the academic literature implies stages. The works of the theorists cited earlier all discuss human development, including adult development, in terms of stages. They imply an evolution, of going somewhere better, more complex, deeper, more organized, more advanced, and more effective.

In this process of advancing as a teacher, research indicates that there are periods of growth and adjustment that have general characteristics distinct from the previous or subsequent periods or stages. Thus, the reader is asked to think of teachers' careers as going through stages as they unfold. They go from a place of lesser capacity and ability to a place of greater capacity and ability as they move through intellectual and emotional periods of adjustment and transformation. Properly nurtured, then, teachers do not fall into periods of stasis, of no growth but are always becoming, stage by stage, more robust, more powerful, and more effective.

HOW DOES TEACHER DEVELOPMENT HAPPEN?

The driving question is how does it happen? Under optimal conditions, how does a novice teacher go from the early stage to the latter stage and become an effective teacher? What happens in between?

To prompt the reader in thinking through this process, it might be helpful now to reinforce two concepts. One, more than any discreet event termed "education" or "professional development," it is local school culture that is the overwhelming influence in animating human development and teacher development.

Two, in spite of the subtlety with which culture asserts it influence, it is possible to identify particular factors in culture that are part of the animation process and how they influence stages of development. Again, asserting one's own self-examination, the reader might want to think about her current stage and what experiences would move him or her to the next stage.

No one has the last word on the best way to describe the stages teachers go through. As previously cited, different theorists have described teacher development in different ways (Evans, 2002; Steffy et al., 2000; Troen & Boles, 2003). On the ground, stages may very well be different in different schools because of the schools' cultures.

The key idea here is that thinking about these stages will, itself, be a productive activity. What does it makes us think about as to how to provide an intentionally developmental culture to all teachers throughout their careers? How will we keep everyone engaged and aspiring to new levels for a full career?

Still, starting from scratch in this thinking may be too much to ask, so a model is going to be presented that depicts the stages of teacher development. This model is not intended to be a contribution to academic theory. Rather, it is a prompt for the reader's thinking. The reader is encouraged to look at it with a critical eye and declare things like "There are too many or too few stages," "This model leaves out an important stage," "This model leaves out an important behavior," or "I would approach these stages in a completely different way."

Again, the point is to get the reader and local schools thinking about how teachers develop and what would be the best way to get them to develop into effective teachers. If we know that it is the culture that teaches teachers how to teach, what does their culture have to provide to steward teachers in the right direction?

It should also be clarified that in spite of the author's declaration that the prompt model to be presented is not to be taken as any kind of considered theory, it has been influenced by important thinkers and scholars with whom readers may be familiar. These include the works of Erickson (1950), Kegan (1983), Kohlberg (1981), Laloux, (2014), Montessori (2011), Piaget (1969), Seligman (2011), and Wilber (2016). But, in spite of the influence of these scholars and researchers, the reader is encouraged to reflect on his or her own experience and study to determine how the stages would be most effectively described.

THE DARK SIDE OF TEACHER DEVELOPMENT

It is a common observation among educators, supported by research (Mirage, 2015; Wolfe, 2000), that teacher development is rapid in early years of their careers but slows considerably after a point. It has further been observed by non-partisan scholars that many teachers enter a period of stasis or even withdrawal (Steffy, 1989). These teachers begin painting by the numbers. There is a sense of coasting, going through the motions without the earlier drive to engage students. These teachers go professionally adrift to varying degrees as they rest on an "adequate skill level" or perform in ways that look to hide their withdrawal from their work.

This book does not blame the teachers. It blames school systems and cultures that do not take responsibility for meeting the learning needs of all of their teachers at the different stages of their development throughout their careers. The traditional school thinking is that schools are for student learning. This is why we need a new school model that is explicitly intended for the education of two populations, students *and* teachers.

Again, inviting the reader to critique the Prompt Stages Model is an idea that will persist throughout this book and is consistent with the notion of teacher development. The idea is that teachers should be properly regarded as thinkers and decision makers. Central to the development of all people is spurring them to think critically and solve problems, then to make organizational changes as needed. Teachers have the capacity to do all of this.

Remember, this book is about teacher development. It is about the reader and becoming a thinker and decision maker in your school. It is not about the right answer coming from just one perspective, even if that perspective is very authoritative or powerful.

At the same time, readers should feel free to consult books and experts about what they think should be done to improve their school. Seeking advice and getting many varied perspectives is part of good thinking. In all of this, however, it is the perspective of this book to protect teachers' roles as thinkers and decision makers. That includes how we think about teacher development.

Parenthetically, please note that as we begin to consider the stages of teacher development, we might become disposed to wonder about the stages of school development. How do schools evolve, if they even do? As you do that, think about what it means for a school's development to start taking ownership of its teachers' development and not leaving it to chance or the direction of higher education or other outside forces.

What follows is the Prompt Stages Model. It will give the reader a concrete idea of what thinking about teacher development looks like. It is intended to get readers thinking about how teachers' capacities might change overtime when they are in an intentionally developmental school in a professional learning community culture.

Please note that this description of stages has a mildly prescriptive quality. It focuses on the stages of teachers who are on the path to success. While teacher apprehensions and missteps are cited, the focus is on what teachers are doing as they evolve from coping to mastering their work. Also note, this description of stages does not include specific classroom instructional techniques. It is assumed that the full array of best practices and other novel techniques will be acquired early on and be a mainstay of learning community work. Rather, this description of stages tries to capture the inner condition of the teacher and how that is manifested in behavior.

THE PROMPT STAGES MODEL

Stage One

Year One: Surviving—and Initiating a Developmental Perspective

At this stage novice teachers run the gamut of skill levels and confidence levels. In most cases observers will see enthusiasm, eagerness, and idealism run high in a new teacher's comments and reports. Apprehension about success may also run high. This may be less manifest. When the high spirits confront some of the hard realities of reluctant learners, the come down can be very harsh. The disappointment can be overwhelming. Research tells us that some of these teachers, including those from elite institutions, may very well quit before the end of the year. Others, perhaps more resilient, will seek out support and advice.

The enthusiasm, idealism, and, to some extent the apprehension, of these novice teachers make them well disposed to becoming a member of a learning community and absorbing the support and optimistic outlook of their colleagues. They are likely going to come for advice and help on a regular basis. Being surrounded by this support and having the value of their enthusiasm and perspective honored, these new teachers will be well disposed to success even when their assignments are challenging. Some are likely to excitedly report big classroom successes or failures to their learning communities.

Being surrounded by members of a caring learning community who are studying and reflecting on their own performance, admitting weaknesses and engaging in various kinds of research, these novice teachers are increasingly aware that their growth as teachers will be a process of many years. They are comforted and bolstered by seeing around them many accomplished teachers who are committed to supporting them in these early years.

Already these novice teachers are getting accustomed to reflecting on their practice and considering how to improve on a personal level. They are also beginning to see their role in helping other teachers, including veterans, improve their practice. They are tuning into their school culture's sense of purpose. Some may announce that their door is open for observation. They showing signs of leadership and are beginning to see that their development as a teacher will be the theme of their career. It will never be finished. Firmly established is the mindset that improvement is expected each year and that it is expected that the teacher will drive his or her own improvement and be able to explain it to other teachers.

Stage Two

Years Two through Four: Becoming an Effective Teacher through Community

Having survived the first year, many second-year teachers see themselves as having a new beginning. Some big mistakes from which they have learned are behind them. Their outlook is positive. They are happy to be working among and enjoying the support of a community of learners whose care they rely on. Some are frank about still having some misgivings about their ability, but they are not yet willing to concede defeat. Their engagement is high.

In that context, these teachers are also beginning to appreciate and becoming more invested in how a learning community's first work is collaboration in understanding and doing what works best in improving student learning. These teachers enjoy reflective discussions with veteran teachers. They are eager to hear and be heard in regular meetings. They are increasingly sensitive to issues of respect, trust, and empathy. As members of professional learning communities, they are learning that effective interaction with students in and out of the instructional contexts is a fine art and craft. They are learning that teachers need each other as they continuously collaborate in order to refine that craft.

Within this developing appreciation, these novice teachers exemplify drive and a fundamental instructional competence. By all accounts they are applying effective methods and kids are learning in their classes. These teachers are increasingly conscious of their strengths and weaknesses and are open to talking about them because they hear the vets talking about theirs. They are actively engaged in examining their own practices and inviting other to help them examine and understand the effectiveness of their instruction. Fellow teachers can easily observe that these teachers get stronger and more effective over time. These teachers become ever more proficient in a variety of instructional and student interaction skills and they see how the protocols of a professional learning community are contributing to them becoming effective teachers. There are more indications of developing leadership. Engagement continues to grow.

Stage Three

Years Five through Ten: Questioning Assumptions and Driving Change

As with the previous two stages, the upper stages of a teacher's development have to do with expanding the teacher's perspective on what influences learning at school and how those influences might be better applied. These teachers are no longer so concerned with developing their own instructional competence.

They are thinking of the school as a whole operation, as a system and culture and the individual teachers role in it. An important aspect of teacher development at this stage is taking a critical eye to the assumptions underlying the practices of classroom instruction, community life, and schooling, itself. Their leadership is blooming. They challenge the people they work with and voicing their concerns and trying to influence their learning community to consider new possibilities.

At this stage of development, teachers may be considered actively undertaking study for an additional academic degree or proficiency certificate. The study areas on which these teachers focus is an expression of a higher sense of educational purpose. They are often driven by a vision of a better school. In that regard, these teachers' creativity and leadership in combination with research will prompt their learning communities to design and drive change to improve teacher learning so it serves the unique characteristics of the population they serve. These teachers will conscientiously avoid central authority, standardized solutions.

Stage Four

Years Ten through Twenty: Leading Research, Leading Change

Teachers at this stage of development have demonstrated in their teaching and academic work a high level of instructional and leadership competence along with a widening perspective on the interaction of instruction, community, and schooling. They may be questioning the very nature of learning itself. They are actively involved in doing, collecting, and synthesizing research that will guide the practice of their professional learning communities and the school. They do their work with a sense of mission. Their leadership is strong. These leaders understand that continuous improvement means continuous change, even of long-held assumptions and structures that are taken for granted by most educators.

At this stage, teachers become scholar-practitioners, and their work may lead to a doctoral degree as granted by their local school in partnership with a university. They are not looking to become administrators. Teachers at this stage have demonstrated high levels of proficiency as scholars, instructors, members of their learning communities, and leaders of school improvement. They are high spirited and may have a following of other teachers who share their sense of purpose or mission. Their participation in innovative initiatives with respect to classroom and school practices will be an important component of their work at this level and a justification of this elite status.

Stage Five

Years Twenty through Thirty-Plus: Becoming a Teacher of Teachers

These teachers have an ever expanding and deepening perspective on education. They embrace its complexity. It is a perspective that at once relishes the cross currents in educational thinking and reform while resisting those who want no change, to return to the good old days, or to only pretend change. These teachers can see over the horizon to a new future for teaching and schooling.

Teachers at this level will likely have some spiritual radiance and share humble tales of personal transformation. They will be those who have demonstrated wisdom in their work and proficiency at helping other teachers move through and up the developmental stages. They exemplify high levels of respect and empathy as they work with others.

In the context of working in community, these teachers have spent their careers focused on self-improvement and personal growth. Their status will be achieved in large measure because it has been attested to via research and reports from those teachers who they have helped and who have described and documented that help and how it worked. They do have a broad following.

Their own work as scholar-practitioners may likely have been in studying and developing the nurturing, coaching, and support skills that inspire those they work with to move to higher levels of development. These individuals have an uncommon depth and accessibility and are at their best when sharing and mentoring.

DISCUSSION OF THE STAGES

There is agreement among a number of theorists that teachers go through stages as their careers unfold. As will be developed, being conscious of these stages and the opportunity to advance will have benefits for individual teachers, their learning communities, and the schools in which they work. This consciousness stands in contrast to most current professional development strategies which are more one-size-fits-all and unconscious of teachers' stages.

Let's review some of the possible benefits of stage consciousness.

1. It makes teachers aware of what behaviors and experiences are appropriate to different parts of their careers.
2. It puts career stasis in a dark light; teachers know growth is always expected of them. It inclines against complacency and withdrawal.

3. It cues newcomers that teacher development will be embedded and career long and is an offering to them from their school.
4. The incline of the stages suggests the value of teacher learning as both a collective and an individual pursuit.
5. It stands to increases teacher aspirations and striving to get to the next level.
6. It contributes to a culture of aspiration and striving; professional development is a cultural emersion experience.
7. It creates a conversation about how to best describe and achieve the stages of teacher development and where it should be headed.
8. It provides opportunities for critical research on the stages of teacher development and how they are best attained.

Remember, one of the basic ideas here is that teachers need a full career of professional development. It is not that it would be nice that they have it; they *need* it. It is integral to high performance. To assume, as many do, that teachers with twenty years of experience don't really need or benefit from professional development ignores what we know about adult development. Adults can and want to develop well into their retirement years (Kegan, 1983).

Now that the reader has had a chance to peruse all of the stages, let's consider each one briefly. Again we must remember that this model is a prompt to get readers to think about the various stages that teachers go through. Your school might develop a different model. It is the process of how a school would come to describe these stages differently that is very important. Hopefully, the reader is now starting that process by making some notes on how to describe these stages that is consistent with *her* own experience.

As this is done, please think about how teachers in general will be affected by reading these descriptions and then inquiring into their own performance. Consider, for example, how a second-year teacher would be affected by the description that says, "They are actively engaged in examining their own practices and inviting other to help them examine and understand the effectiveness of their instruction."

Of course, teachers examining their own practice in a methodical way is highly desirable as would be asking others to give feedback on their teaching. Consider that this explicit description of this stage provides at least one cue to teachers at this stage about what should be happening in their development as a teacher. Such cues become an implicit part of the culture. They make everyone more stage conscious and more developmentally conscious.

While it is not suggested here what the stage descriptions should be, these descriptions will, nevertheless, serve in some degree as statements of expectations. Just as with a child, at some point a description of the child's stage should include expectation statements like, "at this stage the child is taking responsibility for home maintenance like taking out the trash or washing dishes."

Developing stage consciousness in a school culture is very different from a laissez-faire approach to teacher development which suggests that just by being in the classroom teachers get the learning experience they need to develop. It is a traditional school notion of teacher development that it comes from practice, not reflective practice. The wrongness of this idea that teachers grow from their general experience in the classroom will be discussed in greater detail later in this chapter.

A developmental psychologist would never suggest that just being in the world is enough for a child to learn what it needs to learn for healthy development. Rather, they would suggest that children need specific experiences in order to learn specific skills whether they be cognitive-operational or interpersonal. Certain experiences support certain kinds of growth. We should be conscious of providing the right experiences for the right kind of teacher development.

Now imagine if this information about stages was nowhere expressed to the teacher. Imagine that the assumption was that just by teaching another year the teacher would learn enough. Further imagine that from year to year there was nothing in the environment that moved the teacher to consider that she had weaknesses and needed to improve. Imagine that the teacher did not see her performance as something to be shared with a learning community which would be eager to contribute if asked. What this imagining reveals is pretty much what we have in most traditional schools right now. Teachers and school leaders are not developmentally conscious.

How stage consciousness supports a developmental culture for teachers may be discerned in Frederick Laloux's explanation that

> No one can be made to evolve in consciousness, even with the best of intentions—a hard truth for coaches and consultants, who wish they could help organizational leaders adopt a more complex world view by the power of conviction. What can be done is to create *environments* (Waters's emphasis) that are conducive to growing into later stages. When someone is surrounded by peers who already see the world from a more complex perspective, in a context safe enough to explore inner conflicts, chances are higher that the person will make the leap. (Loc. 1040)

DISCUSSION OF STAGE ONE

Year One: Surviving—and Initiating a Developmental Perspective

There is an enormous literature on the first year of teaching. Teachers are urged to access that literature as they consider the first stage of teaching.

There will be no attempt here to rehash that literature. In the context of this book's thesis, however, one point stands out. We want teachers to know that what they learn in that first year is just the beginning of a career-long process. It is the first leg of a long journey where their school will provide them a truly professional career with all of the refinement and growth that it implies.

As observed earlier, teachers want to grow. More than any other factor, professional growth will translate into full engagement and career satisfaction. The trajectory of that growth is best determined by the teacher's early learning experiences in a school.

The optimal experience will be for the new teacher to experience the tug of developmental ideals and expectations while they enjoy a high level of social support from their peers and mentors in a learning community. This is something that just can't be provided in the theoretical discussions on a higher education campus. Properly executed by the culture, teachers develop a consciousness that growing is a personal responsibility pursued among others who have the common purpose of becoming effective teachers.

DISCUSSION OF STAGE TWO

Years Two through Four: Becoming an Effective Teacher through Community

This stage of roughly four years may be thought of as the sweet spot of teacher development. Confidence and instructional competence quickly develop. These young professionals are eager to acquire as many new tools as they can handle from fellow teachers. It is not the purpose of this book to review the particulars of effective teaching. There is a great literature that reviews the research, the art, and the science of teaching. The point is that discussing that literature and experimenting with best practices should be a routine part of this stage and working in an intentionally developmental school derived of learning communities.

In doing this, the community will want to clarify for the novice teachers that the school is a team effort. These teachers will learn most from their interactions within a community of practice where they see, hear, and *do* what they see happening around them. There is within this culture the unspoken, but accepted, notion that teacher development is one of the key purposes of the school and everybody is expected to grow and develop. They will do this for two reasons: (1) It is the best way to improve student learning and (2) It is the best way to improve teacher learning and career satisfaction.

DISCUSSION OF STAGE THREE

What do developing teachers have to do after they have become effective teachers may seem an unnecessary question. If we get novice teachers to become effective teachers by year five, what more is there to do? While a high level of effectiveness should be expected by year five, if professional development were to stop then, it would ignore the needs of mature teachers (Wolfe et al., 2000; Kegan, 1969).

Note that Stage Three says, "taking a critical eye to the assumptions underlying the practices of classroom instruction, community life, and schooling, itself." The fact is that once any practitioner begins to master his or her craft, he or she often looks for more complex challenges (Maslow, 1968; Seligman, 2012) to master. In part this is a function of the effective teacher taking a broader view of his or her work, of looking at the school as a whole and the community around it. Thus, teachers at this stage will likely begin looking at other factors that affect learning and increase learning, including factors from outside their classrooms, maybe outside of the school or local community.

Presumably, teachers at this level will have considered various instructional techniques and schooling routines in a very thorough way. They may even have done some research on such practices and routines. In other words, they have achieved some real expertise. If this research and expertise suggest that there should be changes in instruction or schooling routines, there stands the opportunity to create change to which other teachers will respond. While all teachers should be always involved in creating change, teachers at this level may be thought of as uniquely disposed and qualified to lead such change.

DISCUSSION OF STAGE FOUR

Years Ten through Twenty: Leading Research, Leading Change

It is important to remember that this book advances the idea that schools should be conceived of as centers of teacher education and development. This is the way to effective teachers. But, this is likely not the view of most teachers—that they should be engaged in a thorough routine of professional development as they pass through their thirties, forties, fifties, and beyond. What is the need? Is there real interest?

Two considerations come to bear in this regard. The first is a concern about stasis. There is considerable research that suggests that teachers at the latter stages of their careers do begin to decline in performance (TNTP, 2015; Wolfe et al., 2000). This, regrettably, includes teachers who are at earlier stages of performance. For whatever reason, their engagement becomes stale and their classroom/participatory performance does decline.

The second consideration is that there are also many indications in the research that in these latter stages teachers do have a broadened view of education and school and would jump at opportunities that involved being employed in new ways, ways that drew on their broader view of education. These teachers likely have done a great deal of graduate work and have a sense that they have mastered the classroom all of which leads them to wanting new challenges that draws on their broader view.

These teachers may want to assert some leadership or, at least, the chance to apply their wisdom in new ways. Many policy statements over the years have recognized this need and looked to address it by way of differentiated staffing and/or offering these teachers leadership positions in a variety of areas but particularly in action research, community relations, site-based planning, school reform, and new teacher induction (Holmes Group, 1986).

DISCUSSION OF STAGE FIVE

Years Twenty through Thirty-Plus: Becoming a Teacher of Teachers

Perhaps more than any, this stage will evince the importance of teachers growing as persons as they traverse the stages of teacher development. This growth will provide platforms for continued research on the characteristics of great teachers and help answer the question about the interrelationship of professional growth and personal growth. Most importantly, it will establish in a school's culture that teachers may expect their school to provide for them a full career of professional and personal development.

Among latter stage teachers, there is likely to emerge those who have been especially successful with assisting other teachers in the fulfillment of their potential. These teachers have a deep understanding of the value of bringing people together and they know how to do it. These people have a deeper grasp of the person-to-person aspects of human and professional development. And, they know how to utilize that togetherness to advance teacher development. Apart from the desire of these latter stage teachers to find new areas to assert their gifts, it should be considered that the school, itself, stands to benefit the most in using these teachers as leaders and models in the development of other teachers. They are models of what it is all about.

THE TRANSITION

If educators make the right choice, they will face a transition. Local schools will need to overcome two important and related hurdles in initiating the transition. First, local schools will need to move away from thinking of themselves as primarily for student learning. They will need to move toward popular recognition of schools as places where two groups learn, students *and* teachers.

Yes, for many this will be a stretch, but not an impossible one. The public has other reference points for this concept, such as teaching hospitals, to help them understand the importance of teacher learning on the job. Moreover, the public's own work in various organizations will likely also serve as a basis for understanding that the same is true of teachers. Add to this that the logic of it all is compelling. If novice teachers are telling us that the place they really learn is in schools, it will be hard for the public to ignore this reality.

The second challenge is to devise an approach to teacher learning that actually develops novice teachers into effective teachers, something higher education does not do. Let's be clear, however, that the nuts and bolts of such programs are not the subject of this book. There are many other fine books on that subject.

While many suggestions will be made (especially in the narrative) or implied in this book about *how* this might be accomplished, the core message of this book is the choice. Are educators willing to acknowledge the power of culture over strategy and use culture to create effective teachers? Are they willing to start conceiving of teachers in a different way? Are they willing to start thinking of a new model for the local school?

As this book insists on this one point, it joins those who have already concluded that it is possible to teach teachers how to become effective teachers. It joins those who believe schools can have faculties of *all* strong teachers. The first step in realizing this idea is to place teacher education where it will be internalized by teachers, in a real community of practice in a real local school. Additional transition factors will be developed in an upcoming chapter.

THERE IS NO PRESCRIPTION

As explained, however, this book has no prescription for the reader. This is on purpose. Greater benefit will come to local schools which take the time to think through this process from the roots up. The purpose of this book is to help readers who come from a variety of community and school contexts to think through how a school that operates as a community and has the explicit purpose of developing teachers might be created in their unique context.

Such a stance advances a concept in political science called *subsidiarity*. In affirming the concept for educational applications and citing examples from Finland, Hargreaves and Fullan (2012) explained, "The principal of subsidiarity is one in which issues should be addressed and resolved by the least centralized competent authority among people who are closest to that issue" (p. 175). This book affirms teachers as the "competent authority" best disposed to deal with a community's educational issues.

Having said this, yes, this book will offer some suggestions, some visions, some possibilities. But these should not be taken as a prescription. The concept of subsidiarity is consistent with the promise of this book to protect the decision-making of teachers. It is an affirmation of the idea that there are many roads to Rome and that inviting thousands of school districts to invent their own approach to teacher development stands to increase the thinking educators do and the learning they do from each other. It is a rejection of the idea that the best ideas come from central authorities which implicitly minimized local thinking and imagination.

By not providing a prescription for such a program, this book underscores the importance of teachers, and all school stakeholders, thinking for themselves about the design of a new school model. Every school will have to answer for itself how it will engage the collaborative thinking of their teachers in developing a new school model with a culture that will insure high levels of teacher development to support ever higher levels of student learning.

With this intent, the book will always put the reader's thinking first. Rather than give answers, it will ask questions, draw your attention to the literature, and invite experimentation. Prescriptions and scaled-up policy mandates do little to make educators think critically or creatively. Instead, such mandates most often leave educators feeling left out of the decision-making process. Jaded from years of such experiences, many don't even wonder why they have been left out of the process. They respond by painting by the numbers and instituting programs for which they have little passion or conceptual understanding. They play the game of school—until the funding runs out.

CONCLUSION

Taking a developmental perspective on teacher learning has been the focus of this chapter. Implicit in this view is that teachers will develop by stages throughout their careers, even in the latter years. Also, implicit is the idea that stage consciousness among teachers and school leaders will contribute to schools having a developmental culture.

These stages include the earliest stage when a school is trying to support a novice teacher through the difficult first year. Then, having survived the first year, teachers enter a second stage where they begin eagerly learning the tools of effective instruction and the ways of a professional learning community and how both support becoming an effective teacher.

In the third stage, teachers use their achievement as effective instructors and develop it further with academic research and a broader view of a teacher's work. In the fourth stage, the teacher advances in academic research and school leadership which results in school change and the school developing a unique configuration customized for local application. In the last stage, a teacher becomes a teacher of teachers and advances the school's learning about how we encourage personal and professional growth by coming together as a community of learners.

Chapter 5

The Primacy of Culture and the Promise of Professional Learning Communities

This chapter will review a number of developments that clarify why educators should reconsider the power of culture in teacher development. Having briefly considered the Stages Prompt Model, we face this question: By what devices can a school create a culture that gets its novice teachers up and through the stages? On this question, this book has a clear point of view. It is about culture. *It is the entirety of a school culture that produces effective teachers, and schools with authentic learning communities produce the cultures that produce effective teachers.*

To this end, the following would be among the characteristics of a developmental school culture.

- The purpose is explicit. Just as a youth goes to school understanding that it has been designed for young people to learn, teachers entering this school would understand that it was designed for teacher learning.
- Individual growth and development is an explicit message of the school culture. Everyone knows that beyond delivering instruction, he or she is expected to grow and develop both personally and professionally.
- Leaders in the school model striving for development that should be the behavior of everyone in the school.
- Professional learning communities will be the core cultural structure that invites the reflective and generative practice of teacher thinking, teacher-created knowledge, teacher-generated solutions, and teacher decision-making about the configuration of the school.

So, when we ask ourselves how we can nurture teachers' development up and through the five stages, this book stipulates that we must provide them with the right culture. It all depends on providing them *not* any particular standards, information, professional development activities, or course work but rather actually working in a deliberately developmental culture grounded in professional learning communities committed to reflective practice where continuous professional development is the norm and is embedded in the everyday work of teachers.

With this focus on experience, the evolution of a new school model would depend in large measure on two activities. First, teachers will need to begin to configure their own school in a way that they believe will create a developmental culture. Two, teachers will need to visit demonstration schools, schools that have been declared by themselves and peer schools to be effective in developing teachers and raising student learning levels.

A key point here is that school effectiveness would no longer be about a checklist of standards, guidelines, or practices. Rather, those aspiring to a new school model would focus on what might be called "organic outcomes." These are successful outcomes that may not conform to policy checklists but are, nevertheless, outcomes that educators can see, feel, or experience when visiting a demonstration school. This firsthand experience of the active ingredients that has moved a school to be successful stands to be much more helpful than another set of standards, goals, or guidelines.

Of course, readers still want to know what such a model school looks like. How would it be distinct from a traditional school? What would it sound like? How would it feel? These are great questions, and while this book offers some specifics, it intends to offer only partial direction. The main point here is not so much the specific components of the culture but recognition that more than any other influences it is culture that leads teachers to become effective teachers.

More important than this book giving direct advice about what the components of an intentionally developmental culture should be is raising the question for readers to answer for themselves. What should go on in a new school model that is explicitly designed for both teacher and student learning? What is envisioned here is that once educators arrive at the conclusion that culture is the central issue in teacher development, they will see the need for a new school model.

From there what we should see is that all schools will begin experimenting with developing cultures that actually create effective teachers. With all of this experimentation schools can begin to share what they find effective. Then, teachers should be constantly visiting other schools to experience what has shown itself to be effective in teacher development. The point of "Tina's Story" is to allow the reader such a "visit" to see what such a developmental culture would be like. But more importantly, it is meant to move the reader to think about teacher experiences that they think would be important in such a culture.

Again, a key point here is that we must stop thinking of professional development as discreet events where teachers are provided information by experts in sessions that are set apart from teachers' everyday work. When teacher learning is set apart in this way, it sends an implicit message: Learning and doing can be separated. We can learn how to do our jobs apart from our jobs. (This is the big flaw in higher education teacher preparation.) The message does not prompt teachers to think of themselves as knowledge creators or of the learning community process as a unique means by which teachers create knowledge and develop individually and collectively.

In most traditional schools teachers spend the majority of their time instructing students. Then, occasionally, professional development is provided in the form of one-shot programs that present information to passively seated teachers who may or may not feel the need for the information. In many cases the importance of the information provided was not determined by teachers but by central authorities in state or federal government who are unfamiliar with the needs of a particular school (TNTP, 2015).

THE NEW TEACHERS PROJECT REPORT, *THE MIRAGE*

In this context, a discussion of The New Teachers Project's report (2015), *The Mirage*, is in order. This recent, broadscale, academic study examined the effects of professional development on a large number of teachers across a variety of representative districts. The report set out to identify what experiences in teachers' professional learning showed themselves to be significant factors in the improvement of student learning. In other words, this research sought to identify what Levin, previously referenced, called the "active ingredients" in teacher learning that led to better student learning.

Specifically, researchers wanted to find out if what resulted in better student learning was some type of essential background knowledge. Was it teachers being introduced to new classroom practices or procedures? Was it better understanding of new instructional materials? Was it better use of technology?

Remarkably, this exhaustive study which reviewed extensive and varied quantitative data could not identify one factor in teacher professional development that played a significant role in the improvement of a teacher's performance or student learning. Equally remarkable, the researchers concluded that it was unclear that teacher professional development played any role, at all, in improving student learning (TNTP, 2015). The promise of "professional development," in other words constituted a kind of mirage. What we have always believed was possible if we only taught teachers the right lessons was never there at all. It was a mirage. These findings, unfortunately, found concurrent validation in two other federally funded studies that achieved similar findings (Note 16, p. 2).

While these counterintuitive findings are, at once, startling and disappointing, they did provide some hope in pointing to a way of thinking about teacher professional development that is consistent with the message of this book. Teacher professional development is not about discreet units of learning. It is not about what we directly teach teachers. Rather, *The Mirage* report strongly suggests that it is about the implicit—systems and culture in a school.

Toward the end of the report, there is a section entitled "An Exception to the Rule." In other words, the study did reveal some factors of teacher professional development that did positively influence student achievement. This discovery, however, emerged with the study of a different kind of school system, a "charter management organization," a CMO, which "takes a markedly different approach to teacher improvement" (TNTP, p. 30).

The report notes that data from this district showed "consistently better results" for both students and teachers. It notes that teachers experienced more growth over time, including teachers with many years of experience. The researchers looked for what this CMO was doing differently. They especially wanted to know, per the objective of the overall study, if there were particular strategies that seemed to be having a marked effect on CMO teachers who made greater strides than their peers. Just as with the other districts studied, the answer was no. No particular strategy could be isolated that distinguished one teacher from another. The report explains, "There doesn't seem to be a magic formula of teacher supports that we can link to that growth" (p. 33).

So what accounted for teacher and student improvement in this district? Instead of a formula of specific strategies, the report came to look at "institutional differences," that is differences in culture and systems. In explaining these institutional differences, the authors repeatedly make reference to culture.

They cited, for example, "a network wide culture of high expectations and continuous growth" and "a more disciplined and coherent system of organizing themselves around teacher development" where there is "regular feedback and practice" and teachers working together spending two or three hours a week involved in improving instructional practices in a variety of ways (p. 33).

From this perspective, researchers drew such conclusions as "having a meaningful impact on teacher performance depends as much on the conditions in which the development takes place as on the development itself," and "the evidence suggests that there is promise in the CMO's creating a culture and an organizational structure centered on teacher development," and "the system seems to be doing its part. Their culture of high expectations is met with an equal sense of commitment to helping teachers succeed" (p. 33).

Researchers reinforced this conclusion by highlighting a teacher's testimony. "In focus groups, CMO teachers reflected on the sense that everyone in their school community is constantly working toward better instruction and pushing each other to do their best work." In this context, the report highlighted the testimony of one CMO teacher who said, "What's unique about being at my school is that there is always going to be someone there to push you. I don't think I'll ever be able to stagnate here" (p. 33).

BACK TO THE ALTERNATIVE

This review of *The Mirage* report helps give us perspective on the current approach to professional development that is linear and formulaic. Consider what authorities now consider important parts of the linear formula for teacher success: one part right teacher characteristic, one part testing success, two parts high standards and mandates, three parts special out-of-context higher education programs, and one part incidental discrete experiences acquiring fad knowledge as professional development on the job.

This linear formula stands in contrast to what *The Mirage* report confirms. Teacher learning is more about culture and organizational conditions. Teachers learn to teach not from discrete standards or exercises in professional development whether they be in higher education or in a local school. They learn to teach in the schools where they work because it is in the nature of human being to adapt to cultures.

People have a natural inclination to fit in and become part of their surroundings. This is especially true of novice teachers who are eager to please authority figures and prove themselves to veteran teachers both of which will give newcomers thousands of cues about "how we do things around here." This is how teachers learn and develop.

There is an academic literature that does show that schools with collaborative teacher cultures do improve student learning better than schools where teachers do not work collaboratively. It is a mystery why this research and writing is not referenced in many of the reports on teacher education reviewed in preparation of this book.

THE CASE FOR CULTURES DERIVED OF LEARNING IN COMMUNITIES

It is in this context that we can best appreciate the promise of cultures derived of professional learning communities. As mentioned earlier, in the late 1980s and early 1990s there came two very positive developments in the professional lives of teachers and teacher education: professional learning communities, PLCs, and professional development schools, PDSs. A mountain of books and articles has been published that have explained the value and function of "learning communities," "collaborative cultures," "communities of practice," and "professional learning communities." PLCs and PDSs are largely derived of this line of research, theory, and writing.

Both PLCs and PDSs are founded on much of the same research employed by Sparks and Hirsh (1997), cited earlier, and works by other educators who saw fit to apply organizational theory to schools. These include such works as *Leading for Learning: How to Transform Schools into Learning Organizations Learning Organization* by Schlechty or *Schools that Learn* by Senge et al.

That research emphasized the organizational value and the learning value of higher levels of teacher participation and leadership in the design of student learning and teacher learning. In effect, these movements looked to make teacher thinking and creativity central to school operations. Both PDSs and PLCs are about teachers being involved in and leading schools' decision-making about learning and schooling.

THE END OF TEACHER ISOLATION AND TOP-DOWN AUTHORITY STRUCTURES

Much of the interest in the learning community concept in the 1990s was in reaction to two interrelated cultural conditions in the traditional practice of teaching. One condition was that teachers usually worked in isolation from one another. Behind the closed doors of their classrooms, each teacher largely did his or her own thing to implement the school's curriculum.

Apart from some common requirements of their position as teachers, teachers did not work together. They did not get together for the purpose of reflecting on the effectiveness of the school overall. They did not collaborate on how to improve the practice of teaching in their individual classrooms. Teaching was considered a private matter for teachers to work out for themselves. Each teacher worked his or her magic or lack of it.

Professional development for these isolated teachers was most often one-shot presentations where teachers primarily sat and listened to "whims, fads, opportunism, and ideology" (cited by Schmoker, 2015) in education that had little relationship to what they did everyday behind their classroom doors. Remarkably, the idea of improving student learning by collaborating with one another to change any of the traditional practices, structures, or procedures of the school was rarely considered by teachers. It just wasn't what teachers did.

The second condition was the top-down command and control authority structure in schools where teachers were often excluded from important decision-making about their schools. Decision-making was left to school or central office administrators. This condition is a legacy left over from the design of schools like factories from the industrial age. People at the top did the thinking. People at the bottom followed directions.

As work and research in organizational theory began to find its way into educational circles, the isolation of teachers and their exclusion from decision-making looked increasingly like what they were, anachronisms left over from the industrial age (Senge et al., 2000, 2012). Many publications emerged suggesting to educators that their schools had to offer teachers and other stakeholders greater participation.

THE LEARNING COMMUNITY MODEL PROMISED CHANGE

The advent of the learning community model promised to put an end to teacher isolation and exclusion from decision-making. Briefly put, professional learning communities are formed when teachers get together to share perspectives and work together to solve problems on matters of learning: lesson design, lesson study, evaluation protocols, curriculum development, school structures and design, and/or ad hoc problem solving of all sorts.

A PLC could be in a small group situation where teachers exchange ideas about how social studies and English teachers might work together to teach a Victorian novel. Or, a PLC could be where teachers have come together to talk about how to insert emotional education into scientific lab work.

PLCs can also be large collectives such as an entire school faculty. In these circumstances teachers might discuss the standards, goals, and objectives of the school. Such PLCs invite thinking, reflection, imagination, and broad involvement from all members of a school. Most theorists would agree that PLCs were advocated in order to invite not only teacher input but also teacher leadership (DuFour et al., 2006; Schlechty, 2002; Schmoker, 2006; Wenger et al., 2002).

The learning community concept acknowledges that the real-world workplace in a school is the actual site of teachers learning to teach. Yes, courses and degrees taken and earned at a college or university do affect teachers' frames of reference, but the most important learning for teachers is seen as coming from sharing and learning that is embedded in their everyday work in a school. The concept maintains that if a school operates as a learning community, teacher learning will be propelled to higher levels by the very fact of working and reflecting together.

If a school does not function as a learning community but rather fosters isolation and exclusion from important decision-making, teacher learning will be greatly inhibited or even become negative and lead to teacher disengagement. Recent research by the Gallup organization suggests that teacher disengagement is, in fact, currently at very high levels (Busteed, 2014) and is correlated with teacher's exclusion from decision-making.

The learning community model affirms that the greatest force for a teacher's professional development will come, then, on the job in a learning community where a teacher will likely spend decades developing her or his craft and career. The guiding concept is that in a community of practice all members of a school should come together for collective learning and collective action as a result of that learning.

In such communities teachers are expected to collaborate and act as thinkers, creators, and innovators. Such a scenario acknowledges contemporary organizational theory which sees all members of an organization as agents of change empowered to learn, reflect, and alter the organization for continuous improvement (Deming, 1983; DuFour & Fullan, 2013; Senge, 1991; Senge et al., 2000, 2012).

THE COMPELLING LOGIC OF THE LEARNING COMMUNITY

In contrast to working in isolation or being marginalized from decision-making, the learning community concept posits that learning is deeper and develops faster when it is done in community. The idea follows the common saying that "two heads are better than one." In other words when people are trying to learn together, the sharing of ideas and perspectives and the resulting feedback tend to lead to better thinking and better actions. It is consistent with the academic concept of peer review.

The reader may have noticed in your own experience that when you attempt to explain yourself to others, the very act of explaining helps you understand your own thinking better. At the same time, getting feedback from the people to whom you have tried to explain something also helps refine and push your thinking forward so your ideas become better and better as a result of the process of working as a community. Conversely, listening to the ideas of others and giving feedback also tends to improve everyone's thinking.

This aspect of the learning community model was, of course, very compelling, and in the late 1980s and 1990s the concept was roundly embraced by both policy makers and local school leaders. Around the nation, the term "learning community" became a buzz word for the latest innovation in schooling. It promised teachers more leadership and much greater influence in their schools in the design of student learning and their own learning.

ENDORSED BY NAPDS AND NCATE

It is also notable that the goal of having teachers inducted and developed within communities of learning has also been stipulated as fundamental by two associations that have been primary drivers in teacher education, the National Association of Professional Development Schools and the National Council for Accreditation of Teacher Education (now CAEP). Each has long noted the importance of using the school setting to enhance the clinical basis of teacher education.

Thus, fundamental to the inception of PDSs has been the value of local schools and nearby institutions of higher education forming partnerships to facilitate moving teacher education out of higher education classrooms and into actual schools. In these schools, novice teachers would enter communities of support, inquiry, and practice which provide a concrete basis for conceptualizing effective teaching, observing effective teaching, and being guided in the practice of effective teaching.

Underscoring this commitment to community learning, the NAPDS has, for example, advanced a list of Nine Essentials which guide the Association's work and research. Among them, three make explicit reference to the role of community in teacher learning and development.

> 2. a school-university culture committed to the preparation of future educators that embraces their active engagement in the school community
> 4. a shared commitment to innovative and reflective practice by all participants
> 7. a structure that allows all participants a forum for ongoing governance, reflection, and collaboration. (NAPDS, 2008)

Similarly, NCATE has stipulated an emphasis on school-based learning to enhance the clinical component of teacher education. As a result of convening a Blue Ribbon Panel in 2010, NCATE produced a report, *Transforming Teacher Education Through Clinical Practice: A National Strategy to Prepare Effective Teachers* (NCATE, 2010). The report provided Design Principles for teacher education which included

"Candidates learn in an interactive learning community" (NCATE, 2010). The guidance provided by the NAPDS and NCATE are, of course, very consistent with the proposal of this book.

THE PERSONAL BENEFITS OF THE LEARNING COMMUNITY MODEL

Another aspect of the learning community model was also very compelling. It provided personal benefits to individuals. Along with the benefit of improving the practice of teaching, research into learning communities explained how it addressed the human need for continuous learning and thoughtful, decisive participation in any organization.

Such participation would promise very fulfilling careers to teachers as respected professionals charged with the continuous improvement of their schools. These benefits include

1. A greater sense of belonging, of being a respected member of a team.
2. A greater sense of ownership of the overall institution and its goals.
3. A greater sense of control over one's work.
4. A greater sense of respect and care from one's peers.
5. A greater sense of being respected as a thinker, designer, and decision maker.
6. A greater sense of professional growth and fulfillment.

These personal benefits have been the subject of many a professional treatise on why teachers should adopt the learning community model for their schools. Under the learning community model, teachers not only stand to improve their clinical practice in helping students learn but also stand to enjoy much fuller professional lives working in collaboration with their peers. Such higher levels of teacher engagement have high correlation with student engagement and learning (Busteed, 2014).

With the above information in mind, teachers are asked to take a moment to envision how being a member of a real learning community would be experienced. Imagine you and your colleagues discussing some of the hard issues that teachers face and then making decisions that would change those conditions and your school for the better. That's right, as a result of examining conditions, sharing perspectives, and making decisions, teachers would guide their schools to continuous improvement. They would not depend on outside authorities. How would that feel? How does it compare to having outsiders make the important decisions for your school?

Now if you find yourself thinking, "Oh, that is pie in the sky" or "That's too simplistic or idealistic," you are cautioned. The fact is that such teacher participation and influence is already happening. More than a decade ago Senge, Cambron-McCabe, Lucas, Smith, Dutton, and Kleiner advanced the work *Schools That Learn* (2000, 2012) and explained the concept of schools as learning organizations where the thinking for schools was done in schools.

Most importantly, they gave numerous examples of such schools and their wonderful outcomes.

More recently, Farris-Berg, Dirkswager, and Jung (2012) had their research published in *Trusting Teachers with School Success: What Happens When Teachers Call the Shots*. Their study of teacher-run schools clarifies the many advantages of teacher-run schools and their great promise. It tells the story of many teacher-led schools, their important progress in student learning, and the valuable learning opportunities such schools provide teachers.

Even more recently, the work *Deeper Learning: How Eight Innovative Public Schools Are Transforming Education in the Twenty-First Century* (Martinez & McGrath, 2014) clarified the need for change and how it can be pursued. This research-based work provides a list of model schools that are truly innovating and discusses at length their use of "cohesive, collaborative learning communities that sharply differ from the top-down national norm" (Martinez & McGrath, 2014, p. 14).

Add to this that even the NEA has a *Commission on Effective Teachers and Teaching* and has charged its members to "craft a new vision of a teaching profession that is led by teachers and ensures teaching effectiveness." The point is this: The evolution of teaching is already in progress—and with a sharp focus on teacher participation and leadership.

THE UNREALIZED PROMISE OF THE LEARNING COMMUNITY MODEL

There is a strong likelihood that you have heard the term "learning community" in the course of your academic study or around the school where you work. The learning community concept is often discussed in education textbooks, and many states have endorsed the idea for their schools. If you are very lucky, you may actually work in a school that has real learning communities. The reality, however, is that most teachers do not.

Unfortunately, the learning community concept has gotten more lip service than genuine implementation. This is most often manifested in schools that have pretend learning communities. Because school leaders know that the learning community concept is fashionable, many have been moved to think that any situation where teachers are sharing ideas or collaborating on common projects means that their schools are operating as learning communities. School leaders wrongly call all sorts of situations where teachers get together "learning communities." They are deceptive when they do this.

Still other schools have teacher activities that mirror the reality of a learning community, but these activities are occasional and episodic, and not integral to school operations. They are more of an add-on to traditional school culture. Teachers do not see that their thinking and decision-making exerts any real influence in the school. Mostly, it generates elaborate paperwork which is used as proof of learning communities for central authorities. From all of this teachers have a sense of going through the motions because they see very little in terms of substantial change in their schools.

It is in light of these pretend learning communities that it must be made very clear. The incidental or occasional facilitation of teachers talking with one another, collaborating, or even creating elaborate documents does not constitute true implementation of the learning community model. A review of the literature makes it clear that a genuine implementation of the learning community model constitutes a major and thoroughgoing overhaul of school culture where people's behavior changes, the school's structure changes, the school changes, and student learning improves.

Learning communities are not an appendage to traditional school culture; they replace the traditional school culture (DuFour & Fullan, 2013).

A MAJOR OBSTRUCTION TO DEVELOPING LEARNING COMMUNITIES

Around the same time that the concept of learning communities started to become popular, there was also another emerging concept, school accountability. This concept has persisted and now underlies the demand for better teacher education. Many in society, in business, and in government continue to express disappointment in the outcomes of schooling.

As previously indicated, these critics pointed to low test scores, high dropout rates, unskilled graduates, low graduation rates, and the fact that students in many foreign countries scored better than American students on international standardized tests. These critics understandably want schools to be more accountable for positive results.

One of the outcomes of this disappointment in schools has been that important people in Washington D.C. and in state capitals have lost faith in teachers and local school leaders. These policy makers came to the conclusion that if local school leaders and teachers could not run effective schools by their own devices, it would be necessary to impose on them mandates and standards that would require positive results. Moreover, these mandates and standards would be enforced by a variety of funding and disciplinary devices.

With a genuine desire to get better results from our schools, central policy makers have attempted to take greater control of our schools. To assert this control, states have for a long time been requiring students to pass standardized tests in order to graduate. Authorities were no longer willing to trust teacher evaluation of students as legitimate indicators of learning. All teachers know, of course, that these standardized tests have taken a very imposing presence in our schools.

More recently, the federal government in the *No Child Left Behind* legislation has required schools to show annual improvement in student learning as reflected in standardized test scores. This legislation included some harsh consequences for schools and their leaders if the standardized test results indicate little or no improvement in learning for individual students and for a school overall.

Even more recently, the *Race to the Top* legislation has required that teacher evaluations be at least partly based on the standardized test scores for students in a particular teacher's class. If students in a particular class show little or no improvement in learning, then that teacher could face difficult consequence or be dismissed.

Most recently the passage of *ESSA*, *Every Student Succeeds Act*, has promised to relax some of the controls exerted by the federal government, but not state governments.

As these efforts of central authorities to take control of our schools continue to unfold, the important decision-making for schools has moved away from local school and community stakeholders to central policy makers outside of the school. The decisions made are often made by people who have little experience in classroom teaching and no knowledge of particular schools, their populations, or their unique conditions.

In the face of all of this, teachers find themselves increasingly marginalized as thinkers and decision makers. They see that in spite of their stakeholder status, their influence within their schools is diminished with each new mandate. Teachers watch with frustration as forces outside of schools dictate standards, goals, curricula, lesson design, and even what teachers should say in delivering a lesson. Teachers are even faced with talk among publishers and in policy circles of "teacher proofing" instruction.

Again, this marginalization of teachers as engaged stakeholders in their schools is borne out by research. A recent Gallop poll indicated that "among all occupations tracked in their survey, teachers were the least likely to say that their opinions counted at work" (Busteed, 2014). Moreover, in that same survey teachers were last "in agreeing ... that their supervisors create an open and trusting environment" (Busteed, 2014). This is remarkably dark data considering that it comes more than twenty years after the advent of learning communities was roundly and loudly embraced my many leaders in education, including those in Washington, DC.

So moved by the adversity that contemporary teachers face, Nancy Atwell, winner of the coveted Global Teacher Prize explained in *Education Week* that "public school teachers are so constrained right now by the Common Core Standards and the tests that are developed to monitor what teachers are doing with them" that "if you're a creative, smart young person, I don't think this is the time to go into teaching unless an independent school would suit you" (Moeny, 2015).

Very recently the non-profit Center on Education Policy issued a report (2016), "Listen to Us: Teachers Views and Voices." *Education Week* explained that the report "paints a picture of a profession that has become increasing demanding and discouraging, leaving many teachers who entered the profession for mostly altruistic reasons feeling stressed and discounted." The report goes on to explain that as many as "half of teachers would leave the profession as soon as possible if they could get a higher paying job" (Will, 2016).

Of course, there is a persistent theme that runs through all of these concerns. Teachers are clearly not conceived of as thinkers and decision makers in their schools. What's worse, teachers feel helpless in their situation. There is, apparently, no sense among teachers that they are important players who have the leverage to demand better conditions. They surely do not think of themselves as change agents who are in a position to demand change.

The fact that teachers do not have this self-concept can be laid squarely at the feet of higher education. This is the one institution that has had the opportunity to change the learning trajectory of teachers. Years ago aspiring teachers could have been taught that our schools were obsolete and that it would be up to new teachers to begin to change our schools, but they were not.

It is another perspective on how teacher capacities have been neglected by higher education. Teachers have no sense of their capacity for change as a result of working together. Instead, in a strict adherence to tradition, our new teachers are taught how to be good, individual classroom teachers. Their work together is hardly an afterthought.

It is in the face of such conditions that teachers should consider a different reality as developed in the following table.

MORE CHOICE FOR TEACHERS

When teachers look at table 5.1, would they really consider directing our young, aspiring teachers into the same conditions most of our teachers face today? Would they have them learn to ignore their personal potential and to only expect to be compliant implementers of others' mandates and decisions? Or, would it better to establish the expectation in them that their future in teaching will be one of long-term professional growth as an outcome of their collaboration with others who think of teachers as thinkers, creators, and decision makers bent on change and continuous school improvement.

Table 5.1 A Choice for Teachers

A Career of Frustration Today	A Satisfying Career in the Future
Lack of Self-determination	Self-determination
You lack a sense of control over your work. For the most part, the nature and design of student work, its implementation, and its evaluation is dictated by legacy practices of federal, state, or local officials or publishers with whom you have little contact and who do not ask your opinion.	You have a sense of purpose and feel control over your work. You make important choices and play a key role in the design, execution, and evaluation of your work.
Sortive Evaluation	Supportive Evaluation
You feel little power over your own evaluation. You believe there are criteria included which should not be there and other important factors left out. You see the process as a way of sorting teachers and not very helpful in supporting your improvement as a professional.	You inform how you are evaluated. You have helped design the evaluation process. You play a critical role in how the process is applied. You believe the others involved in your evaluation care about you and are supporting your growth as a professional.
Teacher Technician	Teacher Professional
You see yourself as a worker/technician tasked with implementing standards, goals, curricula, lesson design, and even scripts dictating what you should say in delivering lessons to students. You are never asked to reflect on or give judgment about what is being taught, how it is taught, or the overall assumptions underlying this instructional approach.	You are a Member/Stakeholder: You feel like a respected member of a professional team. You helped the team create a vision for optimal functioning and you work collectively with it to learn and to take action to apply that learning. As part of this, you are often called upon to bring your judgment and imagination to important decision-making.
Lack of Community	Caring Community
The school you work in is large. There are many hundreds, maybe more than a thousand students and over a hundred staff. Many people don't know or care about each other. The friendships that form are part of cliques that are unrelated to the school's goals and culture. There is often animosity between groups. Student and adult behavior often shows disconnection and disregard for others. There is a lot of negative gossiping and complaining. Students' achievement is usually the outcome of compliance or competition not high engagement.	The school you work in is a deliberately designed small community with the stated purpose of creating a culture of caring where both adults and students are committed to a high level of kindness and respect for all members. Members feel connected. They believe that such a caring community is the foundation for human engagement in life and learning. Caring and engagement are seen as the basis for high academic expectations and high student achievement. Members of this community work harder but happier.

(Continued)

Table 5.1   A Choice for Teachers (*Continued*)

A Career of Frustration Today	A Satisfying Career in the Future
Technical Learning	Professional Learning
Your professional learning is focused on the implementation of standards created by others and preparing students for success on an array of standardized proficiency assessments and year-end standardized tests created by others. Neither you nor other teachers are asked to reflect on the value of these standardized tools nor many of the other assumptions and practices of your school. If you disagree with their use, you are regarded with suspicion. A lot of research, including research suggesting the ill-effects of standardized testing is ignored. You experience a high level of frustration and find your thoughts turning to self-protection, not aspirations for personal and professional growth.	You are aware that your school community is heavily invested in your professional learning. There is ongoing reflection on the effectiveness of a broad array of learning and schooling strategies for both students and teachers. Professional learning is embedded in your everyday routines. Research is happening everywhere. There is a collective eagerness to consider imaginative and entrepreneurial ideas for instructional change and overall school improvement. You see and feel your continuous growth as a person and a professional within this culture as you move up the stages and take on new challenges and ever greater responsibilities. You feel respect as a professional.

The importance of teachers experiencing long-term professional growth cannot be overstated. There is in the experience of all educators who have witnessed teacher burnout ample anecdotal information to support the need for career-long professional development. But burnout is not fatigue. Again, according to the famed adult developmental psychologists, Robert Kegan and Lisa Laskow Lahey, "research shows that the single biggest cause of work burnout is not work overload, but working too long without experiencing your own personal development" (Kegan & Lahey et al., 2016, loc. 89). It is an observation that our profession needs to heed.

Think of it this way. Teaching is your profession. You are its steward. Clearly, for lack of asserting ourselves, the teaching profession has gone adrift and now finds itself in troubled waters. Although we clearly did not steer ourselves into this mess, we must take responsibility for getting ourselves out. One way to correct our course is to point the way for the next generation of teachers to a professionalism that is healthy and self-directed. Aspiring teachers need to be pointed in the direction of all of the professional, personal, and student learning benefits inherent in the learning community model. It is a mode of operation that cannot be acquired in higher education.

CONCLUSION

This book attempts to answer the following question: How do we create effective teachers?

It provides an answer derived of research: *It is the entirety of a school culture that produces effective teachers, and schools with authentic learning communities produce the cultures that produce effective teachers.* In developing this idea, the first section of this book, "The Emergence of Teacher as Learner-Collaborator-Leader," took an historical perspective on the concept of teacher learning, particularly developments in the last few decades that have moved the idea of teacher learning away from thinking of professional development as discreet training sessions that were presented to teachers by experts.

Instead, the influence of organizational theory and learning moved many to thinking of teacher learning as a collaborative pursuit that they did for themselves as part of improving teacher learning, student learning, and their school. As part of analyzing how teachers learn, chapter 1, "The Good and Bad of Cultural Learning," reviewed the usually overlooked but powerful influence of cultural learning on teachers and how it can affect teachers in good or bad ways.

Chapter 2, "Cultural Learning, Human Development, and Teacher Development," focused on the need to harness cultural learning to improve teacher learning. It emphasized the value of thinking about teacher development as an explicit purpose of a school where teachers may be observed going through stages supported by positive developmental cultures that support teacher growth for a full career.

Chapter 3, "The Primacy of Culture and the Promise of PLCs," explained that when it comes to the question of creating effective teachers, research points us in one direction. Teachers work most effectively and grow more completely when they work as part of collaborative teams or professional learning communities.

Part II

THE PROMISE OF PROFESSIONAL DEVELOPMENT SCHOOLS

The idea that novice teachers get significant benefit from moving their learning out of college classrooms and into local schools is long-standing. The professional development school movement is, perhaps, the best institutional expression of this idea as it makes students' field experience the centerpiece of teacher preparation. The PDS movement, unquestionably, has the best intellectual product and practice for aspiring teachers of any the professional association. However, its current state of practice reveals significant problems in its reliance on the traditional school model. This section proffers that by focusing its resources on building local schools that do, in fact, create effective teachers the PDS movement may continue its leadership in teacher education.

Chapter 6

Professional Development Schools Interrupted

Along with emergence of the professional learning community model in the 1990s came a related concept, professional development schools. PDSs in the most basic sense are about the mutual benefits of partnerships between local schools and teacher preparation programs in higher education. The principal benefit is the improved induction and preparation of novice teachers in an authentic school setting. PDSs have many precursors but were largely an outcome of a report by the Holmes Group (1986, 1990) which looked to respond to the many critics of our nation's schools and teacher education post the publication of *A Nation at Risk* (1983).

The Holmes Group Report aspired to improve teacher education through such partnerships and basically looked to remake the teaching profession, itself, in the process. Although the professional development school movement has hardly fulfilled the desires of the Holmes Group since then, its limited success has, nevertheless, done much good. Most importantly, it has foreshadowed the emergence of a new model for teacher education which takes place entirely in local schools.

Briefly put, the PDS movement sought to increase the amount of clinical experience (time in schools) for teacher candidates. In effect, it had a premise similar to that of this book—teacher learning would be greatly enhanced by being placed in actual schools. This would be accomplished by striking a new partnership between higher education and nearby local schools which had a constant need for high-quality new teachers. Such a partnership stood to enhance knowledge and practice in both institutions.

Thus, by virtue of the PDS movement, novice teacher learning has moved from the higher-education-classroom theoretical to the in-a-local-school practical. Information about the work of teachers has become more firsthand and precluded all of the problems associated with decontextualized, second-hand information in textbooks or college lectures. In addition to firsthand observation, novice teachers have also been given immediate access to question experienced practitioners, sometimes in the very moment of an event. They were also able to do the same with students.

The concreteness of this participation in a community of practice led, then, to a more personal experience and allowed novice teachers to sort through both the cognitive and emotional meaning of events. Educational theory became more understandable. As previously mentioned, the importance of such participation in a community of practice has been highlighted by NCATE's Blue Ribbon Panel (2010) which placed special importance on the value of clinical exposure and practice in the development of novice teachers.

By having teacher candidates participate in extensive induction programs in a particular school and by designing its own program, local schools could be assured of the completeness and appropriateness of novice teachers' training way before they came in for an interview. And, candidates who demonstrated the most promise as teachers could be given priority when it came time to hire additional teachers.

In the overall, the benefits of such a partnership were numerous, many of which came from the reciprocal relationship where the university learned of the "realities" of teaching from local schools and the local schools learned of recent research and new protocols from the universities for improved teacher induction and development. In the course of this relationship, many institutions of higher education and local schools discovered that their relationship stood to provide still more benefits beyond the induction of new teachers.

THE PROBLEM WITH PROFESSIONAL DEVELOPMENT SCHOOLS

The fact is that these professional development schools did facilitate many improvements in terms of enhancing the professionalism of teaching. Beyond the enhanced induction of new teachers, veteran educators communicated with each other more about what novice teachers needed to get off to a good start. This improved a local school's conceptualization of good teaching.

It elevated professional dialogue and a sense of a school as a learning community. It further translated into other helpful communication and collaboration within local schools and institution of higher education about how to help each other. Many in the PDS movement have reported that this communication has had numerous unintended positive collateral effects on instruction in both institutions.

It is also notable that the growth of the professional development school movement was driven by many "true believers" whose work was enthusiastic and tireless. The movement became a source of needed inspiration for many in the teaching profession, including this author. The idea of improved teacher preparation and helping young teachers get off to a good start was extremely compelling. There was a heroic, pioneering quality to much of this early work of the PDS movement, particularly that of staff at the University of South Carolina which led to the founding of the National Association of Professional Development Schools.

So what was the problem? Again, it was culture. As the vast majority of schools in the United States are traditional schools with traditional school cultures, the schools which formed partnerships with higher education were in most cases traditional schools with traditional cultures. Like most traditional schools, they thought of themselves as having the primary mission of student education. They did not see their mission as extending to teacher education for a full career.

Yes, with the advent of professional development schools, the induction process was greatly improved. Teachers were getting off to a better start and local schools improved their professional climate. But after that better start, it could be observed that early career teachers were acclimating to the old cultures of the traditional school where they started their careers. As newcomers to cultures always do, they looked around them and began to behave and think in accordance with what others did. They imitated the cultural norms of their traditional schools. Thus, most of our novice teachers were doing their formative professional and cultural learning in schools committed to the assumptions, structures, and practices of the nineteenth century.

More specifically, most these schools did not have cultures derived of teaching teams or professional learning communities or anything close to them. Neither did these schools provide teachers with increasing opportunities for collaboration. These schools were not, "settings for mutual exchange between research and practice" (Holmes Group, 1986). They were traditional schools where teachers spent most of their time teaching students and working by themselves in preparation for that duty.

In the overall, most of these teachers were affected more by the dictates of the accountability movement than they were from the spirit of the Holmes Group. How teachers executed their work in these traditional cultures was most often prescribed by outside influences, not teacher thinking. In these schools, professional development was an add-on with occasional rational presentations to teachers deemed important by central office or policy people in remote places.

It was not learning embedded in the everyday work of teachers analogous to that of the teaching hospitals example invoked as a model by the Holmes Group. Most importantly, these schools rarely thought of involving teachers in making changes in their school. What changes did happen were most often the result of policy changes dictated in state capitals or Washington, DC. These schools certainly did not see fit to involve teachers in creating new designs for schools, schools that would better serve the unique learning needs of the populations they served.

All of this is in stark contradiction to what the Holmes Group envisioned. The formation of professional development schools was intended to not only create change in schools but to "change the teaching profession," itself. Central to the Group's vision of change was the heightened priority of teacher learning in local schools. The Holmes Group explained,

> These Professional Development Schools, analogous to teaching hospitals in the medical profession, will bring practicing teachers and administrators together with university faculty in partnership based on the following principles:
>
> - Reciprocity or mutual exchange and benefit between research and practice.
> - Experimentation, or willingness to try new forms of practice and structure.
> - Systematic inquiry, or the requirement that new ideas be subject to careful study and validation, and
> - Student diversity, or commitment to the development of teaching strategies for a broad range of children with different backgrounds, abilities, and learning styles. (*Tomorrow's Teachers: A Report of the Holmes Group*, 1986, p. 67)

What the Holmes Group envisioned, then, were new kinds of schools where teacher learning was central to the operation of the school. But it didn't come to pass. To the extent that higher education and local schools have collaborated, it has been within the bounds of what we know as traditional schools. Professional development schools have not resulted in the transformation of schools but a continuation of the traditional school model.

THE RESULT OF NO CHANGE

The popularization of professional development schools and professional learning communities has now passed three decades. These concepts promised that teachers would participate in important school decision-making and give teachers broad participation and leadership in guiding the learning of students, their own learning, and the learning of novice teachers.

They made this promise because it was the wisdom of our finest organizational thinkers (Argyris, 1980; Deming, 1983, 1986; Senge, 1991; Garvin, 2000; Gruenert & Whitaker, 2015, 2017; Wheatly, 1979) all of whom called for, and still call for, the broad participation of all organizational members in the effort to continuously improve an organization.

Again this thinking has had a much-heralded application to schools supported by many publications and has led to the concepts of professional learning communities and professional development schools becoming widespread. Now, some thirty years later we learn that these programs did not even come close to fulfilling their promise. A 2013 Gallup poll of teachers indicated that among all occupations tracked in their survey, teachers were the least likely to say that their opinions counted at work (Busteed, 2014).

And, our teachers are right. Their opinions count for very little. Most of them are now situated in a school that is not focused on teacher learning, thinking, or decision-making. Our teachers do not follow routines rich in lesson study, reflective practice, or collaborative application of teacher thinking.

Instead, their schools are focused on compliance with the mandates of central authorities. These are the central authorities who are now doing the important thinking with respect to standards, goals, curricula, and standardized assessment. Teachers even find themselves marginalized with respect to lesson design and publishers' "teacher proofing" of lessons and what teachers should say in their delivery.

It is clear evidence that these schools were not designed for collaboration or for the kind teacher learning envisioned by the Holmes Group or advocates of professional learning communities. When you take away teacher participation and decision-making, you take away the most important learning opportunities for teachers.

Rick Breault and Donna Adair Breault refer to this condition in their work *Professional Development Schools: Researching Lessons from the Field*. In confronting issues of culture and innovation and the resulting implementation uncertainties in PDSs, they explain:

> This [implementation] is aggravated by the PDS typically being situated in a regular public school that is distracted by the necessity of its own technocratic preoccupation with state standards and high stakes testing. As a result, whatever idealistic potential there might have been in the NCATE PDS standards is undermined by the bureaucratic, politically situated nature of their sponsoring organization, and the potential for critical reflections and naming PDSs through dialogic process is lost. (Breault & Breault, 2012, p. 23)

There is a reason for this. Without a dedicated mission to innovate, the cultures of the traditional schools where our teachers are employed will not yield. These traditional schools were not designed as places for teachers to think, collaborate, learn, and create change. With their old organizational structures, their old time structures, and their old assumptions about teaching and learning, they were designed to function as top-down authority organizations.

Their intent was to make schools into static learning factories for the mass production of a citizenry who would be provided the basics of what was needed to survive in the industrial age. They were not designed for teachers to collaborate and make critical decisions for continuous school improvement. The current control of our schools by central authorities as they assert state and federal regulation has extended and intensified this legacy condition. Like it or not, the idea of teacher learning has always been and continues to be a side show in these traditional school cultures.

As previously mentioned, the conditions described above fly in the face of important scholarship that has demonstrated that teacher collaboration is essential to high-quality schooling. John Hattie's extensive research demonstrated that teachers working together as evaluators of their impact on student learning have the single greatest effect (by a wide margin) on student learning in comparison to all other variables (Hattie, 2011; www.youtube.com/watch?v=rzwJXUieD0U).

More recently, this conclusion about the importance of teachers working together was also reached by the *National Center on Time and Learning* which underscored the perspective that teachers working in community produce the best learning outcomes for students. As developed by this organization's publication entitled *Time and Teaching* (NCTL, 2015),

> Research shows that schools with the strongest PLCs [professional learning communities] generate higher student performance. Moreover, this working together reaches it optimum effect when teachers are involved in school design that expands the amount of time they have to work together. (Davis, 2015)

Some may resist the idea that the Gallup data apply to PDS schools because they believe PDSs are different. They believe that because of the PDS community's unique history, goals, mission, and induction protocols PDSs have eluded the grip of the traditional school model. But objective data do not support this view. The factors that restrain innovation in traditional schools also restrain it in PDSs.

Senge (1991) points us to a primary restraint on innovation in schools, the persistence of the industrial-age assumptions about learning and schooling (Senge et al., 2000, 2012). The fact is, as will be confirmed shortly, these assumptions drive most schools, PDS or otherwise.

Industrial Age Schools Are Based on Assumptions

About **Time**: Credit for learning is based on teacher evaluation after a student has accumulated the required seat time in an approved course. School will run morning to afternoon 5 days a week except for holidays and weekends for 180 days per school year. There will be a vacation period of about 10 weeks during the summer months.

About **Place**: The primary place of learning is the school and it grounds.

About **Resources**: The school and it programs will be funded by the local board of education as funds are provided by a local municipality via the raising of taxes. These funds may be supplemented by state and federal grants.

About **Teachers**: Teachers are the primary conveyors of knowledge and skills. Credit for learning will follow a student who receives instruction from a teacher in a classroom.

About **Students**: Students are inherently deficient and need to be coerced into having their deficiencies remediated by highly structured school programs.

About **Motivation**: Students will be offered a variety of extrinsic incentives such as grades, rewards, praise, and recognition as the outcome of doing the work prescribed by the school.

About **Context**: The school is dedicated to serving it local community by developing students who are prepared for work, college, and participation in community government and city affairs.

About **How Students Learn**: Certifiable student learning comes primarily from classroom instruction with the use of approved curriculum and textbooks where the students have fulfilled required seat time in a classroom and successfully passed a teacher evaluation process.

About **Knowledge**: It may be thought of as an entity or thing that has quantity and mass. Knowledge can thus be transferred to students by teachers in the way water might be poured into an empty container.

About **What Students Learn**: Students shall learn the approved school curriculum including locally and state required subjects as well as required subjects as stipulated by the many colleges and universities to which students apply. These required courses will be supplemented by elective courses and after school activities.

About **How Students Are Evaluated**: Students will be evaluated by teachers on assignments and given letter grades (A, B, C, D, and F) that certify the completion of work and the level of achievement the work represents.

About **How Learning is Certified**: When students receive passing grades in their courses, they will be certified as having developed the necessary knowledge and skills for that particular course. (Waters, 2014)

Consistent with the unconscious nature of these assumptions, many organizational scholars have explained that these assumptions cause *organizations to continue to do what they have done before* (Hess, 2010; Kelly et al., 2009; Senge, 1991; Tyack & Cuban, 1995; Wagner et al., 2006; Waters, 2014). Add to this that governments and schools, per industrial-age thinking, still rely on *standardization* to maximize the "efficiency" of schools. Schools are prompted to do things as other schools do them, especially to use the same standards and assessment tools.

The number of comparisons of schools to industrial-age factories in the current literature is too many to mention but here are a few (Schlechtey, 2009; Senge et al., 2000, 2012; Wagner et al., 2006; Waters, 2014).

We may also see nineteenth-century standardization protocols in

- **Regional School Evaluations and Accreditation** which have a similar impact on innovation. These evaluations assess school management that results in well-run traditional schools. They do not look for innovation that strives to move away from the traditional school model. (This author has chaired a regional school evaluation and served on an evaluation team for Middle States.)
- **Legacy employment agreements** which have a similar influence. Local associations resist change because it may disrupt or nullify working condition agreements that have taken years to achieve. The influence of negotiated employment agreements is a well-documented restraint on innovation (Chubb, 2012; Moe & Chubb, 2009).
- **College admission standards** such as those asserted by the NCAA also stand as a powerful restraint on innovation as will be developed shortly (Lytle, 2016).

When readers look at this very partial list, they can probably recognize that most schools are affected by these legacy restraints whether or not they are PDSs. The reality is that PDSs, like most traditional schools, are affected by most of these restraints. Given this condition, research on schools in general has much greater application to PDSs than some readers may want to admit.

Yes, the idea of the partnership between universities and schools is a wonderful innovation, but it is self-contradictory if the movement inducts teachers into the structures, practices, and cultures of traditional schools where their participation and voices are restrained. To make this point more concrete, consider James Lytle's January 20, 2016 piece in *Education Week* where he laments the "chokehold" control the NCAA has on secondary schooling and how it restrains the kind of innovation in schools he imagines in this excerpt.

> Imagine a high school offering integrated math courses, Rosetta Stone as an option for foreign languages, dual-enrollment programs with a local community college, massive open online courses, industry and corporate apprenticeships, service learning opportunities, an International Baccalaureate option, performing and visual arts concentrations, and portfolio/competency assessment all taught by highly qualified teachers and others with content expertise. Although such a school might incorporate many of the elements of cutting-edge reforms, it might well have to forgo NCAA review rather than be constrained policies, to the disadvantage of its student-athletes.

Having imagined this innovative school, readers should ask what percentage of PDSs are probably subject to the NCAA regulations that restrain such innovation. It is very likely 100 percent. The reality is that PDSs are subject to the whole gamut of restraints cited above just like all traditional schools. As a result, they are unable to fulfill the aspirations espoused by the Holmes Group.

CONCLUSION

This chapter has reviewed one of the most promising developments in teacher education of the last century, the advent of professional development schools. The formation of professional development schools and the attendant partnership between local schools and higher education have contributed greatly to improving the process by which aspiring teachers enter the profession and become effective teachers.

One can reasonably say, in fact, that the work of the professional development school movement in improving teacher induction foreshadows the coming of schools that provide teachers a full career of learning and development, schools that will fulfill and, perhaps, surpass the aspirations of The Holmes Group. Such schools would, in fact, change the profession.

While the PDS movement foreshadows a new school model, that model is yet to be realized. If the teaching profession is truly going to be changed in the spirit of the Holmes Group, then traditional schools need to change. They need to change to embrace the learning community concept and insure novice teachers have not only a thorough induction but the full career of the professional development they need.

Chapter 7

Professional Development Schools Foreshadow a New School Model

The full promise of professional development schools will be realized by modifying the current model. Yes, professional development schools are a notable success because they have achieved a significant improvement in teacher induction and preparation. As they enhanced the induction process, they have also provided an important ripple effect on the learning of all teachers in PDSs.

While this has been a valuable change in teacher education, it has revealed a problem. The very success of the enhanced induction process has exposed the inadequacy of teacher learning and development after the induction process. The post-induction process needs to be transformed into a more conscious and thoroughgoing process of career-long teacher development.

Instead of being primarily focused on the induction process, PDSs should now be focused on culture development and be designed to provide a full career of teacher development starting in secondary school. Again, this change should not be understood to mean there needs to be more "professional development." Rather, a new school design should be focused on culture building. There is extensive literature on this topic that provides high-quality prescriptive guidance. This literature exists because research tells us that it is culture, not rational learning in "professional development" events, that best accounts for the creation of effective teachers.

Thus, a new school model would be one explicitly designed for teacher learning and have these four components: (1) an academically elite program in secondary schools that invites high-quality, academic students into the teaching profession; (2) a thorough induction process for candidates hired by local schools that is the product of a partnership between higher education and a local school and takes place entirely at the local school; (3) an intentionally developmental school culture grounded in professional learning communities that is also the product of a partnership with higher education and specifically designed to provide career-long development for all teachers at every career stage; and (4) and a disposition to changing traditional schools and to creating model demonstration schools that have a sense of themselves as protean and ready to reconfigure in ways that break with the traditional school model to better meet the learning of teachers and the custom needs of the students and communities they serve.

COMPONENT ONE

Teacher Induction Should Begin in Secondary School

Let's take these components one at a time, starting with secondary school induction. Why institute an elite program that invites high-quality secondary students into the teacher profession? Such an effort, of course, would be consistent with most of the reports reviewed in this book that call for improving teacher candidate quality.

While this book rejects the idea that getting good people is the panacea that will change schools, it does agree that young people who have a good academic and civic background are better candidates for teaching than those who do not. There needs to be formal outreach to such students and the natural place to do that would be in a secondary professional development school.

Beyond improving candidate quality there are a number of other reasons why such a program would improve a professional development school. One reason is that it expands a school's learning community. One of the objectives of a professional development school is to create a community of learners that is constantly focused on a discussion of what is good teaching and how do we create effective teachers. A natural enhancement of that discussion would come from bringing in the student perspective. There is ample research that clarifies how teachers benefit from listening to the voices of students and getting feedback from them on what they see as effective instruction (Cook-Sather, 2002, 2006; Cushman, 2010; Holcomb, 2007; Mitra, 2004, 2008; Rudduck & McIntyre, 2007).

Another reason has to do with the specific benefits for students. Secondary school students are in a unique position to explore what it means to be a teacher. On the one hand they have ready access to teachers to ask about teacher perspectives while they, at the same time, experience what it is like being a student and how that perspective meshes with their desire to be a teacher. This unique student situation presents the teaching profession an opportunity to develop aspiring teachers that should not be missed.

This would be especially true if these aspiring teachers were introduced to the learning community concept in high school. The author has written about how such a scenario would unfold in two works. For teachers, there is this book *Teaching the Next Generation of Teachers: Preparing for the Practice of Professional Learning Communities in Secondary School* (2016). For students there is *Teens to Teachers Leading: Preparing for the Practice of Learning Communities in Secondary School* (2017). The upcoming textbox gives a brief review of the *Teachers Leading* program.

Another reason has to do with adjusting students' concepts of what it means to be a teacher. Most schools are not cultures derived of professional learning communities. Most aspiring teachers likely think of teachers as lone actors who apply their craft in single, isolated classrooms. They do not think of teachers as collaborative. The teaching profession needs to change this conception of teaching by initiating a readjustment in secondary school as it orients aspiring teachers to the idea of teachers performing as members of professional learning communities. Having student practice working as a learning community in secondary school is a good way to accomplish this reorientation.

The final reason has to do with the issue of change. Right now we know that the teaching profession is in an unhappy place. In many ways it is stuck in the past, a condition that contributes to teacher unhappiness (Waters, 2014). This condition was reviewed earlier. If the teaching profession is going to take charge of itself and build for itself more professional conditions via professional learning communities, it is a good idea to begin to orient secondary student to the idea that the traditional school is obsolete, and the profession needs to break away from the assumptions, structures, and cultures of traditional schools. Developing the disposition that teachers need to become dedicated change agents will be best begun in secondary school. It gives them more time to get perspective on the need to let go of the notion that they are going to teach as they once were taught.

Add to this the importance of orienting these secondary students to the need and prospect for change because of their career satisfaction. Right now there are a number of organizations that look to invite students into and prepare them for the teaching profession. These include Tomorrow's Teachers of The College of New Jersey and Educators Rising from Phi Delta Kappa.

Unfortunately, these organizations, like the many reports reviewed for this book, focus on the development of teachers as individual actors, not as collaborators. Their websites or foundational documents give scant attention to the need to change the teaching profession so it is a more collaborative enterprise.

TEACHERS LEADING

A Prompt List for Thinking about and Creating Secondary Programs for Aspiring Teachers

Review these recommendations. Then design your own program.

1. This program would be presented to students as one of elite status. Entry into the program would require at least two qualifications: 1) a record of commitment to doing well in school, and 2) a record of commitment to good citizenship as a steward and helper of young people.
2. The students invited into the course must be committed to completing a program of rigor and significant achievement.
3. It is suggested that whatever name your school chooses for the program that it include the term *Teachers Leading*. For example, the name could be *The Teachers Leading Forum*, or the *Teachers Leading Program*, or the *Teachers Leading Consortium*. The term *Teachers Leading* will indicate that this program is about teachers changing the teaching profession by increasing teacher collaboration and decision making and leading teachers to becoming educational entrepreneurs.
4. Participating schools would commit to installing a *Teachers Leading* program as a major subject to be completed by participating in both a future teachers club and the completion of high level coursework.
5. The course component would involve a student taking at least two major 5 credit courses about teaching. These courses would be treated as major subjects and would involve the rigor that would clarify that an individual student is, in fact, of the high quality that the teaching profession needs.
6. These courses would be taught or guided by teachers or administrators of widely recognized pedagogical distinction.
7. At the core of this course would be orientation to the professional learning community model where students would work in collaborative teams to assess various conditions in their school and work collaboratively to understand them and improve them. The concept of **continuous school improvement** would be a motto of the program.
8. As one of the objectives of *Teachers Leading* would be the recruitment of highly qualified candidates, students in the program would be treated with a high level of deference and the program (including the courses) would provide many of the active experiences which students prize such as class trips, conferences, guest speakers, cultural events, project presentations, panel discussions, inter-school visitations,

action research projects, contributing to research publications, actual teaching in classrooms, apprenticing with veteran teachers and more. *The course would not be textbook-teacher talk centered. It would be student action centered.*

Creating a program such as *Teachers Leading* introduces and orients students to the idea that our traditional schools are obsolete as is the idea of teachers as individual actors. It clarifies for them the need for change as it is accomplished through the learning community concept where teachers are given new voice and regarded as thinkers and decision makers whose responsibility it is to pursue continuous school improvement through continuous change.

COMPONENTS TWO

Continue to Partner with Higher Education for High-Quality Teacher Induction

For nearly three decades now local schools and institutions of higher education have been partnering in the creation professional development schools. These schools have focused on providing novice teachers with a thorough induction process that supported novice teacher success and longer-term teacher retention.

While doing so, these efforts had positive effect on many veteran teachers who became involved in the induction process. Their involvement in helping novice teachers get off to a good start has for many re-invigorated their own careers. It has inspired them to consider further how teacher learning might be enhanced for themselves and other veteran teachers. This positive effect on veteran teachers leads us to consider the next component.

COMPONENT THREE

An Intentionally Developmental School Culture Grounded in Learning Communities

The basic concept here is that becoming a PDS implies that a school's culture would be founded on teachers working in professional learning communities. Thus, schools that are PDSs and schools that aspire to become PDSs (as all should), would embark on developing a school culture derived of professional learning communities. They would do this recognizing two things: one, the research is clear.

Student learning benefits most when teachers work in learning communities. Not choosing to develop collaborative school cultures is done at the peril of student learning. Two, career-long teacher development is implicit in the work of learning communities. Their very purpose is continuous improvement of the work of teachers, a challenge that never ends. Contrary to the isolation of teachers in traditional schools, participation in learning communities unavoidably leads to professional development and that development would implicitly be for a full career.

This of course would begin a real departure from traditional school culture with its inherent teacher isolation and top-down authority structure. How this would come about would probably be best left to the thinking of local schools and their higher education partners. Bottom line, however, is schools would make this transition because it is supported by research.

Implementation of a learning community culture should not be seen as a huge undertaking. There are many, many books which explain the rationale and benefits of learning communities and how to begin implementation. There are also hundreds of schools around the nation that have high-functioning collaborative cultures that can demonstrate the *how* of their success. This is not to suggest that it is a simple process. The literature explains that it is not. That same literature also explains, however, why the improvement of student learning demands that we make the effort.

Again, it is important to remember that the reason for doing all of this is because if research tells us that it is learning communities that produce the best learning outcomes for students, it does not make sense to induct our novice teachers into traditional schools that do not have professional learning communities. The model we now adhere to for our schools needs to change so schools that form these partnerships with institutions of higher education bring novice teachers into school cultures rich in collaborative professional community learning that becomes the foundation for change and continuous school improvement.

COMPONENT FOUR

A Disposition to Change

The purpose of teacher learning is to improve student learning. As teachers learn more and more from their collaborative efforts, the desired outcome is that they come up with ideas about how to improve their instruction, the schooling process, and student learning. Implicit in this process is change, sometimes big change. Teachers and all school stakeholders should have a disposition to accept change as a part of continuous school improvement.

This point needs just a little belaboring. It is hard for everyone to imagine a school that is not like the traditional school that we all know. Our mental models of what a school should be are so strong that often when we embark on change, it ultimately turns out to be not very different from the traditional school (Kelly et al., 2009; Supovitz & Weinbaum, 2008). It is for this reason that creating a disposition to change in our new teachers will not be easy. To accomplish this, our aspiring teachers need to be strongly encouraged to see themselves as leaders in the process of changing our obsolete traditional schools.

Remember, the traditional school we have now is a bad idea for educating youth. Yet, we keep it year after year. This observation is submitted because it is foreseen that teachers might come up with an idea that turns out bad, and some in authority will say "I told you so." Doing so would miss the point. The point is to empower educators to think, imagine, make decisions, and make change, not to insist that their every idea is going to be a great one. Remember, we are already living with a bad idea, the traditional school. Getting away from that bad idea is going to require the freedom to experiment.

So, again, the proposal is to bring the PDS community together in agreeing on a new model for the professional development school, a school that is purposefully designed for a full career of teacher development. That model would include four components:

1. Teacher induction would begin in secondary school with an elite program that invites only students with high-quality academic and civic backgrounds.
2. A teacher induction program for higher education students who are in a teacher preparation program (like what exists now) but all of which would happen in the context of a local school.
3. A commitment to building an intentionally developmental school culture derived of learning communities.
4. Instilling in aspiring teachers a disposition to leading change as part of continuous school improvement.

SOME IMPLICATIONS OF THE NEW MODEL

The important thing to recognize about this model is that it does not prescribe any particular structure for schools. When schools become governed by learning communities, they become protean. They become committed to change when study and evidence indicates change will be better. Right now the evidence indicates that the professional development school movement is stuck in the ditch of the traditional school. The movement needs to make a commitment to a school model that is capable of change, change that will allow many new kinds of school structures that address the unique needs of the populations they serve.

This disposition to change has one other component. Consistent with the ideas previously developed, the situation of teacher preparation should move away from the higher education campus and to local schools. That would include all of the traditional academic work such as reading books, discussing, paper writing, portfolio developing, and everything else. It is proffered that the objectives of all these activities would be better achieved if conducted in the context of a school where the theoretical has the best chance of interfacing with the practical.

As part of this relocation, local schools will have to rethink how school facilities are used and their hours of operation in order to accommodate their teachers working with higher education staff during and after "school hours." Higher education scholars would now have expanded opportunities for research that is grounded in the work of local schools. All of these changes would, of course, acknowledge the irrefutable reality that the real places that teachers learn to teach are in local schools. Thus, the importance of keeping teacher learning in the context of a school would become a fundamental of the PDS construct.

For the teachers' part, this arrangement would mean no longer having to drive for thirty or forty minutes every week to a remote campus to take generic graduate classes that do not have relevance to local school conditions. Instead, higher education teachers would work with local teachers to design experiences, courses, and degree programs that synthesize and execute the appropriate scholarship while it all takes place within the context of the school and address challenges that teachers face on the ground in their daily work. Teacher education would no longer be decontextualized in remote campus locations. Learning to be an effective teacher would happen where it happens best, on the job.

THE LOCAL SCHOOL TAKES CONTROL OF TEACHER DEVELOPMENT

To get more perspective on the changes that are possible, local schools and districts should consider the issue of control. The proposed reconfiguration of PDSs is about local schools taking control of the process by which teachers are developed so those teachers meet the needs of local schools. It is a rejection of the one-size-fits-all, generic approach provided by higher education.

The implication is that when districts and schools determine what unique qualification they want in their teachers, they can start to design programs that will enculturate the skills and values that are desired. They will not have to depend on the disparate programs of higher education or the alternatives to prepare teachers. The overall effect of such an approach will be to get local schools more focused on the cultures they need to build in order to develop the teachers they believe they need.

Without this local control, what is there? There is what we have now: Local schools receive novice teachers from a cross-section of colleges and universities which produce candidates of unpredictable quality from generic preparation programs which are very different from the other. Then these new teachers have to be inducted into a school and learn a new set of values and protocols.

Consider, if you would, what it would be like for a school to have greater control over the teacher development process so the novice teachers coming into full service at a school are ready to meet the needs of a local school's population and the community it serves. It is hard to believe that any school leader would not want to have control over how their new teachers are inducted and prepared. School leaders can consult with whoever they wish, and they should consult. But decision-making should ultimately come from within school. The thinking for schools should be done in schools by teachers.

What follows then is to think about what such a program might look like or be like. How can a local school create a culture that creates effective teachers? What experiences would members of your school community think to be important to the development of its teachers? As you think about this, also note that your school community is now charged with doing some serious thinking about learning. It is charged with thinking and acting critically and creatively. It is being charged with innovating for school improvement. It is not just following and coping with central authority directions. Isn't that what a school should be, a center for thinking?

THE PATTERN OF COMING TOGETHER

At this stage of the book, the reader is asked to observe a pattern, separate entities keep coming together. Leaders of higher education and local schools come together in partnership. Teachers in higher education join with teachers at all levels in local schools. Teachers who previously worked in isolation from each other will come together to work in learning communities. Teachers and students come together to share perspectives on learning and instruction. Veteran teachers and aspiring teachers in secondary schools come together to re-chart the pathway of aspiring teachers as they learn to work in professional learning communities and become practicing teachers. Novice teachers and local schools come together in new ways to form intentionally developmental schools where teachers learn from cultures, not presentations.

The readers should note the pattern of elements of our profession moving from isolation to unification. It is old knowledge that people do better when they come together with purpose. From the family who sits around the kitchen table and talks about how to handle a situation to the United Nations where countries sit together to do the same thing, coming together always works better.

The idea of compartmentalizing in schools and having teachers work in isolation are ideas left over from the industrial age. So is the idea of using factories as models for schools. Compartmentalizing, standardizing, and top-down authority are all old concepts of how organizations should work. While those old ideas about organizations had value in their time, we now realize that organizations do better when unity is emphasized over compartmentalizing. We have learned over the years that the future of organizations is about bringing everyone in, giving everyone ownership.

Organizations function at higher levels when all of their members feel ownership, feel charged with making things better, not just waiting passively to listen to recommendations or orders from the top. The direction of our learning over the decades beckons us to affirm the importance of teachers as thinkers and decision makers who work in community. The PDS community should affirm a new school model with the components discussed because teacher learning has a causal relationship to student learning, and it is culture, not rational learning, that accounts for the creation of effective teachers.

CONCLUSION

The full promise of professional development schools will be realized by modifying the current design of PDSs. Instead of being primarily focused on the new teacher induction process, PDSs should become school specifically designed for teacher learning which have four components: (1) an academically elite program in secondary schools that invites high-quality students into the teaching profession; (2) a thorough induction process for locally hired novice teachers that is the product of a partnership between higher education and a local school; (3) an intentionally developmental school culture grounded in learning communities that is also the product of a partnership with higher education, all of which would provide career-long development for all teachers at every career stage; and (4) a disposition to creating schools that have a sense of themselves as protean and ready to reconfigure in ways that breaks with the traditional school model to better meet the custom needs of the populations and communities they serve.

Chapter 8

The Path to a New School Model
Teacher Development through School Development

The idea of teachers developing in stages naturally brings us to the idea of schools developing in stages. This chapter is about how schools, like individual teachers, might see themselves as in an evolutionary process. It will suggest that there are stages in school development and that those stages are an expression of culture and how people collaborate to create a unique school that is customized to address the unique strengths and needs of the population it serves.

But the idea of school development as analogous to human development is not a common concept for most educators. Even when schools have goals, as most do, we know that these goals almost never translate into a traditional school changing its basic structures and practices. Most schools are static. Their basic structures and practices are pretty much what they have been for decades.

Few educators reflect on their school and say "Well our school is in this stage or that stage." If their traditional schools are functioning smoothly, if everything is orderly and reasonably okay, there is no expectation that the school will go through significant changes as a natural matter of evolution or development. As in most traditional schools, there is stasis where what has been done before goes on and on for years and decades.

This chapter explores the antithesis of this state. It explores what it means when a school is in evolution, constantly developing to a higher stage, continuously changing to improve teacher learning and student achievement. All of this comes as a result of a school culture focused on the individual and collective development of teachers, mindful of how growth and development looks and unfolds and improves student learning.

But what does the growth and development of a school look like? What are the developmental stages a school might go through? Many scholars and education writers have described school conditions in terms of their cultural conditions and the resulting student achievement (Fullan & Heargraves, 2012; Deal & Peterson, 2013). Although they have not offered these descriptions in terms of stages, per se, they have presented these conditions in evaluative terms which assess effectiveness.

The point here is not to stipulate that there are clearly delineated stages that schools go through although there may be. Rather, the point is to inspire reflection. If we acknowledge the well-accepted notion that people go through developmental stages, can we also see that institutions and schools go through such stages?

Reflection is the key point. When we step back and look at our schools, how would we describe their effectiveness? How is one school more evolved than the school in the next town? How is the school less evolved than a school in the next county? Most importantly, what is the right criterion for making such judgments? Coming up with final answers to these questions is not the point. The point is thinking about the condition of your school, not just accepting that it is just a school like so many others and does what others do.

Of course, teachers are not used to thinking about the evolution of their school. This is most likely attributable to the fact that traditional schools were not designed to change and evolve. They were designed to do the same thing year after year after year. Stakeholders were not charged with thinking of themselves as change agents, and, as we know, our schools have changed very little over the last one hundred years. Most of the schools teachers work in have the same assumptions, structures, and cultures that they had a hundred years ago (Senge et al., 2000, 2012; Kelly et al., 2009).

By contrast, inherent in developmental theory is the notion that all things in the universe go through stages of development (Wilber, 2016). Each stage lays the groundwork for the next stage. While schools in the United States have demonstrated little evolutionary change in the last hundred years, it is still reasonable to speculate on how schools might develop should educators decide to adopt a new school model based on learning communities where teachers are important decision makers and continuous school improvement through change is the norm.

SCHOOLS EVOLVING, SCHOOL NOT EVOLVING

The reasons for this persistent failure of schools to change developed an aura of mystery. Why haven't the most capable and dedicated of school leaders been able accomplish real change? In his pivotal work, *The Fifth Discipline*, Senge (1991) attempted to address the mystery with a concept he called "mental models" (p. 163).

Mental models are like pictures in one's mind derived from past experience of what something is or should look like. By this line of thinking, when education leaders attempted to change, they began with the only mental models of a school they had, the traditional school. The outcome was that the new programs leaders attempted to implement always came out looking like something from a traditional school.

The consequence was that anything innovative failed to materialize and merely reflected traditional concepts. Senge (1991) explained that "new insights fail to get put into practice because of the conflict with deeply held internal images of how the world works, images that limit us to familiar ways of thinking and acting." He further says, "Our mental models determine not only how we make sense of the world, but how we take action" (p. 163, 4). Thus, attempts to change most often resulted in more of the same.

What complicated the problem of leaders being constrained by old mental models was that few school leaders had a vision of what a school would look like which did not resemble a traditional school. Techers should think about that. What would a school look like if it did not resemble the schools that we teachers know from the past? On what basis would teachers design such a different school? What assumptions and concepts would guide the design of a different kind of school?

These are not easy questions to answer. But the fact remains that they do need to be considered. They need to be considered by all involved because to date student learning continues to lag (Institute of Educational Sciences, 2012). Student engagement and teacher engagement continue to lag (Yazzie-Mintz, 2007, 2009; Met Life, 2013). These questions stand to be especially important for early career teachers because how they are answered stands to radically change the nature of teaching. The answers will affect their careers and the professional growth they will or will not enjoy.

In this regard, some nuance needs to be injected. In the broadest sense what is being explained here is true: Schools are not changing. There are, nevertheless, some important exceptions. Teachers and other school stakeholders are experimenting with new school structures. Throughout our society, experimental schools, online schools, charter schools, and a variety of unique learning programs are springing up. Although these experiments serve a small percentage of all students, they are starting to have an impact on how people think about schools.

With these new programs in sight, there is increasing interest on the part of parents to be able to choose the schools to which their children go. This includes public schools. So, as consideration is given to the need for change and the rightness of change, there must also be consideration given to what is happening around traditional schools. Is the environment of our traditional schools changing? Are public schools encountering competition? How should teachers think about these developments?

In their work, *Teaching the Digital Generation: No More Cookie Cutter High Schools*, Kelly et al. (2009) are more pointed in attributing educators' inability to change to the force of habit. They capture this force of habit in a concept they call "TTWWADI . . . That's The Way We've Always Done It." They explain,

> How can you explain the steadfast refusal of most people in education to embrace anything more than superficial changes to the way schools operate? We perceived that the school system is under the influence of a powerful force that compels it to continue on its current course. This is a force so potent that few have been able to break free of its grasp. What is this force that makes education so impervious to change? It's TTWWADI, and it has awesome power over people . . . a mindset that develops as people form habits of behavior, both personally and professionally. (Kelly et al., 2009, p. 3)

The application of this concept of habit rings true on a number of levels. Certainly most of us know this to be true in our personal lives. Habits are hard to break. New Year's resolutions are always a struggle, particularly when they come in conflict with habit. Veteran teachers have probably also seen this to be true in their own schools. They have seen so many innovative programs come and go, only to have schools return to long-standing practices that were established decades prior. Kelly et al. (2009) are probably right that institutional habits are even harder to break than individual habits. There are so many more wills resisting change.

While it is not clear that this concept of school going through developmental stages has ever been explored by theorists or researchers, the concept has definite application in this book's argument. As leaning communities study their performance, learn, and make appropriate changes in practices and school structures, they will transform their schools from the traditional, industrial-age model to a new model based on teachers working in learning communities. It implies a new culture for schools where change and development for individuals and the collective "school" is the norm as both move to ever higher stages of development.

As in the case of teacher development, reflecting on it was assisted by reviewing a prompt model about which the readers were invited to critique and change. The same will be true with respect to school development. Again, the stages described shortly do not represent an attempt to contribute to academic theory. Rather, the stages represent a prompt model to assist the reader in considering how any school might evolve to new and more productive levels where the culture of the school creates effective teachers.

The criterion that drives this model is teacher and student learning. Every stage represents an advancement in teacher learning

Having said this, the stages described below have in some measure been informed by current organizational theory which has been applied to schools by many other educators and writers (Demings, 1983, 1986; Lalaux, 2014; Senge, 1991; Senge et al., 2000, 2012). Of particular note is the work of Peter Senge and his discussion of the learning organization and the steps that members of an organization need to follow in order to become what Senge has termed "a learning organization." This concept found it fullest educational application in the book *Schools that Learn* (Senge et al., 2000, 2012), a work where Senge collaborated with Nelda Cambron-Mccabe, TimothyLucas, Bryan Smith, Janis Dutton, and Art Kleiner.

THE SCHOOL PROMPT STAGES MODEL

Stage One

Bringing People Together. In the context of a traditional school, an early sign of evolution is bring stakeholders together for reflection. This idea to bring stakeholders together for reflection is often expressed in creating a site-based planning committee made up of teachers, administrators, community members, and students.

In such groups, people have gotten together primarily to listen to each other's concerns and perspectives on problems or opportunities in schooling. Striving for authenticity, there is a strong interest in making sure that people are heard, that their voices are validated. Some refer to such committees as "distributed power" suggesting the increased power of all stakeholders to influence what happens at the school.

Those schools with leaders truly intent on change invite people to join in who have shown themselves to also be open to or want change. They do not impose the concepts of site-based planning or learning communities on those who are not interested and do not share their sense of urgency. The formation of such a group may involve a pointed discussion or the reading and discussing of an article or book. While there are many variations on how people are brought together, the key idea is that people come together for sharing perspectives, learning, and possibly to take action.

The important thing here is that there is no effort to force change on veteran teachers who don't want it. This avoids all of the foot dragging and subversion that goes with change that is forced on teachers by overenthusiastic school leaders. At the same time, it provides for the learning community group to conduct business knowing everybody that sits in their group is onboard with the basic concept of sharing perspectives, learning, and taking action. No time would have to be devoted to defending the concept, just discussing its implementation.

Stage Two

Make a Commitment to Change. A common outcome of bringing people together is that people begin to see new possibilities and begin to envision change. One realization that often comes to such groups is that, in spite of the difficulties associated with change, it is a good thing. It is how people and institutions move forward. It is how continuous improvement happens. Thus, a group can make a commitment to change, itself. There is recognition among members of the group that people working together reflecting, learning, and changing things is a normal part of continuous school improvement.

Stage Three

Focus on Student Achievement Outcomes. An important sign of evolution in a school is a renewed commitment to the core purpose of the school, student achievement. Based on this renewed commitment, traditional schools move away from the idea that delivery of curriculum and instruction is the primary responsibility of schools. They move to thinking that the school's primary responsibility is assuring that all students learn and making all adjustments necessary to insure better outcomes.

With this central purpose, schools begin to focus on evaluating how well what the school does advances student learning. Stakeholders no longer take comfort in the fact that the school may be orderly or that people are doing what they are supposed to do. Instead, they are constantly assessing whether or not students are really engaged and learning more and more each year. Achievement is always on the incline.

This focus on student achievement may be seen as having five conceptual building blocks.

1. Teacher learning is highly correlated with student learning.
2. Effective teachers advance student learning
3. There are not enough effective teachers
4. Schools are responsible for creating their own effective teachers.
5. Research makes it clear that effective teaching comes from school cultures derived of collaborative learning communities.

Stage Four

Learning Communities Are Established. When schools renew their commitment to student achievement, there is a natural inclination for teachers to ask the following question: How can we be more effective? As this book has and will assert over and over again, the research points us in one direction. Schools and teachers are more effective when teachers work together, when they collaborate in professional learning communities. Thus, evidence of a school's development comes when schools make a commitment to creating authentic learning communities.

Because the research supports it, parties are brought together to discuss the nuts and bolts of the transition to genuine learning communities. More and more people are invited in, but no one is forced in. The school is advancing on a tipping point. The purpose is to create a school that creates effective teachers. Knowing that this is an outcome of culture, all involved are thinking about what the change involves. What needs to be added to the school culture? What needs to be removed? All stakeholders are kept informed and invited to be involved.

All stakeholders are prompted to learn as much as possible on how to implement PLCs as the core element of culture in the school. Why, because research tells us that teachers in collaboration have a distinctly greater positive impact on student achievement. People read and seek advice widely. They talk with each other frequently.

People go to conferences. Higher education is invited in to both advice on the transition and to add activities and procedures that contribute to an intentionally developmental culture. A *Teachers Leading* program is formed that bring students into the learning community and prepares them in the procedures of learning community culture and gets them to anticipate teaching in only a school that is highly collaborative.

As this process unfolds, teachers regularly monitor student engagement and achievement. They identify problems in student learning and find ways to collaborate on their solutions. Teachers are constantly evaluating their performance by getting feedback from students and other stakeholders. In all of this, teacher learning is increasingly embedded in the everyday teaching, study, and research of teachers and not the result of discreet professional development events presented by "authorities."

Teachers will spend more time creating their own knowledge and coming up with ways to increase their collaborative time. They will undertake some small projects at first. They will celebrate their success. At this stage that might include more lesson study on areas of instruction that do not seem to make the mark in terms of student achievement assessment data. They read a book together. They conduct some small-scale action research. They investigate student engagement. They review research with a member of higher education.

Observing the school in broad terms, one sees that more and more elements of the school's culture have a developmental theme. Measures of student achievement go to higher levels. Teachers see themselves achieving higher stages of professional performance. As a culture, the school is all about personal and professional growth.

Stage Five

Begin the Formal Induction of New Teachers. At this stage, two things are evident. First, the function of the learning communities is improving. New and veteran teachers are maturing in their grasp of the dynamics of their work in communities of learning and the professional literature that informs it. Learning communities have become a cultural norm, and school personnel have high level of confidence in the effectiveness of their operation.

The second evident condition is a move to become a site for demonstration and teacher induction. This is, again, a reflection of staff confidence that they are on top of their game. The school no longer needs to depend on remote, decontextualized programs of preparation at institutions of higher education, or the alternative programs. Further, there is recognition that announcing the school as a center for teacher preparation, a PDS 2.0, will raise the consciousness of all stakeholders with respect to how the school assures high levels of student and teacher learning. There is, yet, more review and reflection on the thoroughness of a school's supportive culture.

Stage Six

Advancing, Sharing, Becoming a Unique Demonstration School. At this stage the school has matured as a learning community culture. People thrive on working together and all of the informal, personal, and human activity that contribute to community. There is a deepening relationship between the members of the local school, the school and members of higher education institutions, and the school and the community. As a result of these growing relationships, everyone feels more satisfied with what they are doing and accomplishing.

All involved understand the importance of the school being a place for teacher education, a place that creates effective teachers. The school has become a place of study, reflection, and research. It also makes a point of advancing the concept of learning communities by inviting in many visitors from surrounding schools, communities, and higher education. Members hold local conferences and contribute at regional and national conferences. They publish in local media and academic journals.

The school is now a full-blown intentionally developmental organization. The learning community work dominates teachers' thinking about how to teach well. Teachers see themselves as entrepreneurial innovators who are continuously recreating their school. Teachers are very stage conscious. They routinely tell aspiring teachers how great their teacher development opportunities are. The school is always poised to change, reconfigure, and become a new kind of school.

One implication of the last stage is that a particular school may evolve in such a way that it will be very different from other schools. It will have done this because as a result of stakeholders, especially teachers, working together and determining that certain changes would better serve student and teacher learning in a particular community. Thus, the configuration of the school breaks with the traditional school model. The outlook of the teachers and other stakeholders is that the school will likely continue to change as learning indicates that change will make the school better.

There is another element to this uniqueness. When teachers have the power to change their schools, it affirms diversity and inclines away from one-size-fits-all. With this affirmation, schools can feel intellectual and practical comfort in making changes that serve the unique needs, talents, and potentials of the populations they serve. Schools can focus on individuals instead of being driven by the one-size-fits-all standards and demands of central authorities.

When a school accepts its uniqueness and affirms the power of diversity, it has truly taken an evolutionary step. This value is attested to in Scott Page's book (2007) *The Difference: How the Power of Diversity Creates Better Groups, Firms, Schools, and Societies*. In these circumstances, a powerful combination comes together: (1) the opportunity for teachers and stakeholders to think and assert their judgment, thus, go in new, entrepreneurial directions and (2) the thinking and judgment of stakeholders is able to affirm and develop important strengths in a community that might otherwise be ignored. All of this is much better for teachers and, by implication, for their students.

CONCLUSION

This chapter has dealt with an unfamiliar concept, the evolutionary stages of a school. Traditional schools have maintained the same configuration for so long—over hundred years—that it is hard for most to even imagine that a school might function and even look very differently from those of the past. Nevertheless, this chapter has detailed the possible stages of a school's development as a way to get the reader to imagine how such change might unfold, how it would result in the creation of effective teachers.

Chapter 9

Tina's Story

Aspiring Teachers Shop for Professional Learning at Local Schools

The culture of a school specifically designed for teacher development is best conveyed through a story that doesn't say what a teacher education school would be like but *shows* it. The subject of this narrative is Tina. The narrative describes Tina's induction into teaching from secondary school through her college years and her eventual acceptance of a teaching position at a PDS 2.0, Beacon Ridge High School.

TINA'S SECONDARY SCHOOL EXPERIENCE

This is Tina's story. Tina had been dreaming of becoming a teacher for many years. She first acknowledged those dreams in the fifth grade where she found her teacher, Mrs. Flowers, particularly inspiring. Tina remembers that she and Mrs. Flowers formed a warm relationship around a project Tina did which involved teaching origami to third graders. Tina explained that after the fifth grade, she had persistent thoughts about becoming a teacher and being like Mrs. Flowers.

In both middle school and high school Tina became a member of the **Teachers Leading Conference**, as her school called it. As part of this program, Tina was acknowledged as an outstanding student and a prime candidate for becoming a teacher. Her acceptance into the **Teachers Leading Conference** was based on her excellent achievement in school and her work with the Girl Scouts and her church where she was aspiring to become a Sunday school teacher.

Tina remembers that after being accepted into the *Conference*, she was recognized at school assemblies, in the school newspaper, and at various community events as being a member of the elite **Teachers Leading Conference**. Tina also explained that "many students and my friends showed me a lot of respect after I was accepted into the program. It made me feel special."

The **Teachers Leading Conference** was not just an after-school club. It was an academic program which invited application from a diverse group of students but did not accept all students. While it did involve many after-school activities, a large part of the program was during school and included some demanding academic classes which required a lot of work on various projects that simulated her future work as a teacher in a learning community.

What Tina liked about the program, and many outside students envied, was that it was very active. There was very little sitting and listening to teachers talk. One of Tina's friends who was not part of the program observed to her, "You guys seem like you are always doing stuff, going places, having special events."

It was true. Tina's program was made up mostly of active projects involving all kinds of research about her school and how to solve problems that she and her classmates observed in classrooms and in the school. On top of that, it seemed her class was always going to conferences, panel discussions, and trips of all sorts related to becoming a teacher.

As part of this, the **Teachers Leading Conference** introduced Tina to the idea that in the future the work of teachers would depart from many past practices and would be grounded in the collaborative work of professional learning communities. In Tina's school, her formal classes were entitled "Perspectives on Learning and Achievement" and "The Goal of Teacher Development and School Development."

In her classes and during after-school activities, Tina did her classwork as part of a team that clarified problems in student learning, researched solutions, and proposed new practices for better student learning. She was often asked to make good use of her perspective as a student and the perspective of teachers, whom she frequently consulted, as she analyzed conditions and situations at school.

Through all of this Tina was an excellent student. She graduated fourth in her class from a high school that was highly regarded for its academic rigor and the success of its graduates. Tina often attributes here success in high school to her participation in the **Teachers Leading Conference** which gave her the feeling that she was on the cutting edge of big changes in teaching and schooling. She felt like a pioneer and felt deeply satisfied that she was part of something that did and would do so much social good.

TINA'S APPLICATION TO LOCAL SCHOOLS FOR ASSOCIATE STATUS

In Tina's junior year of high school she and her classmates undertook two big projects: For Tina this meant applying to college to study biological sciences and applying to several high schools near her first choice university for associate status. This associated status meant that while Tina was studying for her bachelor degree in biology she would not take education or teacher preparation classes at her university.

Rather, she would begin her teacher preparation right in an actual school. There she would learn how that unique school approached serving its unique community. It was understood that this induction into the unique culture of a local school was much more productive than generic preparation in higher education much of which often didn't apply to the needs or practices of local schools.

Tina has known since middle school that her preparation and development as a teacher could go in two possible directions. She could get her teacher preparation at an institution of higher education or she could go to one of the increasingly popular local schools that prepare their own teachers. These schools were informally called PDSs, but formally, they were known as Professional Development Schools 2.0. The word among students was that the local schools were a better deal. Among others, two factors figured prominently in their calculation, cost and outcome.

The cost of getting one's teacher preparation at a local school was clearly cheaper. While there were some additional costs, there was no extra year required after one gets their degree in their chosen field. This is partly because as an associate at the local school, teacher candidates work for the school. They do an assortment of jobs as part of their learning. In their junior and senior years, they will very likely do a lot of teaching as part of apprenticing with a teacher at this school. There is the added benefit that certain assignments in the local school would even be paid for by the local district. Substitute teaching is just one example.

With respect to outcomes, student opinions also figured strongly in Tina's decision to work with a local PDS. The skinny that came from students that Tina spoke with indicated that you learned "way more" at the local schools.

> Why? Because you are there. You see what is really going on. There are no surprises when you go in for student teaching or actually start teaching. By the time you finish your program with a local school, you are used to everything there. You are part of the team. You have learned what the school that wants to hire you thinks you need to know.

Bottom line: the outcome is better.

Back at her high school, Tina's teachers explained what they saw as an emerging reality: Schools that became centers for teacher preparation, PDSs, looked to deliver to their students higher-quality professional learning. Why? Because, it was a way to attract great new teachers to their school. They understood how word of mouth spreads, so when schools became PDSs, they would want to create programs that attract the best possible teacher candidates. This placed schools in a position to compete for candidates by offering them the best possible induction programs.

Thus, near the end of her junior year in high school, Tina contacted six PDSs to get the brochures on their programs of teacher preparation and development. She studied all of them to see how their offerings compared and differed. She also talked to as many people as possible about what they had heard about the various programs at the different schools.

Because she chose to enter a PDS instead of a traditional teacher preparation program in higher education, Tina knew that fulfilling this choice would depend on her developing an association with a particular secondary school in the right geographic choice area close to her university. So, while still in high school, Tina started investigating what was offered by local schools which were now declaring themselves to be Professional Development Schools 2.0.

As part of getting associate status at a local high school, Tina would be responsible for spending five hours a week at the school in her freshmen year of college, ten hours a week in her second year, fifteen hours a week in her third year, and twenty hours a week in her final year.

Tina's college years would, then, have two components. At college she would pursue a liberal education with a focus on extensive lab work in the biological sciences. The second component of her college years would be her participation at a PDS. There Tina would participate in an induction program that would prepare her to a high level of skill by the time she graduated from college and was ready to become a full-service teacher.

It is noteworthy that Tina institution of higher education had a partnership with the high school she chose for her induction. The university, in fact, had such a partnership with a number of local schools, and many members of the university faculty either spent a great deal of time in the local school or they had offices at the local school or in the district. The partnership reflected the belief that collaboration between the local school and higher education would have the best outcomes for teacher preparation and it would all work best when situated in an actual school.

Being given associate status by a local high school involved a commitment from both Tina and the school. For Tina's part, she was making a commitment to the requirements of full participation throughout her college years and then becoming a teacher at the school if a position was available.

For their part, the local school offered Tina what she judged to be an outstanding program of induction and preparation during all of the hours she would spend at the school over the course of four years. She was assured by her prospective schools that her participation in the school's operation during her pre-service years would be authentic, not one of marginal observation. Because Tina was a high-quality candidate and because the school had a high-quality program, both felt their investment in the other was warranted.

An added incentive for Tina was the fact that Beacon Ridge had recently been designated a demonstration school by the National Association of Professional Development Schools. Beacon Ridge was, thus, going to become a school where other schools visited to learn how to develop a culture like BR's that was specifically designed for a full career of teacher development.

As part of this arrangement, local schools were conscious that if they were going to attract the teacher candidates they most wanted, they would have to provide them the kind of professional development and support that such candidates expected. PDSs also saw it as their responsibility to develop these high-quality candidates and make them into effective teachers. While in recent years teacher candidate quality was on the rise, teacher candidates on Tina's level were considered especially desirable. Tina was aware of this and had high expectations.

When Tina entered college, she did not enter a teacher preparation program, but she was designated as an education major. This meant that she worked with her adviser at the university to arrange her schedule of classes so as to accommodate her preparation work at a nearby school. All of the reading and paper writing she would do in connection with her teacher preparation would come out of her work with the local school where university teachers and local teachers worked together to devise a program for incoming pre-service teachers.

It is noteworthy that while in high school, Tina's school was in the process of becoming a professional developmental school 2.0. The secondary induction program Tina experienced focused on the formation of learning communities as the new basis of teacher preparation and development. As part of this program, veteran teachers provided presentations and discussion groups on how to evaluate and choose a high-quality teacher education school for her preparation after high school.

TINA'S INDUCTION AT BEACON RIDGE HIGH SCHOOL

Tina remembers her first day at Beacon Ridge which started with a meeting with five other college students, all freshmen at their respective institutions.

At the meeting were the high school principal, a professor from Tina's university, and a lead teacher who taught history at Beacon Ridge. The purpose of the meeting was to introduce the group of five novice teachers to each other and to the full array of experiences they would have as they began their induction and their participation in Beacon High's school culture.

It should be emphasized that the participation of the students at BR was going to be authentic. The students would not be in observation mode most of the time. It was expressed to Tina that while observation was very important, what was more important was participation, becoming part of the school. Tina was told that regardless of what kinds of assignments she received, the most important thing was to go all in and get fully involved.

Students like Tina would be asked to do things that were important to the function of the school and particular classrooms. As a matter of entry into the school's community, all five of the novice teachers had applied for a certificate as a substitute teacher and were, thereby, eligible for supervising students when the school needed their services. Still, there were many possible assignments.

These new inductees might be used for

- Instructional support in classrooms (Tina would often help with lab work.)
- Student research support for students in the media center
- Direct instruction when a teacher was needed in another area
- Substitute teaching
- General supervision throughout the school
- Help in a homework center
- Action Research assistants
- Testing monitors
- Composition lab support
- Club membership
- Theater production support
- Athletic team support
- Helping in the attendance office
- Participation in administrative meetings
- Sharing her college assignments with students
- Helping the *Teachers Leading* program
- Arranging assembly programs
- Policing school grounds
- Work with Community Partners

WORKING WITH COMMUNITY PARTNERS

One of the most highly regarded innovations at Beacon Ridge High School was their Community Partners Initiative. This meant that the High School involved a large array of people, businesses, municipal agencies, and corporations in providing students both instruction and hands-on learning experiences. As of Tina's entry date as a pre-service teacher, secondary school courses were offered on their home sites by the police department (two courses), the fire department (two courses), the local hospital (three courses), the city manager's office (one course), the mayor's office (one course), the Office of Animal Control (two courses), and the Chamber of Commerce (two courses).

In addition, courses were offered by professionals who live in the community and came to students' homes to teach courses in law, veterinary medicine, stocks and bonds, antiques, child guidance, government, local history, local geology, beach ecology, microbiology, professional music recording, gardening, small business start-up, writing professionally, ballooning, kite art, home construction, cabinet making, and Victorian home restoration. When Tina was first introduced to the Community Partners Initiative, she felt she was beginning to see how teaching and schooling had change since she was in Mrs. Flowers class.

AUTHENTIC PARTICIPATION

In addition to her work with community partners, the avenues of authentic participation were supplemented by a novice teachers' participation in the work of the various professional learning communities in the school. During the course of the first day's meeting, the lead teacher tried to clarify how much was going on in professional development. She provided each novice teacher with a calendar of that month's PLC activities. And, on an electronic billboard, the lead teacher showed the events going on for that day and the rest of the week. They included the following:

- A demonstration lesson on authenticating survey responses
- A demonstration lesson on flipped instruction
- A lesson design study group on the "flipped" lesson
- A science PLC meeting on "Authentic Assessment Using Parents"
- The presentation of research results on school discipline outcomes
- A fishbowl of BR students for novice teachers
- A conferences of athletic coaches and dance teachers on Community Leadership
- A student feedback session on multiple choice testing
- A student feedback session determining the length of projects
- A reading circle discussing the book *Most Likely to Succeed*
- A reading circle discussing the book *Deeper Learning*
- A first day feedback meeting with the new novice teacher cohort

The list impressed Tina with how much was going on and got her to wondering how teachers fit in actual teaching with so much happening. She also felt immediately drawn to a couple of the sessions, Authentic Assessment Using Parents and the one on project length. She was happy to see that so much thinking was going on and elated to think that she was soon going to be a part of it all.

During the meeting each of the school representatives, including the principal, spoke for about six to seven minutes. Each spoke on the work of their professional learning communities, past and present, and the research he or she had done or was doing at the time. Each, including Tina's mentor, also elaborated on his or her stage of development now and what she or he aspired to achieve as an educator in the future. There was an emphasis on each individual owning and taking responsibility for his or her own growth. Everyone was expected to have a professional growth agenda.

What impressed Tina most about this session was that the lead teacher and the principal spoke at some length about his and her personal and professional weaknesses and their journeys in trying to overcome them. Tina was also somewhat taken aback by this. She asked in her thoughts, "We're going to talk about our weaknesses?" As she thought about it, she couldn't help but confirm that it was a good idea, but also knew that doing it would likely be a stretch for her and her peers.

A key impression Tina got from this meeting was that it wasn't what she expected. There was a lot that was new. The discussion of teachers' developmental stages and teacher research in combination with the personal confessions about weaknesses and aspirations for personal development were not what Tina thought would happen. Where were the curriculum manuals and textbooks, the standards and the guidelines?

What added to it all were some posters around the room. One announced IF YOU THINK YOU KNOW HOW TO TEACH BECAUSE YOU ONCE WENT TO SCHOOL, THINK AGAIN. It was like the school leadership was trying to send a clear message about something, but Tina wasn't sure she knew exactly what the message was.

Another prominent poster read, ONE OF THE BIGGEST PROBLEMS IN LEARNING HOW TO TEACH IS UNLEARNING WHAT YOU THOUGHT YOU KNEW ABOUT HOW TO TEACH. And another read: IT'S NOT WHAT YOU KNOW. IT'S WHO YOU ARE

And then there was the one that hung over the room's whiteboard which read TEACHING IS NOT ABOUT TALKING. LEARNING IS NOT ABOUT LISTENING. YOUR MOVE. All of these posters left Tina feeling stumped. When Tina read this last one, she put her head down for a moment to think. All she could think was that she didn't know what to think. Everyone was so warm and nice, but the idea of teaching, which seemed so familiar to her, now was beginning to seem mysterious like there really was a new adventure ahead.

Tina and all of the novice teachers got the message quickly. This school was not like a traditional school where teachers taught their classes and their work was done. Before the end of the meeting all of the students in Tina's novice teacher cohort were encouraged to write about their initial impressions in their "A Teacher's Journey" journal which Tina and others had been keeping since they were in ninth grade as part of the *Teachers Leading* program. There were, in fact, two Ph.D.s from a local university who were keeping track of novice teachers' early impressions as part of research they were doing on "changing teacher mindsets."

That first day, Tina was assigned a mentor for this first year at Beacon Ridge. They had lunch by themselves so they could get to know each other. Because she was not yet a teacher, Tina's relationship with her mentor had more to do with Tina's adjustment to the school's culture than dealing specifically with classroom management or instructional issues. That would come in due course as Tina received more assignments inside classrooms.

In the early days as an associate at the high school, Tina met with her mentor after school as often as possible. In that course, Tina observed her mentor working with students after school as they pursued various projects in the school laboratories. Eventually, Tina got involved in helping her adviser's students, and the students began to seek Tina out for help, too.

Tina's mentor was also involved in Beacon High School's *Teachers Leading* **Program,** and one of Tina's first assignments was to make a brief presentation to the group of aspiring teachers. Tina tried to be as encouraging as possible and told about her own journey and the profound influence she felt from her fifth-grade teacher, Mrs. Flowers.

TINA FEELS THE CULTURE

For that first year, every time Tina went to BR, she found herself involved in some new aspect of the school's operations. One effect of this was that Tina became known around the school. People recognized her and readily greeted her in different situations.

As their familiarity and closeness increased, Tina found herself getting an up-close perspective on all of these people and how they did their jobs, what they talked about, what they laughed about, what they whispered about, who they trusted, who they didn't, and how they talked about kids. Tina also wondered about how knowing that she was observing them affected their behavior. The bottom line for Tina, however, was a realization: She was fitting in. She was becoming part of this school.

When she visited different classrooms, it was rarely to just sit and listen. Her mentor would ask her to look for certain teacher or student behaviors. She was asked to examine and be critical of how things were working. Tina was encouraged to assess what she was seeing in terms of this question: Would I like to be a student in this class? Later Tina would be asked to give her perspective. She would be asked at a meeting, "Tell us about a class that you observed that you really enjoyed and why, but please don't mention the teacher's name."

Of great interest to Tina were the meetings of the various learning communities. Some were focused on instructional issues but not all. One discussion that had been ongoing in her learning community had been going on for nearly two years. It concerned the question of competencies. That is, should learning at school be more focused on students attaining competencies as opposed to earning credit for having been in a class for a certain amount of time?

Another ongoing issue concerned homework. The school had been conducting action research on homework. The research question was, "Do students who do homework assignments learn more than those who do not?" The data collected so far was the subject of much discussion within the learning community. Tina found herself reflecting on her own homework completion in high school and how it figured into her real learning.

As Tina's involvement with the learning communities developed she came to understand that the communities were not over invested in any particular technique or standard as the answer to creating effective teachers. Rather, the communities wanted to build a school around cultures of continuous striving and improvement. Pursuing this theme, Tina saw that the learning communities did the following:

1. Devised and refined classroom instructional strategies
2. Devised and refined individualized learning and project learning strategies
3. Investigated the outcomes of instructional strategies
4. Reviewed their mission statement and other foundational documents
5. Facilitated new teacher induction
6. Facilitated secondary school student induction of new teachers
7. Demonstrated instructional approaches for each other and other staff
8. Presented research and practical discoveries for all staff
9. Consulted with students on how to improve instruction
10. Met with all school stakeholders
11. Considered and re-considered the purpose of the school
12. Evaluated themselves as school leaders
13. Evaluated their enrichment of the school as a community
14. Evaluated the relationship of school procedures to classroom practices

15. Evaluated professional development programs delivered by outsiders
16. Conducted research, wrote reports, submitted articles for publication
17. Attended conferences
18. Continuously updated communities effective use of technology
19. Responded to student concerns about learning and schooling
20. Brought students into learning community on ad hoc basis
21. Conferred with nearby schools
22. Hosted visitors to see their school operation
23. Visited other schools with learning community cultures
24. Read and discussed books and papers together
25. Held local conferences
26. Discussed failed projects
27. Reflected on their communities effectiveness and efficiency
28. Engaged in self-evaluation procedures by individuals
29. Engaged in peer-review procedures among learning communities
30. Facilitated simulation exercises for all staff

One important function of the learning communities that developed over the years was the provision of simulation exercises. In these exercises, there were demonstrations and guidance on deal with unique instructional challenges. For example, staff was invited to participate and demonstrate skills such as discussing with students why undesired work is necessary or helpful, how to handle classroom debate that becomes angry or hostile, how to interrupt instruction for a tangential teachable moment, or understanding how the game of school hurts learning.

Three times a year, Tina's science learning community conducted student focus groups. In these focus groups the faculty met with students to get feedback from them on instruction. One of the community's favorite questions was, "What do teachers do that make you want to learn?" Another focus group was wider in scope and dealt with the structures of schooling. A favorite leading question for this group was "What kinds of changes here at school would make you happier as a student?" The third set of focus groups had to do with students' sense of developing self-direction. The learning community was interested in how students assessed their own developing self-direction and how that self-direction was supported by school. The lead question was usually, "What at school supports your sense of self-direction?"

Most of these focus groups were conducted as fishbowls. Students would sit in a circle with one adult who was the facilitator. Around the students would sit adults who would take notes but not participate. It was up to the facilitator to elicit as much valuable data as possible. There was time, however, after the sessions where participants and spectators had an opportunity to interact.

One of the things Tina noticed was that all learning communities reported to all other learning communities. Part of the school's routine was to occasionally provide teachers one hour of time to read other learning communities' reports. This, however, was only part of the teachers' reading responsibilities. Every year the entire school would read one book together, and each learning community would read one book together. The book this year for the entire school was Tony Wagner and Ted Dintersmith's *Most Likely to Succeed*. In her science learning community they were reading Jon Bashmun's book, *Smaller and Smaller*, on nano-theory and the teaching of the earth sciences.

THE PRIORITY OF TEACHER COLLABORATION AND PROFESSIONAL LEARNING

And, unlike when she was in secondary school, BR made time arrangements that allowed teachers to design the school calendar for more time to collaborate. Some days were entirely devoted to teacher collaboration and students were not present. In other cases, only one or two departments were given time to collaborate for two or three hours at a time.

Providing this extra time for teachers to collaborate was the outcome of the staff and community's affirmation of the importance of teacher collaboration and learning and how to make the time available for it. This did not necessarily mean that students had the day off. Sometimes entire grades reported to different venues around town where there would be required cultural events, discussions, and participation requirements.

Yes, this sometimes meant less seat time for students in routine classes. This was arranged, however, so it did not mean less learning. The staff had worked with students and parents to develop an array of activities that both groups agreed were educational and worth the time. A teacher and a community member were joint chairs of the Collateral Learning Team. Whether it was watching a thoughtful movie or presentation in a large group setting, there had to be a consensus that the event was not "busy work" and had real value.

The value of giving teachers time to work together became evident to Tina in her own science learning community where a number of the veteran teachers had been to conferences on "discovery learning" in science classes. They had become advocates of discovery learning, and their attitudes had strong impact on the entire learning community.

One of the intentions of these teachers was to draw students' attention to discovery learning, things that were discovered even though one was not trying to find them out. Tina was so happy that her work allowed her to collaborate with these pioneering teachers who were looking to make changes.

In another instance, veteran teachers were now conducting some instructional experiments with how lab partners communicated with one another before, during, and after lab work. They wanted to find out more about what students were expressing in terms of discovery learning. Did they ever say things like, "Did you notice . . . which I wasn't expecting?"

An important part of teacher learning at Beacon High was the opportunity to work on additional certificates and degrees as part of one's work at the school. With a cadre of university scholars on site, classes were held at the school where most, but not all, of the graduate students were teachers from Beacon High.

Book reading, paper writing, and research were usually all related to what was happening in the school or had emerged as an issue in a learning community. Many teachers were working on master degrees and some on doctoral degrees. Most teachers belonged to at least one professional organization, read its journal, and participated in an annual conference.

At the time of Tina's arrival, four graduate courses were being offered at the school in the early evenings. In every case the courses were designed by a collaborative team from higher education and the teachers at Beacon High. While all teachers were allowed to take graduate courses and proficiency courses if they chose, every teacher was expected to be matriculated in a master degree program by their fifth year of teaching.

In her first year, Tina was also exposed to a number of research projects as presented by the researchers in her department. She became involved in one. It was explained in this way: In a control group, lab partners did not have a pre-lab work discussion about expectations. In the experimental group, partners were directed to have a discussion about what they thought their lab work would produce.

Partners would then record the basics of their pre-lab work discussion in a journal before beginning their work. Later, both groups would evaluate the outcomes of their work and whether their expectations were met. The science teachers wanted to find out how much verbalizing of lab work intentions affected the quality of the lab work and its outcomes. To what extent was effective lab work an outcome of communication between the people doing the lab work?

Teachers ran this experiment for more than a month, and reported their finding at a special learning community meeting. As Tina helped execute this experiment, she also made observations about three other instructional techniques which her learning community had become interested in: (1) having lab partners start by taking time to review the lab work protocols and purposes among themselves instead of having the teacher do it from the front of the room; (2) the teacher walking around the room during the lab work—what did it mean to the students?—and (3) the teacher being social and friendly while the students were focused on executing lab protocols—was it distracting or motivating? Tina and the other members of her learning community reported on their finding after each did twenty observations.

BY THE END OF HER FIRST YEAR

At the end of Tina's first year, a meeting was held where the five members of Tina's cohort were asked to reflect on their first year at Beacon High and evaluate the program they had experienced. Those running the meeting made two strong points during the meeting. One, they explained in detail how what Tina's group experienced was superior to what students experienced in traditional teacher preparation programs. These school leaders were still selling their program.

The second was that the evaluation team wanted to know from the students how they would change the program in order to improve it. They provided the novice teachers an anonymous way of doing this on computers in the school's computer lab. They explained that just as in the high school, they were intent on changing their program from year to year depending on how it was reviewed by the inductees who experienced it.

Over the course of the next three years, Tina's involvement in BR's culture became deeper and deeper. When she looked back, she could see that she had been involved in nearly every aspect of the school. In the course of this involvement, Tina had gotten to know many of her colleagues on a deep level and had started to feel a lot of ownership of the school's success. She had a strong sense of how people wanted to help her meet the school's expectations for continuous professional growth. When she had the opportunity, she would tell other aspiring teachers in secondary school that professional development schools 2.0 were a much better choice than teacher preparation in higher education.

Part III

TINA BETRAYED

HIGHER EDUCATION'S REFUSAL TO CHANGE

Chapter 10

Understanding Higher Education's Betrayal as Revealed in Low Student Achievement

Tina's story gives a practical view of a path to a new school model, one designed to educate and develop both students and teachers in the place where we know teachers really learn to teach, in local schools. But, consistent with the title of this book, higher education has chosen to stay with its obsolete model. It has done this in the face of abundant scholarship and the successful practice of many different learning organizations, including schools. This choice and higher education's behavior constitutes a blatant betrayal of both teachers and their students. While impeding the professional growth of teachers, it has also worked to undermine student achievement. What follows is a deeper dive into how higher education teacher preparation destines our nation's teachers to ineffectiveness. It is, in effect, the behind-the-scenes story of that ineffectiveness.

As in all such stories, many of the players at fault have gone to great lengths to obscure the truth. Thus, the necessity of this book. The issue comes to the fore as our nation's report card, the National Assessment of Educational Progress, and the media have again positioned student learning in our nation to be faced with such descriptions as "stagnant, flat-lined, static, and intractable."

Translated these descriptions indicate that there has been little progress in student achievement in American classrooms since the 1970s when the testing of our nation's students first began. This reaction comes to us yet again because on October 30, 2019, the U.S. Department of Education released the latest round of disappointing NAEP scores. Following is a new understanding of why our schools are failing and higher education's long-standing role in the underachievement of our schools. It is yet another tale of how adults often make choices that are better for adults in the name of doing better for the kids.

This new understanding of the persistent underachievement of American students starts with the reader considering the teachers you worked with in your own personal schooling. Consider the ones you loved and the ones whose incompetence insulted you. The reader should ask why did these teachers teach or fail to teach in the ways that they did. And even if you had an elite education, consider the possibility that the teachers who seemed awesome or exceptional then may have seemed that way for reasons other than instructional effectiveness. After all, as a youth, when you got passed whether or not you liked your teacher, did you have any sense of what instructional effectiveness was? This book should lead us to question what instructional effectiveness is, why it is missing in most of our schools, and why we have refused to fix the problem.

To achieve this understanding, this book will continue to ask the reader to reference your personal experiences with teachers and the variability in their quality. But, in spite of this request, this book about the relationship of teacher preparation to poor student achievement will also ask you to do something difficult for most educated people. It was for this author, a teacher of more than thirty years. The request: to suspend the notion that you really know much about effective teaching and student learning. Like most of the teachers you worked with over the years, both good and bad, average and elite, the ones you liked and the ones you disliked, it is unlikely that you really understand some of the most basic factors in effective teaching and student learning. Recent research suggests that few of the teachers who we liked or who we thought were great were nearly as good as we thought. Most were certainly not effective.

But before we get down to the details, some clarifications are necessary. First of all, this book *is*, again, intended to be an act of whistleblowing. The overriding intention is to expose wrong doing. It is a wrong doing that exceeds academic differences of interpretation. The wrong doing is not like the controversies around new math or old math, phonics or whole language. Rather it involves choices that enter the arena of malpractice. That is, higher education has, for selfish reasons, knowingly done the wrong thing in teacher preparation when a better, more effective alternative was clear. Thus, for decades higher education has not been providing students who aspire to be teachers what they were promised, a research-based induction process that sets them on a developmental path to becoming effective teachers.

As the violation of laws will not be explored here, this book should be taken as a professional indictment and a confessional complaint. The author, who was slow to realize it, will show that higher education has taken a decidedly self-serving stance of *no change* on teacher education. It is this refusal to change that higher education will continue to create a flood of ineffective teachers for the most expensive system of schooling in the world.

This author is a career high school teacher and teacher education insider. He considers himself a teacher advocate, and was once president of his local union and settled two contracts. As a career high school teacher and Ph.D., he has been active in the induction, preparation, and development of teachers for several decades.

In the mid-1990s his involvement in teacher education went to another level when he became involved in the professional development school movement. Professional development schools, PDSs, are local schools that make an elaborate program commitment to teacher induction and preparation in partnership with nearby universities which then send teacher interns to these local partner schools for a variety of induction experiences. The primary objective of PDSs is to give aspiring teachers such a good start in teaching that the teacher will not fall victim to teaching's many frustrations and ultimately leave teaching.

Professional development schools are a great idea. A lot of good has come of them for both higher education and local schools. In partnership with a local university, the high school where the author taught became the first high school professional development school in the State of New Jersey. He was one of its co-coordinators and later became a founding member of the National Association of Professional Development Schools. He believes the professional development school movement stands to be the lever whereby our nation can properly reorient teacher education, but, at this time, the outlook is not good. As will be detailed, higher education has shown itself to be unwilling to change its teacher preparation model in the face of better alternatives, alternatives which are supported by research and which the PDS movement, itself, has caused to emerge.

As suggested earlier, to best appreciate what is going to be explained here, the reader should revisit personal schooling experiences. It is this personal experience with teachers and how they affected you that should serve as the entry route to understanding teacher effectiveness and distinguishing that effectiveness from teacher affect and all the other reasons students come to like their teachers.

As you consider this, also consider that apart from the lagging student achievement in our nation, research suggests a compounding factor: Only about 30 percent of our students are highly engaged at school. And when you further consider the rampant reality of gaming in school, particularly among high achievers, readers should all be moved to wonder what our schools are doing and what is really being taught and learned. Hopefully, it should move all readers to want to fix what is wrong for the sake of the young people they know.

To fully understand the situation under discussion, the reader is also going to be asked to process some nuance. The fact is that many of the teachers who you may have enjoyed, including in higher education, were very likely not effective teachers by the standard to be presented shortly. This may have been the grand orator, the ardent activist, the fun teacher, the deeply caring teacher, or any variety of teachers who were affecting and engaging but who, in the end, did not employ research-based strategies that would help you learn or grow as you might have. What may be most difficult for the reader to face is that you are completely unaware of the resulting gaps in your own learning and how those gaps have affected your thinking and development as a person.

Let's begin by reviewing the old story. Educational achievement and engagement in our nation's schools continues to lag, and ineffective teaching has been and is still the problem. It is a story revived by news outlets every couple of years when the nation's report card, the National Assessment of Educational Progress, is issued by the U.S. Department of Education. This is followed by experts telling us, repeatedly, that the problem is ineffective teaching.

It's true. A great deal of often-cited research tells us conclusively that the single most important variable in students learning at school is the quality of the teaching. If students are not learning at school as they should, then the problem is the teaching. The data are clear. That's an old and tired story, and you probably already knew it. You probably knew it on some level as a student in elementary school.

The reader probably also knows that dating back to 1983 and the publication of *A Nation at Risk*, the nation's efforts to solve the problem of ineffective teaching have included several major pieces of national legislation, *No Child Left Behind*, *Race to the Top*, the *Common Core Curriculum Standards*, and the *Every Student Succeeds Act*, all of which have focused on the quality of teaching and teacher accountability in our schools.

Efforts to raise the quality of teaching have included raising admission standards to schools of education, making coursework more demanding during teacher preparation, providing novice teachers more clinical practice, heightening teacher licensing requirements, making teacher evaluation more frequent and more stringent, providing more teacher professional development, instituting more teacher-specific accountability testing of students, firing weak teachers, incentivizing teachers who successfully raise test scores, increasing the number of subjects tested, and extending the probationary period before tenor is granted.

The reader probably thinks it all sounds like a reasonable effort. Most people do. But in these efforts we may see the first layer of scandal. The effects of all of these efforts have been researched by the universities themselves, and not one of these initiatives correlates with improved student learning. That is, when these changes were instituted, it didn't change student learning outcomes. And here's the kicker. Those who claim to prepare our nation's teachers have known for years about the ineffectiveness of these efforts. They have known for a long time that higher education teacher preparation, with all of its "improvements," has had no correlation with improved student learning. That is part of the reason why the nation's report card has not indicated meaningful improvement in student achievement over the last forty to fifty years.

The traditional teacher preparation formula goes something like this: Aspiring teachers become education majors in college and, along with a subject major, they take a variety of courses that are related to teaching. Over a four-year period they will visit schools and engage in what is now called *clinical practice*. Clinical practice is a minor variation on what used to be called *student teaching*. It means novice teachers will spend time in schools observing master teachers and teaching students.

During clinical practice an effort is made to introduce student teachers to best practices and connect the clinical experience with the theory that is being studied in the on-campus courses. In recent years there has been increasing emphasis on clinical practice, and novice teachers are spending even more time in local schools.

Unfortunately, as with the other changes, there is scant evidence that this increased focus on clinical practice has made a difference in the learning outcomes of the students that these pre-service teachers will eventually serve as licensed teachers. More on that shortly. But again, the problem: although many will deny this, most teacher education teachers in higher education have known about this lack of correlation and have known it for a long time.

In 2006, the eminent Arthur Levine, former dean of Columbia Teachers College, explained in his report on teacher education for the American Educational Research Association that there was no evidence that university teacher preparation correlated with improved student learning. Twenty-five years later, there has been no notable change in that reality.

The failure of university teacher education to make a difference in student learning has been more recently explained by the frequently cited researcher Dr. John Hattie. In his famous book *Visible Learning*, Dr. Hattie tells of his review of eight hundred meta-analyses related to student achievement which included those for teacher education. The inquiry found "the meta-analyses relating to teacher education show the effect size of teacher education on subsequent student outcomes is negligible (about 0.10)." Hattie further cites Qu and Becker (2003) who also "reported a very small effect size from twenty-four studies." So small was the effect size that "the effects of four-year college training compared with the effects of alternative certification is d= -0.01and, compared with emergency licenses, d=0.14." These data were consistent with Sparks (2004), also cited by Hattie, who reported "fully certified teachers had slightly more effect on student achievement than those with probationary or emergency licenses (across mathematics, science, and reading; d=0.12)."

While these data should give us pause, there is even more reason for concern about the effects of higher education teacher preparation. Noted educational researcher and writer Lee Teitle, author of *Professional Development Schools Handbook* (2003), helps us understand still more about the ineffectiveness of higher education teacher preparation with the observation that what aspiring teachers learn in their preparation programs eventually will "wash off."

The essence of this concept is that what teachers "learn" in their teacher preparation programs eventually washes off when teachers settle into a regular teaching job in a particular school. Novice teachers, then, drift away from what was learned in their higher education classrooms and begin to adopt the ways of the school culture where they work. That is, these new teachers begin to do things in the way they see them being done by the teachers around them in their workplace. It is a natural phenomenon. Anyone involved in teacher preparation knows that this wash off is routine among new teachers. The inflated ideals and course titles of university teacher preparation and graduate school fade away, replaced by cultural learning, good or bad, at the job site.

When this author and his colleagues first observed this "wash off," neither did we have a word for it nor did we want to believe it. After having provided an intensive induction process for our pre-service teachers that emphasized copious mentoring in conjunction with introduction to a variety of best practices in teaching, we saw our newly hired teacher interns begin sinking into what we thought of as the "old culture" of our school. It was a culture we wanted to leave in the rearview mirror.

In that old culture, too many teachers undertook, in varying degrees, what can only be called a cynical view of teaching. These teachers would withdraw from the challenges of teaching and sink into a pro forma approach to getting their work done. These teachers would complete all of the outward requirements of teaching but at the same time begin to withdraw emotionally from their work. Their performance took on a gaming quality.

Student compliance, more than learning, became a basis for passing a class. The challenges in teaching our students became a basis for complaining in the common areas of the school building instead of opportunities to seek solutions in professional conversations. It was exactly the opposite of what we had hoped for in starting a professional development school.

It was also something we really didn't like talking about. It was judgmental and felt disloyal, like an assault on our colleagues, a family of sorts whose professional hardships could not be underestimated. We all knew in ourselves how easy it was to become cynical. Our society and the school would give us lots of reasons to become one on a regular basis. So, pointing a finger of blame at many "old-culture" teachers seemed unfair and too easy. This author feels it in this writing. At the same time, it was too true to be ignored. The cynicism and withdrawal was like an infection that we didn't want to acknowledge but ultimately could not deny.

While it is granted that teachers are rightly disposed to complain about a lot in how our nation's schools are run, we became distressed because the whole point of a professional development school was to give teachers so much support and such a comprehensive induction that they would not be disposed to withdrawal or taking on a cynical view of their work. Unfortunately, we came to see that the practical reality turned out to be that the old culture of our school trumped our intensive and idealistic induction process.

Facing the reality of this "wash off" phenomenon raises a variety of questions about why so many teachers eventually get turned off or, to use the more common expression, burned out. Assuming the reader is not a teacher, it may be surprising to learn that burnout is such a powerful force in the cultures of so many schools. If the reader *is* a teacher this reality may not be a surprise, but it still may be very difficult to acknowledge.

This book does not look to undertake the broad question of how teachers burn out, but it does mean to emphasize that the professional development school movement was intended to counteract such burnout and to increase teacher retention through a more comprehensive and supportive induction. It meant to put an end to the stressful "you're own your own, sink or swim" approach that so many teachers experience at the start of their careers.

The reader is probably aware that nearly half of all new teachers leave teaching within five years of beginning their work. The reality is that teaching, done right or not done right, is very challenging work. In some schools it can feel impossible, even to otherwise very competent people with high-quality educations. Teachers have to have an exceptional commitment and resilience. How teachers come to cope with the demands and frustrations of teaching are various, but it was the intent of the professional school movement to support teachers to such an extent and in such a way that their effectiveness as teachers would gradually overcome the expected frustrations and their temptations to bail out.

There was one especially important reason for this. Without high levels of support, we knew that teacher would likely leave teaching or, even worse, stay and begin to adopt coping mechanisms that were contrary to effective teaching. The unfortunate reality is that many do. Teaching becomes just a job, and the coping mechanisms, often not acknowledged as such, get the teacher through the day with fewer incidents and less frustration.

A lot of these mechanisms may keep classrooms orderly and give them the look of proper procedure but, in the end, they do not translate into effective teaching and student learning. Like this author, the reader may be able to remember many such classrooms. But we are not just talking about "busy work" here. The reality is that a lot of strong direct instruction is not effective instruction.

Having read this, the reader may now begin to recognize that some of your teachers who were compelling speakers, had powerful authority, were very caring or were just fun may have been employing, in some measure, coping mechanisms and may not have been giving you what you really needed in terms of guided instruction that led to real learning. It may be that you didn't really care at the time. Like your teachers, you may have just wanted to get to three o'clock without complications.

But now the data and the prospect of your own children being affected may give you a different perspective. While in the arena of instruction there are still many roads to Rome, some of the roads are supported by research and others are just contrivances of people trying to deal with the pressures of classroom control and curriculum coverage and just doing their best to cope. It is not effective teaching that produces high levels of learning.

Why did teachers gravitate to the cynical old culture? It was concluded that it was not because the new teachers were seeking cynicism but because they were seeking inclusion. Every new member of a culture wants to become a full member. The same was true for the new teachers coming in to our school. They wanted to be accepted into their new environment. But as they merged, they were exposed to a lot of negative, sometimes toxic talk and they witnessed teachers performing in varying states of withdrawal. Eventually, we began to see many of our new teachers become increasingly disposed to negative attitudes and showing the early signs of withdrawal.

The principal of our professional development school at Rahway High School reported special concern about exposing intern teachers to veteran teachers who had over the years become toxic. While he was grateful for the teachers who volunteered to be supervising teachers, he came to realize that some of these teachers were toxic and spent a good deal of time sharing their toxic views with their interns. Some of these teachers eventually shared that they saw their sharing as giving the intern teacher a reality check.

They believed these new teachers needed to know the reality of the school experience. On top of sharing their "reality check" toxicity, some supervising teachers appeared to be using their arrangement with a student-teacher as a coping mechanism to lighten their own workload. As a result, high school principal, Edward Yergalonis, felt the need to assess the toxicity quotient of any teacher who expressed interest in being a supervising teacher with the hope of not placing an intern teacher with them.

Leaders of the professional development school eventually came to face that although we wanted our teachers to be guided by all of our high-minded induction programs, we could not control their daily social interactions in the hallways, the teachers' lounge, the parking lot, or the cafeteria. Their exposure to negativity was inevitable. Then came a realization: There was no counterinfluence to this negativity. Our school did not have professional learning communities so when our new teachers had "prep time," they did not convene for professional conversations with other teachers to seek solutions. More often they entered into social situations where teachers were likely complaining, mocking, or joking about a variety of problematic conditions at school. And, of course, there was a lot to mock.

The basis of this chapter is that after years of study and observation, it became clear that it was the culture of the school, the whole school, that was the key ingredient in an effective and positive teacher induction. It was the only pathway to higher student achievement. What aspiring teachers needed was the cultural experience of a community working together for professional and personal growth, not a broad assortment of independent teachers exercising individually contrived coping mechanisms. It took years to come to this conclusion, but it was a conclusion supported by recent research that applied cultural studies to schools and isolated culture as the most important variable in creating effective teachers. It adhered to historian David Brooks's observation, "Never underestimate the power of the environment you work in to gradually transform who you are."

This application of cultural studies to schools has been developed in works such as Deal and Peterson's *Shaping School Culture* and Gruenert and Whitaker's *School Culture Rewired* and *School Culture Recharged*. Distinctive among these works is the research done by The New Teacher Project that was published in their report entitled *The Mirage*. This report gave particular emphasis to their researchers' discovery of the ineffectiveness of "professional development" and other rational learning sessions that school leaders occasionally insert into the routines of teachers in a traditional school.

This new understanding about the overwhelming power of school culture then led members of the PDS at Rahway High School to ask new questions: When new teachers met veteran teachers at our or any school, what rubs off? When new teachers met a new school's norms, programs, procedures, what rubs off, what signals were received? And the big question: Would new teachers get the message that effectiveness was important or that coping was an acceptable default?

After a review of the literature on school culture, it became clear to us that without proper guidance and support, new teachers could turn their coping mechanisms into a career in teaching, and a school's culture could become largely derived of teachers independently contriving their own quasi-instructional coping mechanisms none of which had any basis in professional sharing with other teachers or educational research. In this context, the reader is asked to recall: If as a student you ever wondered about how your teachers selected their instructional techniques? Why did they choose one technique over another?

This learning about school culture highlighted another reality. It largely nullified our long-held belief about how to improve teaching. It was not specific information, programs, books read, or professional development that led to greater teacher effectiveness. It was culture. If the culture of the school did not somehow signal to new teachers that teacher development was a core focus of the school and each teacher in it, then no amount of university courses or in-school professional programs would make a difference.

The precise lesson we learned then became this: We couldn't change teaching by bringing a new program like that of a professional development school into the old culture of our school. We had to change the culture of our school first, and it had to be done in such a way that participation in the school, in and of itself, led teachers to effectiveness.

For a variety of selfish reasons to be discussed, few in higher education, however, will admit to this reality. But, Teitle's observation about the "wash off" effect is consistent with the research. Teachers really learn to teach in the schools where they work, not in the remote, decontextualized classrooms of higher education. This observation is critical so it needs to be repeated. Abundant research tells us that as a result of cultural adaptation, teachers really learn to teach in the schools where they work, not in the remote, decontextualized, campus classrooms of higher education. The student achievement data cited earlier should be taken as conclusive proof. Higher education has seen student achievement flatline for over fifty years and during that time it has refused to change its model.

Chapter 11

Understanding the Betrayal as Revealed in Higher Education's Fraud

So, the question becomes this: If teachers really learn to teach in the schools where they work, why has higher education not moved teacher preparation to the places where teachers work? That is, could schools be changed so that they are not only places for the education of students but also for the induction and development of teachers? And, couldn't higher education move its stewardship of teacher induction to the place where it has the greatest effect, the local school?

Yes, while this idea would require some substantial change in traditional schools, is it unreasonable that schools would change so they create the teachers they need right in the place where they are needed? Remember, research tells us that teacher effectiveness is the single most important variable in student learning at school.

Consider this: What good is teacher preparation in one university program, no matter how "powerful," if the novice teacher is going to go off to employment at a school where she will eventually learn very different protocols, priorities, and norms? The answer is that such a system renders what happens in university teacher preparation a waste of time. But this is what happens in all teacher preparation. What is learned is washed off by the culture of the school where the teacher ultimately takes a full-service position.

What pushes these conditions into the arena of betrayal is the fact that the leaders of university teacher preparation have faced these questions. They have faced them knowing that, as Arthur Levine asserted, what they were already doing had no correlation with improved student learning. And, they were also well aware of the wash off effect. In spite of this, leaders of university teacher preparation programs made a conscious decision to continue to do what they have been doing for decades.

Why did higher education make this decision? The answer to this question drills to the heart of the scandal, and it brings us to the most unseemly part, money. The reader probably does not know that most of a university's programs cost much more than they take in from student tuition and fees. One of the big exceptions to this norm is teacher preparation. Of all the academic programs at a university, teacher preparation is probably the biggest money maker, and is often referred to by insiders as the "cash cow" of many universities.

So substantial is the money produced by the on-campus component of teacher preparation that it is used to support many other programs at the university. So, if universities were to lose this source of cash, they would be deeply affected. Other programs would suffer too.

Bottom line, deans of schools of education across America have been told in no uncertain terms by university leaders to do what is necessary to maintain their state accreditation, keep their teacher preparation programs alive, and keep the money coming in. Suffice it to say that given this charge, schools of education have pulled out all of the stops to make sure they do not lose their teacher preparation programs.

But this absolute need to maintain the teacher preparation programs presented schools of education with a dilemma. On the one hand these schools had to maintain their traditional teacher preparation programs with all of their fee charging, on-campus components. On the other hand, university teacher preparation had to appear to be making substantial changes that addressed the problem of how to improve student learning. Their solution to this dilemma comprises another layer of scandal.

How higher education dealt with its dilemma is a study in fraud and what has been called "more of the same change." Based on numerous highly critical studies on teacher education in recent years, higher education knew in clear terms that it had a problem and that change was in order. The honest observation at this point is that higher education did face its problem. It just didn't respond honestly to it. This could be seen in how it responded to a report from the National Council for the Accreditation of Teacher Education, NCATE, which commissioned a Blue Ribbon Panel for the study of teacher preparation and issued a highly critical but highly regarded report. The report was emphatic about the need for significant change saying

> The education of teachers in the United States needs to be turned up-side down. To prepare effective teachers for the 21st century classrooms, teacher education must shift away from a norm which emphasizes academic preparation and course work loosely linked to school-based experiences. Rather, it must move to programs that are fully grounded in clinical practice and interwoven with academic content and professional courses. (NCATE, 2010, p. ii)

The operative concept here is "fully grounded clinical practice." In other words, teacher educators who prepared this report seemed to face the fact that aspiring teachers benefited most from "school-based experiences" as opposed to on-campus coursework. But the report also emphasized that the school-based experiences need to be collaborative. So, NCATE's report came to emphasize two specific areas for improvement: one, novice teachers needed more "fully grounded" clinical practice and, two, that clinical practice would be optimal in the context of collaborative school cultures and professional learning communities.

These were excellent recommendations. They showed some realism and honesty at work. There is substantial academic literature that supports the value of novice teachers having more practical experience in schools and the superior student learning outcomes in schools with collaborative cultures. After the Blue Ribbon Panel's report, teacher preparation institutions entered into a frenzy to elevate the concepts of clinical practice and professional learning communities. These terms became part of every conversation, every report, every grant application, and every evaluation criterion.

But the ugly reality is that these concepts got scant application. Or, one might say that they got just enough application to create the right appearance without causing any major changes in the traditional teacher preparation programs. Most importantly, *on-campus components remained the centerpiece of teacher preparation*.

Two developments are notable in this regard. First, schools of education put a new emphasis on clinical practice. Some, for maximum spin, started to call it "intensive clinical practice." For many schools of education this meant that a teacher's clinical exposure in an actual school would be expanded from the traditional one semester of student teaching to two semesters or more. The appearance of this was perfect because it responded directly to NCATE's recommendation for "more fully grounded clinical practice."

The second development has to do with professional learning communities. The hard reality was that higher education could not do much about getting local schools to institute authentic professional learning communities. The difficult truth was that, in spite of the documented efficacy of PLCs, leaders in both local schools and universities did not have a good, practical understanding of the concept. Both were stuck in the traditional school frame of reference.

For higher education to demand that local schools have authentic learning communities to qualify for a school-university partnership was just too great of a demand. Teacher preparation would grind to a halt while leaders in local schools and higher education figured out just what professional learning communities were and how they might support teacher development. This was largely because PLCs are not just teachers having meetings. PLCs have very precise protocols that require significant training and changes in traditional school culture, particularly how teachers spend their time. Both local schools and universities stood to be disrupted in significant ways if PLCs became a hard requirement.

But in this context, let the reader be reminded: The research tells us that schools with PLCs produce better student learning outcomes than schools without them. It should also be noted that the reader probably never went to a school with a culture derived of professional learning communities. But this research tells us that this working together is critical. John Hattie's research, previously cited, found that when teachers work together as evaluators of their impact on student learning, it has a distinctly powerful effect on student learning in comparison to all other school influences (https://www.youtube.com/watch?v=rzwJXUieD0U).

The work and research of the *National Center on Time and Learning* underscores this perspective. It found that teachers working in community produce the best outcomes for students.

> As developed by this organization's publication entitled *Time and Teaching* (NCTL, 2015), Research shows that schools with the strongest PLCs [professional learning communities] generate higher student performance. Moreover, this working together reaches it optimum effect when teachers are involved in school design that expands the amount of time they have to work together. (Davis, 2015)

Facing the difficulty in establishing PLCs in local schools, higher education's solution was to obfuscate, to just talk a lot about PLCs, and to call all sorts of teacher meetings PLC meetings even though they were not. This, at least, created the appearance of heightened collaboration in response to NCATE's Blue Ribbon Panel Report. Thus, the traditional formula for teacher preparation with university coursework as a centerpiece was allowed to persist with only minor modifications. Most regrettably, a long-term developmental path to teacher effectiveness, which is parcel to teachers working together in PLCs, has never been established.

In case you missed it. Neither of these changes, the extended clinical practice nor the increased talk about collaboration and professional learning communities, in any way interfered with the cash-cow coursework at the university campus. Thus, higher education achieved its goal of maintaining the coursework that has been a big source of income. It did this while ostensibly seeking change. It is this successful sleight of hand that may explain how and why higher education's role in persistent teacher ineffectiveness has not been perceived for the outright scandal that it is.

Keeping in mind the primary objective of higher education was to maintain its cash-cow teacher preparation programs, there is still the need to see the scandal in even more dreaded terms. Higher education actually maintained its cash-cow agenda while knowing it could do a better job if it changed. As you will see shortly, much has been written about how teacher education and schools might change and move schools in the direction of what is called a "learning organization" where all teachers can become effective teachers.

Before we consider the learning organization model, however, it is important to emphasize that people in teacher education knew all about the learning organization concept. It was not some marginal mystery. Countless books and articles have developed the concept of the learning organization. Many of these books were written specifically for an audience of educators. This awareness clarifies the lie that creating effective teachers is some kind of deep mystery. It is not. That is one of the key points of this story and a pillar of this scandal. In fact, abundant research tells us that we can have schools with all effective teachers, everyone. The wonderful reality is that we do know how to create effective teachers. The scandal is, ala higher education teacher preparation, we just don't do it. That would require a big change in the cash-cow model.

In this regard, it is important to point out that while higher education is the primary culprit, the associations that represent higher education teacher preparation also have responsibility and should be named. These are associations such as the Association of Teacher Educators, the American Association of Colleges for Teacher Education, and the National Association of Professional Development Schools. Their resistance has been adamant.

Together these institutions and associations constitute a professional front for the status quo in teacher education. They want to stick to the traditional formula described earlier. They do not want to turn teacher education upside down as suggested by NCATE. As will be documented shortly, they want to maintain on-campus coursework as the centerpiece of teacher preparation. In doing this, they have refused to acknowledge the research that beckons a new direction in teacher education and making schools learning organizations.

Higher education's obstruction in the use of professional learning communities and the development of a new school model has another financial component, jobs. In the preparation of this book and sharing the manuscript with other teacher educators, a common response was how disruptive this change would be to higher education teachers involved with teacher education. If local schools became the centerpiece of teacher education, what would happen to all those on-campus teaching jobs? What would happen to faculty offices, parking spaces, and seniority if higher education staff actually had to move in to local schools? How would tenor be affected?

This is not to diminish these working condition issues. They are not unimportant. But the emergence of these concerns in the context of the broader issue of teacher effectiveness and student achievement does belie a misplaced priority. In the overall, higher education teachers who reviewed this manuscript were quick to object to how what is proposed here would disrupt their traditional relationship with their higher education employers. It gives more insight into how financial issues influenced the thinking of these higher educators involved in teacher preparation.

The fact is that in a broader sense, educators themselves, both at the local school level and in higher education, have resisted change to the traditional school model and how it inducts and develops teachers, but the bulk of this resistance has been financially inspired under the leadership of higher education. What has been lost in all of the wrangling that has gone on with respect to teacher compensation and working conditions over the years is that if higher education had led schools in transitioning to learning community cultures, it would have eliminated many of teachers' complaints particularly regarding how teachers' opinions influenced their school. In effect, under the traditional school model, teachers were not trusted with school success.

It is in this context that we are right to look at the single variable that has not changed in teacher preparation over the last century, higher education on-campus teacher preparation. Then we must look to the leaders in teacher education to ask why there has been no change. The answer is that higher education has made it part of its mission to keep teacher preparation as an on-campus cash cow while going to great lengths to disguise this recalcitrance behind an ostentatious parade of more stringent requirements for teachers which they knew did not raise student achievement. It has all been a fraud.

Chapter 12

Understanding the Betrayal in Higher Education's Willful Blindness

In the context of framing higher education's betrayal of students and teachers through fraud, it would now be helpful to take an even more careful look at the research on effective teaching and how it has been ignored by higher education. At this point the reader might be questioning the premise of this book. Can higher education teacher preparation really be that bad? What they have done sounds reasonable. And what is this secret sauce of effective teaching that might reverse this betrayal? How can it be that higher education does not want to use it and that no one is talking about it?

The next layer of the betrayal is that the secret sauce is not a secret at all. There is a mountain of popular and academic literature about the secret sauce. The literature is actually popular among educators although it is derived of research usually done outside the field of education. That research has taken place in fields like systems theory, organizational theory, or organizational learning although there has been much done in the field of education, too.

The research has to do with how organizations maximize their effectiveness by increasing member involvement and leadership. In the reader's own professional work, you have probably read an array of both academic and popular articles about how organizations achieve greater effectiveness through member or employee involvement by way of teaming and collaboration both on the whole organization and small group levels. It has been a popular theme in many business and academic fields for decades, including education. Simply put, teamwork works.

Research over the last half century tells about progress in our understanding of how organizations learn and how organizations have advanced their own learning internally and greatly improved the effectiveness of many for-profit and not-for-profit organizations. The reader may recognize the names of such scholars and business leaders as W. Edwards Deming, Peter Drucker,

Chris Argyris, Jim Collins, Peter Senge, or Phyllis Wheatley. The essence of the learning these scholars and practitioners have tried to share is this: hierarchical organizations are less effective than those where there is broad member collaboration, member ownership, and all members work to learn and make decisions together on how to improve performance and increase organizational capacity.

This idea of making organizations collaborative is now commonplace in the corporate world. It has reached the point where people think of it as just common sense. Unfortunately, application of the important lessons that have come from the field of organizational learning has occurred in only a limited number of schools as most local schools have adamantly adhered to the traditional school model with its top-down authority structure.

It is a structure where teachers are isolated from one another in privatized classrooms. Per this structure, teachers rarely collaborate and important decision-making for a school comes not from teachers but from a hierarchy within the school, district, county, state, or nation. Teachers are not asked to study and think through the challenges in their schools. They are not asked to participate in studying their own effectiveness or in making important decisions for their school.

Rather, teachers are asked to follow the directions that come from a hierarchy often distant from their schools and flowing from people in federal or state agencies who are not teachers. This control from a distance has been the thrust of much of the national legislation previously cited. Per these conditions, it should be easier to see why teachers often don't feel personally invested in what they are told to do; they don't feel ownership or a sense of professional or personal efficacy in the grand plans that come from above. Many experience withdrawal, and their work becomes pro forma.

These feelings among teachers illustrate another important lesson for schools that comes from organization theory: When members of an organization begin to collaborate and work together, it changes the culture of the organization. Lots of research tell us that when everyone is asked to be a thinking participant in the organization, it has the effect of increasing trust, ownership, drive, and, especially, learning.

In fact, it is the conclusion of much recent research that it is, in fact, the culture of an organization that is the real driver of learning and effectiveness, not explicit rational strategies such as five-year strategic plans or "professional development." As Peter Drucker has famously noted, "Culture eats strategy for breakfast." In other words, organizations can have all sorts of wonderful missions, plans, and strategies, but if the organization's culture does not support these, then the culture will always win out.

In this regard, it is also very telling that Senge et al. (2000) published the monumental work entitled *Schools that Learn*. The book discussed the application of learning organization theory to schools. It is the same thinking outlined in Senge's famous work *The Fifth Discipline*. *Schools that Learn* gives a thorough explanation of what organizational learning means for school improvement and how the cited example schools have already become learning organizations. It is inconceivable that this much-heralded work was missed by those that have been leading in teacher education. One can only conclude that it was not missed but ignored.

A more recent work charts the transition of a school from teachers working independently to a collaborative culture. *Trusting Teachers with School Success* (Farris-Berg, 2012) tells the story of how teachers were first reluctant to enter into a collaborative model but later came to realize that they would not want to return to the isolation of traditional teaching.

Similarly, an even more recent work on collaborative culture has also been ignored. It is the 2018 publication entitled *Leading a High Reliability School* by Marzano, Warrick, Rains, and DuFour, all leaders in the teacher collaboration movement. As *Schools that Learn* was a by-product of research and scholarship initially intended to help big commercial organizations become more effective, *Leading a High Reliability School* is derived of research and study of organizations which by their nature have little tolerance for failure. One example is a nuclear power plant.

As our public schools have become notorious for their tolerance of failure, that failure became a standing invitation to educators for a strategy that would stop the failure. The research and study of high-reliability organizations presented in *Leading a High Reliability School* provides a blue print for highly collaborative schools that, like those organizations cited in *An Everyone Culture*, virtually guarantee a growth culture that insures teacher effectiveness and student success. Significantly, application of the concept requires high levels of member collaboration and, as a cornerstone, teachers working in professional learning communities.

Like the others, this reference is presented because it clarifies the place professional learning communities have in the research literature but also to emphasize that it is part of a research literature ignored by higher education teacher preparation.

Mindful of how these lessons on the benefits of collaborative organizations and organizational learning were ignored, let's look again at our schools and how we continue to prepare teachers. The big take away is this: Higher education does not prepare teachers for learning organizations with professional learning communities. Rather, they prepare teachers for old-style traditional schools where teachers operate as lone actors in privatized classrooms where they learn to "figure it out for yourself," do their own thing and, unfortunately, come to love their independence. Then when teachers are brought together, ala the aforementioned national legislation, it is usually to receive direction on how outside people think teachers should to do their jobs.

This brief review of the learning organization concept brings us back to the heart of the scandal. In spite of all we have learned about how organizations become effective, higher education continues to conceive of and prepare teachers to be lone actors who practice in independent, privatized, closed-door classrooms. The isolating effects of preparing teachers to be lone actors have been written about extensively.

The enormous literature on professional learning communities describes the negative effects of teacher isolation ad nauseam along with the generative effects of professional learning communities. Still, year after year our nation's teachers are prepared to work in schools that are not collaborative. It all constitutes an example of willful blindness.

The works cited above were not incidental publications that were hard to differentiate within a crowd of similar publications. Rather, they were high-profile publications by noted scholar/authors who had a significant publication history. So, why were they ignored in the nationwide effort to create more effective teachers? The only explanation is that they did not fit the financial model steadfastly defended by higher education.

Besides the financial incentive, another way to understand higher education's unwillingness to change how we prepare teachers may be found in a mindset. The reality is that just about every teacher and school leader has been prepared to adopt the mindset that conceptualizes teaching as largely an independent endeavor. Consider the ones who become the leaders of schools. It is teachers—teachers who were trained to think of school as the traditional school with teachers as independent actors. The mindset extends back to the day when these school leaders entered a traditional school as small children.

Most inferred the traditional school mindset as they observed that their teachers worked independently. Then, for those students who aspired to be teachers, there was nothing in their direct preparation at universities that suggested that change was needed, that the research demanded that schools be restructured so teachers became more collaborative and begin to function as learning communities.

In higher education teacher preparation, there is no attention to the research that clearly demonstrates that school cultures derived of learning communities produce better student learning outcomes than schools where teachers function as lone actors. This is, of course, compounded by the fact that when teachers go for graduate credits that would allow them to become school leaders, they go to the same schools of education that saw no point in suggesting to their education majors that the traditional school needed to change to become a collaborative learning organization.

In this mindset we get a clue to another motive. While higher education understandably wanted to protect the handsome income it gets from teacher preparation, couldn't it have changed its preparation model and still maintained the income? For example, couldn't it have invented courses on professional learning communities or how schools become learning organizations? Of course, the answer is yes.

But it is only a faint yes.

The real answer is no. If we again remind ourselves that it is school culture that is the primary variable in creating effective teachers, then it dawns on us why a lot of on-campus coursework has been shown to be ineffective. Coursework just does not have the effect of culture. The same would be true if students took courses on professional learning communities or organizational learning. The reading about and discussing these topics does not have the same learning effect as experiencing them and living them in an actual school.

Then the final reality comes forth: Higher education really does not have the capacity to provide aspiring teachers with the cultural experience of a collaborative school derived of professional learning communities. Only a local school has that capacity—providing the school does have a collaborative culture derived of professional learning communities. Higher education is then faced with the uncomfortable reality that its primary product, on-campus coursework, is ineffective and irrelevant.

Then another realization hardens: When our society prepares teachers, it should prepare them by facilitating their participation in a school with a collaborative school culture derived of professional learning communities. It is the most effective way. The idea of cooperative cultures appeals to both common sense and the observations of those who have studied how organizations thrive and succeed. What's more, the literature is popular, even trendy. Yet, higher education has seen fit to turn a blind eye to it.

Not applying this literature betrays teachers by depriving them of the career-long personal and professional growth inherent in the learning community experience. Regrettably, higher education has known about the concept of professional learning communities for a long time. Its blindness to how application of the concept would improve student learning can only be understood as being willful.

Chapter 13

Understanding Higher Education's Betrayal in Poor Teacher Development

Having laid out this indictment, let's pause for a moment to look even more closely at long-term teacher development. Consider this contrast: On the one hand, a new teacher enters the teaching profession as a traditional independent teacher who develops her lessons on her own year after year. This teacher is periodically given "professional development" that is offered on a school and district basis. Sometimes this professional development is inspired by teachers, but more often it comes to teachers as part of an edict from federal, state, county, or the local district. As such the requirement of this professional development has come from people who are not teachers and are resolute about one thing: They know better than classroom teachers.

Now consider the contrast. A new teacher enters the teaching profession by way of a local school that has a learning community culture. While this new teacher will deliver daily lessons to her classes, the substructure of the lessons will have been curated via a professional learning community. What does that mean? The answer to that question bring us to the superiority of this teachers long-term personal and professional development. For example, let's say that a professional learning community decides to focus on how best to teach about the Civil War. Consider the following possibilities within the learning community:

1. All the teachers present their points of view on instructional possibilities.
2. Some teachers decide to voluntarily do an assessment of what students currently know.
3. Some teachers decide to review the literature about the Civil War "Teaching Best Practices on Teaching about the Civil War."
4. Some teachers want to make sure that students can be active during the teaching so they brainstorm possibilities.

5. Some teachers want to make sure that often debated topics are presented to students.
6. All teachers decide to read a short book together on "The Causes of the Civil War."
7. On and on.

Now let's ask this question: Which new teacher will likely learn the most over the course of a career? Is it the one working independently or the one who works in a PLC?

It would be very hard to make the case that the teacher working independently will learn the most. Of course, an entire book could be written on what a traditional teacher might miss learning in comparison to a teacher who is developed over year while participating in a professional learning community. But there are three that are critical. One is school culture, itself. Another is the substructure of instruction and, finally, the game of school.

THE POWER OF SCHOOL CULTURE

It is understood that these claims for the power of culture have a nebulous quality to them. Although an understanding of the power of culture is not new, it is fairly new in its application to schools. Not necessarily involving prescribed content, organizational structures, or new job descriptions, seeing the customs and norms of culture as the primary vehicle for teacher learning is a significant departure from the notion of professional learning from books, instruction, courses, degrees, and "professional development" that is purported to happen on the campuses of higher education. It also stands in sharp contrast to the approaches used in the aforementioned legislation which called for many prescribed teacher behaviors, teacher controls, teacher-proof lesson design, and testing for strict data creation ala teacher accountability.

By contrast, the idea of culture invites skepticism because the concept, itself, is so inclusive of wide-ranging phenomena, much of which is neither easily described nor measured. Scholars and everyone are right to ask, what particulars are we talking about here, and how can we measure and/or be sure of any of the causes or effects?

While this line of questioning is reasonable, it must be balanced with another perspective. The research on the efficacy of rational learning verses cultural learning is increasingly clear. Many recent studies, with hard data, have shown rational learning approaches, particularly "professional development" to have little or no effect on teacher performance or student learning. One carefully focused study in particular by The New Teacher Project found that

School systems are not helping teachers understand how to improve—or even that they have room to improve at all. Teachers need clear information about their strengths and weaknesses to improve instruction, but many don't seem to be getting that information. The vast majority of teachers in the districts we studied are rated Effective or Meeting Expectations or higher even as student outcomes in these districts fall far short of where they need to be. Perhaps it is no surprise, then, that less than half of teachers surveyed agreed they had weaknesses in their instruction. Even the few teachers who did earn low ratings seemed to reject them; more than 60 percent of low-rated teachers still gave themselves high performance ratings. Together, this suggests a pervasive culture of low expectations for teacher development and performance. These low expectations extend to teachers' satisfaction with the development they received. While two-thirds reported feeling relatively satisfied with their development experiences, only 40 percent reported that their professional development activities were a good use of their time.

By contrast, an increasing number of recent studies, including that of TNTP, have demonstrated the power of culture as it influences members to adjust to organizational norms and, unavoidably, learn what Deal and Kennedy have famously termed "the way we do things around here." Of course, such learning can be for better or worse. School cultures can invite teachers into high-development, stasis, withdrawal, or even toxicity. That reality notwithstanding, many recent studies with hard data point to the power of properly designed cultures as having very positive outcomes—outcomes which have exceeded that of rational strategies for teacher development.

There are numerous studies, but one such study was conducted by eminent developmental psychologists Robert Kegan and Lisa Laskow Lahey. The findings of this study are now detailed in a book entitled *An Everyone Culture: Becoming a Deliberately Developmental Organization*. The book reviews the study of three for-profit and not-for-profit organizational cultures that were explicitly designed for member development and shown to be effective at spurring that development.

To be clear, Kegan and Laskow Lahey's study reveals how various organizational cultures were explicitly designed to engender member development. That is, just by virtue of membership in these organizations, the members automatically became engaged in a developmental process. No activities were either added or elected. Just through everyday operations personal and professional know-how of members deepened and grew. Stasis and/or withdrawal into pro forma work practices declined since they were largely impossible because of the push of cultural norms. Development, itself, defined these cultures as they pushed member performance to move in an upward direction toward expertise.

It is noteworthy in this context that many teachers have implicitly recognized the shallowness of their school cultures and deliberately sought professional enhancement from other sources. Across our nation thousands of teachers have undertaken efforts to get National Board Certification. This is a rigorous program requiring a high level of dedication to personal and professional improvement in a variety of skill areas related to schooling.

It is a clear indication of teachers' desire for higher levels of professional development. And consistent with this argument, it is noteworthy that The National Board also emphasizes culture in its five core principles and stipulates that teachers, once certified, work within professional learning communities.

This desire for professional improvement is also evident in Kegan and Lahey's (2016) study which is rich in personal testimony about how individuals had deep desires to attain professional refinement. The book offers many examples of how these highly varied organizations created cultures that put their members on a long-term developmental path. So, yes, this notion of the power of culture does have a nebulous quality, but readers of this book and Kegan and Laskow Lahey's work should be reassured that the study was conducted by scholars of high reputation. Their data are rich and scientifically derived. Add to this that along with the works already cited, *An Everyone Culture* is only one of a growing number of studies that have investigated how to engineer the positive impact of culture.

Of course, the big point here is that schools could do this, too. Schools could move away from the notion that rational instruction can be occasionally injected into old-school cultures of teacher isolation and that it will make a difference. It does not. The scholarship on this point is quite clear. What makes a difference in teacher development is the long-term involvement with a growth culture. Now it should be the new work of teacher preparation institutions, particularly the National Association of Professional Development Schools, to lead the teacher preparation community set up shop right in local schools and begin the work of helping local schools create the cultures that create effective teachers.

The reality is that the schools we have now were never designed for teacher learning and development. Even the most naive observer should be able to see this. As teachers work in isolation from each other, a collaborative culture cannot develop. There is no norm of professional discussions and peer review. Teachers do their own thing. And, dare it be said, teachers actually learn to devise ways to hide behind the closed doors of their classrooms in order to protect their autonomy from the insane government agents that presume they can from afar order teachers and schools to change by fiat.

THE SUBSTRUCTURE OF INSTRUCTION

Higher education's aversion to preparing teachers for collaborative school cultures invites another insight, perhaps the most concerning. Failing to prepare our teachers for professional learning communities precludes even more critical teacher learning about the substructure of teaching. While most of our teachers are unfamiliar with the term "substructure of teaching," failing to educate our teachers about the substructure of teaching should be seen as a fundamental source of teacher ineffectiveness.

In effect, it is in this issue that one can see how teachers have been betrayed by higher education. By sending teacher off to think of themselves as independent actors in isolated classrooms, higher education restricts teacher development. It says that teachers are actually on their own in devising curriculum and how to teach it.

This term "substructure of teaching" is not a term common in the educators' lexicon, although it should be. The substructure of teaching means what goes on behind the scenes of instruction that determines why teachers choose what to teach and in the ways they do it. For example, an intern teacher may see how the master teacher teaches, but will she see how and why the master teacher chooses her topics and methods? Where does the master teacher's thinking and lesson design come from? Does it come from teachers sharing designs and learning outcomes with other teachers? Does it come from action research? Does it come from consulting academic research? Do teachers work together to find evidence for why one method is more effective than another? Most importantly, does the school have formal structures for teachers to collaborate and perform these tasks on a routine basis?

No surprise: In the vast majority of cases, our nation's intern teachers will not learn about this substructure of teaching, and they will never learn that schools should have formal structures to facilitate it. They will never learn that the most effective schools are schools that are derived of a learning community culture. They will never learn that their teacher preparation is second rate for ignoring the concept professional learning communities and their value in schools.

Instead, they will learn what traditional school cultures teach, that every teacher is responsible for doing his or her own planning, short term and long term. They will learn that teachers work in isolation in privatized classroom. Yes, there is a written curriculum, but it is the culture of most traditional schools that each teacher loosely follows the curriculum in her own way. And, yes, teachers will talk and share, but the hard reality is that this talking and sharing is incidental. In such cultures, teachers learn to prize their independence. Especially, in the era of accountability, teachers cry out, "Leave me alone. I know what I'm doing."

So, in most schools, this examination of the substructure does not happen. There is no community of practice. There are no formal structures for teachers to routinely have professional conversations about evidence of method effectiveness. Most of our schools are made up of teachers who are operating as lone actors unaware that this is the source of their ineffectiveness. After trying very hard to improve student learning, most teachers are left scratching their heads wondering why they could not move the needle on student learning. This was so true in this author's case. Thanks to higher education, teachers don't know what they don't know. And for the most part, neither does the public.

What compounds this scandal is that while the academics teaching in our schools of education may not know how to implement professional learning communities, they are well aware of the concept, and they also know that schools with learning communities produce superior student learning. They have seen the literature and the data. They know that when teachers work together and share perspectives, instruction improves, and when multiple perspectives are suppressed, as has been the case in reading instruction, instruction flounders.

But still higher education teacher preparation ignores the learning community concept because universities simply do not have the capacity to engender the cultural learning that should be part of every new teacher's preparation. Higher education cannot sell a product that it does not have.

What must be emphasized here is the long-term effect of teachers not working together. Imagine the growth of a teacher who works with other teachers for years dealing with the problems of both instructional effectiveness and institutional effectiveness. Then compare that to the teacher who spends an entire career working independently with no sense of responsibility for the entire school program. It is this comparison that underscores the betrayal of teachers. The traditional school structure actually restricts teacher growth.

If, again, you recall your days with weak teachers at whatever level, this is one way to explain why there were weak teachers in your school. There was no inherent program of teacher development in the school. Teachers were left to their own devices to get control, manage the class, and teach the curriculum. For too many that meant teacher talk, teacher talk, teacher talk. While these teachers had occasional professional development sessions, they almost never had substantial professional conversations among themselves about how to do a better job. It just was not done. The focus was on class control and information transfer to students. Cover the material.

The idea of the school being for teacher development and teachers' examination of how learning happens was marginal or pie in the sky. It just wasn't part of a traditional school's culture. The author would further note that the absence of such professional conversations was an implicit message to all teachers: Your work is not worthy of such conscientious review. Just keep doing what teachers have always done. Keep moving the ball forward and, as best you can, keep order and get through your days without incident.

FACING THE GAME OF SCHOOL

For perspective, let's consider what we all know about the cultures that develop in most traditional schools. They are variation on the often written about cultural phenomenon called the *game of school*. It is the opposite of a deliberately developmental organization. Instead of focusing on learning or professional growth, the goal of the game of school is to create the appearance of doing what one is supposed to be doing, achieving, while one actually does something else.

For students the goal is to create the appearance of learning by getting good grades all the while knowing that their "learning" is founded on memory and will soon be forgotten. For teachers it is the act of teaching. The teachers make sure that they are seen delivering instruction from the front of the class and that all of the ostensible requirements of teaching such as lesson planning, attendance, instruction, student participation, and progress reports are in place. Most students learn to give the teacher what she wants and, just in case, to understand the magic of extra credit in maintaining one's academic status. And we all know that authentic student learning becomes overshadowed by such critical appearances.

We all have played the game of school as youths when we pretended to learn by memorizing or downright cheating and gave the teacher what we believed the teacher wanted, and then we forgot it shortly after the test. Ala traditional school culture, teachers knew this and went along with it. You can lead a horse to water and all that. There are many variations on this pretense. Compliance with school requirements is mostly ostensible, not real. It is an understandable development for teachers considering how stressful teaching can be combined with teachers' sense of being unsupported by conduct standards and being on their own to sink or swim.

More than any other concept, the game of school accounts for the mediocrity and averageness of schooling outcomes. It has, in fact, been called by another name, the *contract for mediocrity*. And, it is like alcoholism in a family. Everybody knows about it, but nobody talks about it. Even now, you may feel resistance to even thinking about the pervasiveness of this sham, unwilling to acknowledge that you may have carried what you learned from the game of school into your professional work. But for this discussion, what is most important is that the game of school is the default culture that develops when schools are designed for teachers to function as lone actors deprived of professional conversations.

It is worth noting that in an organization dedicated to professional growth, the game of school has no foundation. It can't thrive. Members are continuously having professional conversations about the success or failure of their work. They review each other's work. And they talk openly about gaming their work and the opposite, how learning might be made more authentic and personal. Members cannot give in to the impulse to withdraw into toxic complaining as part of an independent existence behind the classroom doors that protects them from peer review.

Chapter 14

The Future Darkens for Tina
Higher Education's Plan for the Future

BACK TO THE SCANDAL

This digression into imagining what teacher preparation could be is important. It is this vision and similar ones that higher education continues to reject in favor of the traditional formula with its focus on-campus coursework. It has not done this without resistance, however. The fact is that the universities have received major criticism for their inability to improve student achievement. And the idea of preparing teachers in actual local schools has been floated many times. In fact, accusations of the irrelevance of university teacher preparation became so common in recent decades that it served, at least in part, as a basis for two developments. One, many shortcut approaches to teacher induction emerged and many of these eventually received accreditation by state governments. The failure of these shortcut approaches will be dealt with shortly.

The other noteworthy development came from the renowned Linda Darling-Hammond's famous essay, "In Defense of University Teacher Education," and her book *Powerful Teacher Education*. Both the essay and the book make the case for university teacher preparation. From the standpoint of this expose, the relevance of Darling-Hammond's defense of university teacher preparation can be summed up by the fact that neither the essay nor the book pays much attention to the idea of professional learning communities as a critical part of teacher preparation. And, as might be expected, both give great emphasis to what happens on campus at the university.

But a key component of Darling-Hammond's argument is something that is true. Local schools do not have the capacity to be training centers for new teachers. Our traditional schools were never designed for teacher development, and because the vast majority of our schools are committed to conceiving of teachers as independent actors, the idea of inducting new teachers in actual schools with cultures derived of a learning community and designed for continuous, career-long teacher development is way beyond the frame of reference of most of our school leaders.

When leaders of local schools are asked about developing a learning community culture they, of course, decline the offer seeing that it means change and disruption. Like those in higher education, local school leaders prefer to keep doing things the way they have always done them.

The reality, however, is that Darling-Hammond and like thinkers have always had a choice. They could have made an argument for change so our schools became good places for our teachers to learn their profession in a learning community context. Or they could stick with tradition and continue to prepare our teachers out of context in higher education classrooms so these new teachers would be destined to think of themselves as traditional independent teachers. Can we be surprised that higher education's choice was *to not change our schools and to not change higher education teacher preparation*?

Unfortunately, Darling-Hammond's neglect of the PLC concept is indicative of the broad mindset of university teacher educators. Most regrettably, it is strongly indicated in higher education's plans for the future. A first example of this misconception of a good teacher as a lone actor comes from the National Conference on Teacher Quality and its 2018 Report. Remarkably, this report's recent review of teacher preparation programs finds these programs' focus entirely on preparation of teachers as lone actors and how their preparation defines them as individual classroom managers and instructors. Nowhere in the report is there a consideration of teacher involvement in professional learning communities as fundamental to effective teaching.

But, if at this point the reader has any doubt about this thesis and higher education's selfish intentions, we need only to review the American Association of Colleges for Teacher Education's plan for the future of teacher preparation as presented in the report from their Commission on Clinical Practice.

This report is one about which the National Association of Professional Development Schools and other education groups have expressed much excitement and confidence. They see it as representing higher education's best thinking and a strong answer to the previously cited 2010 indictment of teacher education which came from NCATE.

Unfortunately, a careful look at this new document from the Commission on Clinical Practice reveals that the real intent of higher education continues to be to keep the on-campus component of teacher preparation in place while it ostensibly advances the concept of clinical practice which, the reader is again reminded, still has no correlation with improved student learning. All the while, it is as if the research on the effectiveness of schools with professional learning communities did not exist.

As it is a response to NCATE's recommendations, it would be reasonable to expect that the Commission's renewed thinking on teacher preparation would heavily reference the research on collaborative school cultures and professional learning communities, but it does not. For example, the Clinical Practice Commission Report gives only a token mention of collaboration and, most tellingly, *suggests no formal structures for professional conversations and teacher collaboration.* The token mention of collaboration comes in the report section entitled "Design Principles." This section calls for "Candidate engagement in interactive professional learning communities," but, as will be detailed, *this concept is never developed in the report. It is an example of how inflated language about PLCs is used to distract from the fact that there is no intent to use them.*

The report also presents a Guiding Conceptual Model. But again, there is no mention of professional learning communities or any formal structures necessary for teacher collaboration. Yes, the report is replete with lofty language about reflection and teachers communicating, but *no formal structures are suggested.* This absence of formal structures is very telling. Any organizational leader knows that getting things done requires plans and formal structures to achieve those plans. Organizations cannot depend on lofty language and good intentions to achieve key organizational goals.

The failure of the Guiding Conceptual Model to stipulate a formal structure for teacher collaboration is at once glaring but also typical of most schools. Because of the buzz quality of PLCs is so strong in education, many school leaders would rather call any meeting teachers have a "professional learning community" than actually restructure their schools to provide the time and training to institute the formal arrangements necessary to have authentic professional learning communities. Richard DuFour and Robert J. Marzano, two scholars eminent in the field of teacher collaboration, have called attention to this persistent condition explaining, "It is perplexing to see the number of districts that proclaim the importance of staff members working collaboratively that provide neither the time not the structure vital to collaboration" (p. 73). But the reality is that DuFour and Marzano's comment is unduly polite and restrained. The on-the-ground reality in most traditional schools is that PLCs are seen as too intrusive, complicated, disruptive, and time consuming so it is just easier to fake it.

The even bolder headline here is that this failure to provide formal structures is not only true of most districts but also true of the professional associations that lead higher education teacher preparation. It truly is a united front against change. But what is most important about this is that it is clear evidence of fault. Given the NCTQ Report and the Clinical Practice Commission Report, it should be clear that higher education teacher preparation must bear major responsibility for this mindset that resists formalizing teacher collaboration and keeps teachers sidelined as critical thinkers who investigate their instructional effectiveness and manage the direction of their schools.

There is another implication which should be very concerning to all educators. Resisting the formalization of professional learning communities diminishes local schools as centers of thinking where teachers investigate the effectiveness of teaching and schooling and then make considered, evidence-based decisions for change. When teachers are involved in school decision-making, schools become thought centers that are less reliant on distant authorities in Washington, DC, state capitals, or higher education. Under this scenario, teachers do research, hone convictions, and are less available to faddish external manipulation. An observer has to wonder if turning local schools into bona fide centers of thought might be seen as a threat to higher education by higher education. Do we really want to turn our teachers into thinkers who insist on being listened to as opposed to being compliant implementers of policy decisions made far from their schools?

Further evidence of higher education's real agenda for the future of teacher preparation comes in the Clinical Practice Commission's Guiding Conceptual Model, which has six parts. Not surprisingly, five of the six parts focus on on-campus coursework. It is a program design which hardly reflects an intention to ground teacher preparation in schools or turn teacher education upside down.

The university-centric slant of the Commission's report is further evident in its Lexicon of Practice wherein the role of professional learning communities is not mentioned at all, and neither is professional learning communities even defined as a critical term in the teacher preparation process. Most critically, PLCs are nowhere mentioned in the Central Proclamations about how clinical practice is essential to high-quality teacher preparation. These Proclamations are given the highest profile in the report and include a Pedagogical Proclamation, but, amazingly, there is no mention of the importance of professional learning communities within it.

This brief review of how higher education's plan for the future of teacher preparation has avoided a full grounding of teacher preparation along with the value of professional learning communities in that preparation should make it clear that higher education is not only culpable for ineffective teaching but is still clinging to its ineffective model from the past. It is hard evidence of how Tina and all of her young colleagues are being betrayed. It continues to prepare teachers as lone actors via decontextualized, campus coursework while it ignores the substructure of effective teaching, that critical part of teaching that takes place in professional conversations, teacher investigations into instructional effectiveness, and the process of teacher decision-making that underscores the visible behavior of teachers in the classroom and takes place in PLCs.

TEACHERS WORKING TOGETHER FOR CAREER-LONG TEACHER DEVELOPMENT

If higher education were to get behind the idea that teacher preparation can only be long term and must involve teachers working together in an actual school, it would make complete sense to the public, politicians, and future teachers. It makes common sense to make schools the places where teachers learn to become effective teachers. Where else could they do it? But common sense finds an unexpected ally in academia where extensive research has concluded that organizations achieve optimal functioning when they function as communities.

Should higher education embrace the idea that teacher education must be about long-term immersion working in a learning community, it would give our nation's teachers what they want: more opportunities to interact professionally and a professional growth trajectory that empowers teachers to fulfill their potential and retake charge of their schools. This is a win-win scenario in a school-university partnership.

In their recent book, *An Everyone Culture: Becoming a Deliberately Developmental Organization*, developmental psychologists Robert Kegan and Lisa Laskow Lahey make a critical point when they observe that "research shows that the single biggest cause of work burnout is not work overload, but working too long without experiencing your own personal development" (Loc. 687). Their research and that of many other scholars who are applying cultural studies to schools should tell us that such personal and professional development as it comes from school cultures where teachers work together is the frontier most worthy of the teacher education community's redefined mission.

References

PREFACE

Levine, A. (2006). *Educating school teachers.* Washington, D.C.: The Education Schools Project.

INTRODUCTION

ACT. (2015). *The conditions of future educators.* www.act.org/research.
Carnegie Forum on Education and the Economy & Task Force on Teaching as a Profession. (1986). *A nation prepared: Teachers for the 21st century.*
Cochran-Smith, M., & Zeichner, K. M. (Eds.). (2005). *Studying teacher education: The report of the AERA panel or research and teacher education.* Mahwah, NJ: Lawrence Erlbaum Associates Publishers for American Educational Research Council.
Curtis, Rachel for the Aspen Institute Education and Society Program. (2013). *Finding a new way: Leveraging teacher leadership to meet unprecedented demand.* Washington, D.C.: The Aspen Institute.
Darling-Hammond, L. (2000). How teacher education matters. *Journal of Teacher Education*, 51(3), 166–173.
Kanstoroom, M., & Finn, C. E., Jr. (Eds.). (1999). *Better teachers better schools.* Thomas B. Fordham Foundation. Washington, D. C.
Kelly, F., McCain, T., & Jukes, I. (2009). *Teaching the digital generation: No more cookie-cutter high schools.* Thousand Oaks, CA: Corwin Press.
Levine, A. (2006). *Educating school teachers.* Washington, D.C.: The Education Schools Project.
National Commission on Teaching and America's Future. (1996a). *What matters most: Teaching for America's future.* New York: Carnegie Foundation.

National Commission on Teaching and America's Future. (1996b). *What matters most: Teaching for America's future*. Woodbridge, VI: National Commission on Teaching and America's Future.

NCATE. (2010). *Transforming teacher education through clinical practice: A national strategy to prepare effective teachers: Report of the blue ribbon panel on clinical preparation AND partnerships FOR improved student learning.* http://www.ncate.org/LinkClick.aspx?fileticket=zzeiB1OoqPk%3D&tabid=7.

Senge, P. (1990). *The fifth discipline: The art and practice of the learning organization*. New York: Doubleday, a Division of Random House.

Sopovitz, E. H., & Weinbaum, E. H. (2008). *Implementation gap: Understanding reform in high schools*. New York: Teachers College Press.

The Holmes Group. (1986). *Tomorrow's teachers: A report of the Holmes Group*. East Lansing, MI: The Holmes Group, Inc.

The Holmes Group. (1995). *Tomorrow's schools of education*. East Lansing, MI: The Holmes Group, Inc.

The New Teacher Project. (2015). *The mirage: Confronting the hard truths about our quest for teacher development*. New York, New York (500 7th Ave).

CHAPTER ONE

Busteed, B. (2014, October 9). Make a difference: Show students you care. *Business Journal*.

Darling-Hammond, L. (1999). The case for university-based teacher education. In M. Cochran-Smith, S. Feiman-Nemser, & D. John McIntyre (Eds.), *Handbook of research on teacher education: Enduring questions in changing context* (3rd ed.). New York & London: Routledge, Taylor & Francis Group.

Deal, T., & Kennedy, A. (1982). *Corporate cultures: The rites and rituals of corporate life*. New York: Addison-Wesley.

Deal, T., & Peterson, K. (2016). *Shaping school culture* (3rd ed.). San Francisco, CA: John Wiley & Sons.

Dewey, J. (1904) The relationship of theory to practice. *The Middle Works*. https://people.ucsc.edu/~ktellez/dewey_relation.pdf.

Farris-Berg, K., & Dirkswager, E. (2012). *Trusting teachers with school success*. New York: Rowman & Littlefield Education.

Garvin, D. (2000). *Learning in action: A guide to putting the learning organization to work*. Boston, MA: Harvard Business School Press.

Goodlad, J. I. (1984). *A place called school*. New York: McGraw-Hill Education.

Gruenert, S., & Whitaker, T. (2015). *School culture rewired: How to define, assess, and transform it*. Alexandria, VA: ASCD.

Gruenert, S., & Whitaker, T. (2017). *School culture recharged: Strategies to energize your staff and culture*. Alexandria, VA: ASCD.

Kegan, R., LaHey, L. L. (2016). *An everyone culture: Becoming a deliberately developmental organization*. Boston, MA: Harvard Business School Publishing.

Senge, P. (1991). *The fifth discipline: The art and practice of the learning organization*. New York: Doubleday, a Division of Random House.
Senge, P., Cambron-McCabe, N., Lucas, T., Smith, B., Dutton, J., & Kleiner, A. (2000). *Schools that Learn: A fifth discipline fieldbook for educators, parents, and everyone who cares about education*. New York: Doubleday.
Senge, P., Cambron-McCabe, N., Lucas, T., Smith, B., Dutton, J., & Kleiner, A. (2012). *Schools that learn: A fifth discipline fieldbook for educators, parents, and everyone who cares about education*. New York: Doubleday.
Teitel, L. (2003). *The professional development schools handbook: Starting, sustaining, and assessing partnerships that improve student learning* (p. 1). Thousand Oaks, CA: Corwin.
Will, M. (2016, May 4). Teachers feel their voices aren't heard in policy discussion, survey finds. *Education Week*.

CHAPTER TWO

Anderson, R. C. (2016). The makers: Creativity and entrepreneurial spirit. In Y. Zhao (Ed.), *Counting what counts: Reframing educational evaluation* (p. 86). Bloomington, IN: Solution Tree Press.
Brill, S. (2011). *Class warfare: Inside the fight to fix America's schools*. New York: Simon & Schuster.
Corcoran, T. (1995). Helping teachers teach well: Transforming professional development. *Policy Brief*. Consortium for Policy Research in Education, Penn Graduate School of Education.
Darling-Hammond, L. (2006). *Powerful teacher education: Lessons from exemplary programs*. San Francisco: Jossey-Bass.
Deal, T., & Kennedy, A. (1982). *Corporate cultures: The rites and rituals of corporate life*. New York: Addison-Wesley.
Deming, W. E. (1983). *The new economics*. Cambridge, MA: Massachusetts Institute of Technology, Center for Advanced Engineering Study.
Fischer, G., Giaccardi, E., Eden, H., Sugimoto, M., & Ye, Y. (2005). Beyond binary choices: Integrating individual and social creativity. *International Journal of Human-Computer Studies*, *63*(4–5), 482–512.
Gallimore, R., Emerling, B. A., Saunders, W. M., & Goldenberg, C. (2009). Moving the learning of teaching closer to practice: Implications of school-based inquiry teams. *Elementary School Journal*, *109*(5).
Green, E. (2012). *Building a better teacher: How teaching works (and how to teach it to everyone)*. New York: W. W. Norton & Company.
Gruenert, S., & Whitaker, T. (2015). *School culture rewired: How to define, assess, and transform it*. Alexandria, VA: ASCD.
Gruenert, S., & Whitaker, T. (2017). *School culture recharged: Strategies to energize your staff and culture*. Alexandria, VA: ASCD.

Hanks, L. J., & Wenger, E. (1991). *Situated learning: Legitimate peripheral participation.* New York: Cambridge University Press.

Hanushek, E. (2011). Recognizing the value of good teachers. *Education Week, 30*(27), 35.

Lave, J., & Wenger, E. (1991). *Situated learning: Legitimate peripheral participation.* New York: Cambridge University Press.

Levine, A. (2006). *Educating school teachers.* Washington, D.C.: The Education Schools Project.

Morris, A. K., & Hiebert, J. (2011). Creating shared instructional products: An alternative approach to improving teaching. *Educational Researcher, 40,* 5.

Morris, A. K., & Hiebert, J. (2012). Teaching, rather than teachers, as a path toward improving classroom instruction. *Journal of Teacher Education, 63*(2), 92–102.

Schein, E. (2010). *Organizational culture and leadership* (4th ed.). San Francisco, CA: John Wiley & Sons.

Schlechty, P. (2009). *Leading for learning: How to transform schools into learning organizations.* San Francisco, CA: Jossey-Bass.

Senge, P. (1991). *The fifth discipline: The art and practice of the learning organization.* New York: Doubleday, a Division of Random House.

Senge, P., Cambron-McCabe, N., Lucas, T., Smith, B., Dutton, J., & Kleiner, A. (2000). *Schools that learn: A fifth discipline fieldbook for educators, parents, and everyone who cares about education.* New York: Doubleday.

Senge, P., Cambron-McCabe, N., Lucas, T., Smith, B., Dutton, J., & Kleiner, A. (2012). *Schools that learn: A fifth discipline fieldbook for educators, parents, and everyone who cares about education.* New York: Doubleday.

Sparks, D., & Hirsh, S. (1997). *A new vision for staff development.* Alexandria, VA: ASCD.

The New Teacher Project. (2015). *The Mirage: Confronting the hard truths about our quest for teacher development.* New York, New York (500 7th Ave).

CHAPTER THREE

Bain, K. (2012). *What the best college students do.* Cambridge, MA: Belknap Press.

Brown, J. S., & Adler, R. P. (2008). Minds on fire: Open education, the long tail, and learning 2.0. *EDUCAUSE Review, 43*(1), 16–32.

Busteed, B. (2014, October 9). Make a difference: Show students you care. *Business Journal.*

Cochran-Smith, M., Feiman-Nemser, S., & McIntyre, D. J. (Eds.). *Handbook of research on teacher education: Enduring questions in changing context* (3rd ed.). New York & London: Routledge, Taylor & Francis Group.

Collins, J. (2011). *Good to great: Why some companies make the leap . . . and others don't.* New York: Harper Business.

Colvin, G. (2008). *Talent is overrated: What really separates world-class performers from everybody else.* New York: Geoffrey Colvin.

Corcran-Smith, M., & Lytle, S. (2008). *Teaching as Stance: Practitioner research for the next generation.* New York: Teachers College Press.

Davis, J. (2015). *Time and teaching.* Boston: National Center on Time and Learning.

Deal, T. E., & Peterson, K. D. (2016). *Shaping school culture* (3rd ed.). San Francisco: Jossey-Bass.

Deming, W. E. (1983). *The new economics.* Cambridge, MA: Massachusetts Institute of Technology, Center for Advanced Engineering Study.

Dovey, K. (2009). The role of trust in innovation. *The Learning Organization, 16,* 4.

Dufour, R., DuFour, R., Eaker, R., & Many, T. (2006). *Learning by doing: A handbook for professional learning communities at work.* Bloomington, IN: Solution Tree.

Farris-Berg, K., & Dirkswager, E. (2012). *Trusting teachers with school success.* New York: Rowman & Littlefield Education.

Fullan, M., & Heargraves, A. (2012). *Professional capital: Transforming teaching in every school.* New York and London: Teachers College, Columbia University; Toronto, ON: Ontario Principals Council.

Gallimore, R., Emerling, B. A., Saunders, W. M., & Goldenberg, C. (2009). Moving the learning of teaching closer to practice: Implications of school-based inquiry teams. *Elementary School Journal, 109*(5).

Gladwell, M. (2011). *Outliers: The story of success.* New York: Little Brown & Company.

Gruenert, S. (2005). Correlations of school culture and student achievement. *NASSP Bulletin, 84*(645), 43–55.

Gruenert, S., & Whitaker, T. (2015). *School culture rewired: How to define, assess, and transform it.* Alexandria, VA: ASCD.

Hanushek, E. (2011). Recognizing the value of good teachers. *Education Week, 30*(27), 35.

Hattie, J. (2012). *Visible learning for teachers: Maximizing impact on learning.* New York: Routledge and The Taylor Francis Group.

Hofstede, G., & Hofstede, G. J. (2004). *Cultures and organizations: Software of the mind.* New York: McGraw-Hill Education.

Hord, S. M. (1991). *Professional learning communities: Communities of continuous inquiry and improvement.* Austin, TX: Southwest Educational Development Laboratory.

Institute of Education Sciences. (2012). *NAEP long term trends.* http://ies.ed.gov/.

Johnson, D. W., & Johnson, R. T. (1999). *Learning together and alone: Cooperative, competitive, and individualistic learning.* Boston: Allyn and Bacon.

Kegan, R., & LaHey, L. L. (2016). *An everyone culture: Becoming a deliberately developmental organization.* Boston, MA: Harvard Business School Publishing.

Kelly, F., McCain, T., & Jukes, I. (2009). *Teaching the digital generation: No more cookie-cutter high schools.* Thousand Oaks, CA: Corwin Press.

Lave, J., & Wenger, E. (1991). *Situated learning: Legitimate peripheral participation.* New York: Cambridge University Press.

Levine, A. (2006). *Educating school teachers.* Washington, D.C.: The Education Schools Project.

Littles, J. W. (1982). Norms of collegiality and experimentation: Workplace conditions of school success. *American Educational Research Journal, 19*, 325–340.

May, M. A., & Doob, L. W. (1937). *A report of the sub-committee on competitive-cooperative habits, of the committee on personality and culture.* New York: Social Science and Research Council.

Moffett, J., & Wagner, B. J. (1968). *Student centered language arts K-12.* New York: Heinemann.

Morris, A. K., & Hiebert, J. (2012). Teaching, rather than teachers, as a path toward improving classroom instruction. *Journal of Teacher Education, 63*(2), 92–102.

National Commission on Teaching and America's Future. (1996). *What matters most: Teaching for America's future.* Woodbridge, VI: National Commission on Teaching and America's Future.

NCATE. (2010). *Transforming teacher education through clinical practice: A national strategy to prepare effective teachers.* Report of the blue ribbon panel on clinical preparation AND partnerships FOR improved student learning. http://www.ncate.org/LinkClick.aspx?fileticket=zzeiB1OoqPk%3D&tabid=7.

Polanyi, M. (1969). *Knowing and being.* Chicago, IL: University of Chicago Press.

Reeves, D. B. (2010). *Transforming professional development into student results.* Alexandria, VA: ASCD.

Schein, E. (2010). *Organizational culture and leadership* (4th ed.). San Francisco, CA: John Wiley & Sons.

Schmoker, M. (2016a, October 21). It's time to restructure teacher professional development. *Education Week.*

Schmoker, M. (2006b). *Results now: How we can achieve unprecedented improvement in teaching and learning.* Alexandria, VA: ASCD.

Senge, P. (1991). *The fifth discipline: The art and practice of the learning organization.* New York: Doubleday, a Division of Random House.

Senge, P., Cambron-McCabe, N., Lucas, T., Smith, B., Dutton, J., & Kleiner, A. (2000). *Schools that learn: A fifth discipline fieldbook for educators, parents, and everyone who cares about education.* New York: Doubleday.

Senge, P., Cambron-McCabe, N., Lucas, T., Smith, B., Dutton, J., & Kleiner, A. (2012). *Schools that learn: A fifth discipline fieldbook for educators, parents, and everyone who cares about education.* New York: Doubleday.

Song, H. J., Kim, H. M., & Kolb, J. (2009). The effect of learning organization culture on the relationship of interpersonal trust and organizational commitment. *Human Resource Development Quarterly, 20*, 2.

Sopovitz, E. H., & Weinbaum, E. H. (2008). *Implementation gap: Understanding reform in high schools.* New York: Teachers College Press.

The Holmes Group. (1986). *Tomorrow's teachers: A report of the Holmes Group.* East Lansing, MI: The Holmes Group, Inc.

The Holmes Group. (1990). *Tomorrow's schools of education: A report of the Holmes Group.* East Lansing, MI: The Holmes Group, Inc.

The New Teacher Project. (2015). *The mirage: Confronting the hard truths about our quest for teacher development.* The New Teacher Project. New York, New York (500 7th Ave).

Tilin, F., & Wheelan, S. A. (1999). The relationship between faculty group development and school productivity. *Small Group Research, 30*(1), 59.
Trimble, S. B., Peterson, G. W., & Gary, W. (2000). *Multiple team structures and student learning in a high risk middle school.* Paper Presented at the Annual Meeting at the American Educational Research Association, New Orleans, LA.
United States: National Commission on Excellence in Education. (1983). *A nation at risk: The imperative for educational reform: A report to the nation and the Secretary of Education, United States Department of Education* (Vol. 2). Ann Arbor, MI: University of Michigan Library.
Vesio, V., Ross, D., & Adams, A. (2008). A review of the research on the impact of professional learning communities on teaching practice and student learning. *Teaching and Teacher Education, 24*, 80–91.
Waters, R. (2012). *Secondary students' transitioning from compliance to intentional learning* (Doctoral Dissertation). UMI ProQuest (Order No: 3504071). Minneapolis, MN: Walden University.
Wenger, E., Mc Dermott, R., & Snyder, W. (2002). *Cultivating communities of practice.* Cambridge, MA: Harvard Business Review Press.
Yergalonis, E. (2016). *Expecting excellence.* http://www.expectingexcellence.net.

CHAPTER FOUR

Cook-Gruetner, S. (2004). Making the case for a developmental perspective. *Industrial and Commercial Training, 36*(7), 275–281. MA: Harvard Business Review Press.
Cook-Gruetner, S. R. (1985). *Ego development: Nine levels of increasing embrace.* MA: Harvard Business Review Press.
Erickson, E. (1950). *Childhood and society.* New York: W. W. Norton & Company.
Evans, L. (2002). What is teacher development? *Oxford Review of Education, 28*(1), 123–137.
Fowler, J. W. (1981). *Stages of faith: The psychology of human development and the quest for meaning.* San Francisco: Harper & Row.
Fullan, M., & Heargraves, A. (2012). *Professional capital: Transforming teaching in every school.* New York and London: Teachers College, Columbia University; Toronto, ON: Ontario Principals Council.
Gebser, J. (1986). *The ever present origin.* Athens, OH: Ohio University Press.
Graves, C. W. (2004). *Levels of human existence.* ISBN-10: 097247420X.
Kegan, R. (1983). *The evolving self: Problem and process in human development.* Cambridge, MA: Harvard University Press.
Kegan, R., & LaHey, L. L. (2016). *An everyone culture: Becoming a deliberately developmental organization.* Boston, MA: Harvard Business School Publishing.
Kohlberg, L. (1981). *The philosophy of moral development: Moral stages and the idea of justice.* San Francisco: Harper & Row.
Lalloux, F. (2014). *Reinventing organizations: A guide to creating organizations inspired by the next stage of human consciousness.* Brussels, Belgium: Nelson Parker.

Loevinger, J. (1976). *Ego development: Conceptions and theories*. Thousand Oaks, CA: Jossey-Bass.

Maslow, A. (1968). *Toward a psychology of being* (2nd ed.). New York: Van Nostrand.

Montessori, M. (2011). *The Montessori method*. Amazon Digital Services. www.amazon.com

Piaget, J., & Inhelder, B. (1969). *The psychology of the child*. New York: Basic Books.

Selligman, M. (2011). *Flourish: A visionary new understanding of happiness and well being*. New York: Free Press, a Division of Simon and Schuster, Inc.

Steffy, B. E., Wolfe, M. P., Pasch, S. H., & Enz, B. J. (2000). *Life cycle of the career teacher*. Thousand Oaks, CA: Kappa Delta Pi & Corwin Press, Inc.

The Holmes Group. (1986). *Tomorrow's teachers: A report of the Holmes Group*. East Lansing, MI: The Holemes Group, Inc.

The New Teacher Project. (2015). *The mirage: Confronting the hard truths about our quest for teacher development*. The New Teacher Project. New York, New York (500 7th Ave).

Torbert, W. R. (2004). *Action inquiry: The secret of timely and transforming leadership*. San Francisco: Barrett-Koehler Publishers.

Troen, V., & Boles, K. C. (2003). *Who's teaching your children?: Why the teacher crisis is worse than you think and what can be done about it*. New Haven, CN: Yale University Press.

Wilber, K. (2016). *Integral meditation: Mindfulness as a way to grow up, wake up, and show up in your life*. Boulder, CO: Shambhala Publications, Inc.

CHAPTER FIVE

Busteed, B. (2014, October 9). Make a difference: Show students you care. *Business Journal*.

Dufour, R., DuFour, R., Eaker, R., & Many, T. (2006). *Learning by doing: A handbook for professional learning communities at work*. Bloomington, IN: Solution Tree.

Dufour, R., & Fullan, M. (2013). *Cultures built to last: Systemic PLCs at work*. Bloomington, IN: Solution Tree Press.

Farris-Berg, K., & Dirkswager, E. (2012). *Trusting teachers with school success*. New York: Rowman & Littlefield Education.

Kegan, R., & LaHey, L. L. (2016). *An everyone culture: Becoming a deliberately developmental organization*. Boston, MA: Harvard Business School Publishing.

Martinez, M., & McGrath, D. (2014). *Deeper learning: How eight innovative public schools are transforming education in the twenty-first century*. New York: The New Press.

Money, J. (2015, April 1). Don't become a teacher advises award-winner Nancy Atwell. *Education Week Teacher*, 4(26).

NCATE. (2010). *Transforming teacher education through clinical practice: A national strategy to prepare effective teachers*. Report of the blue ribbon panel on

clinical preparation AND partnerships FOR improved student learning. http://www.ncate.org/LinkClick.aspx?fileticket=zzeiB1OoqPk%3D&tabid=7.
Schlechty, P. (2002). *Working on the work: An action plan for teachers, principals, and superintendents.* San Francisco, CA: Jossey-Bass.
Schlechty, P. (2009). *Leading for learning: How to transform schools into learning organizations.* San Francisco, CA: Jossey-Bass.
Schmoker, M. (2006). *Results now: How we can achieve unprecedented improvements in teaching and learning.* Alexandria, VA: Association of Supervision and Curriculum Development.
Schmoker, M. (2016, October 21). It's time to restructure teacher professional development. *Education Week.*
Senge, P. (1991). *The fifth discipline: The art and practice of the learning organization.* New York: Doubleday, a Division of Random House.
Senge, P., Cambron-McCabe, N., Lucas, T., Smith, B., Dutton, J., & Kleiner, A. (2000). *Schools that learn: A fifth discipline fieldbook for educators, parents, and everyone who cares about education.* New York: Doubleday.
Senge, P., Cambron-McCabe, N., Lucas, T., Smith, B., Dutton, J., & Kleiner, A. (2012). *Schools that learn: A fifth discipline fieldbook for educators, parents, and everyone who cares about education.* New York: Doubleday.
Sparks, D., & Hirsh, S. (1997). *A new vision for staff development.* Alexandria, VA: ASCD.
The New Teacher Project. (2015). *The mirage: Confronting the hard truths about our quest for teacher development.* The New Teacher Project. New York, New York (500 7th Ave).
Wenger, E., Mc Dermott, R., & Snyder, W. (2002). *Cultivating communities of practice.* Cambridge, MA: Harvard Business Review Press.
Will, M. (2016, May 4). Teachers feel their voices aren't heard in policy discussion, survey finds. *Education Week.*

CHAPTER SIX

Argyris, C. (2012). *Organizational traps: Leadership, culture, and organizational design.* New York: Oxford University Press.
Breault, R., & Breault, D. A. (2012). *Professional development schools: Researching lessons from the field.* Lanham, MD: Rowman & Littlefield Education.
Busteed, B. (2014, October 9). Make a difference. Show students you care. *Business Journal.*
Chubb, J. (2012). Overcoming the governance challenge. In C. Finn & D. R. Fairchild (Eds.), *Education reform for the digital era.* Washington, D. C.: Thomas B. Fordham Institute.
Davis, J. (2015). *Time and teaching.* Boston: National Center on Time and Learning.
Deming, W. E. (1983). *The new economics.* Cambridge, MA: Massachusetts Institute of Technology, Center for Advanced Engineering Study.

Garvin, D. (2000). *Learning in action: A guide to putting the learning organization to work.* Boston, MA: Harvard Business School Press.

Gruenert, S., & Whitaker, T. (2015). *School culture rewired: How to define, assess, and transform it.* Alexandria, VA: ASCD.

Gruenert, S., & Whitaker, T. (2017). *School culture recharged: Strategies to energize your staff and culture.* Alexandria, VA: ASCD.

Hattie, J. (2011). *Visible learning for teachers: Maximizing impact on learning.* New York: Routledge, The Taylor Francis Group.

Hess, F. M. (2010). *The same thing over and over: How school reformers get stuck in yesterday's ideas.* Cambridge, MA: The President and Fellows of Harvard College.

Hess, F. M., & Manno, B. V. (Eds.). (2011). *Customized schooling: Beyond whole school reform.* Cambridge, MA: Harvard Education Press.

Kelly, F., McCain, T., & Jukes, I. (2009). *Teaching the digital generation: No more cookie-cutter high schools.* Thousand Oaks, CA: Corwin Press.

Lytle, J. (2016, January 20). The NCAA's chokehold on secondary schooling. *Education Week.*

Moe, T., & Chubb, J. (2009). *Liberating learning: Technology, politics, and the future of American education.* Thousand Oaks, CA: Jossey-Bass.

NCATE. (2010). *Transforming teacher education through clinical practice: A national strategy to prepare effective teachers.* Report of the blue ribbon panel on clinical preparation AND partnerships FOR improved student learning. http://www.ncate.org/LinkClick.aspx?fileticket=zzeiB1OoqPk%3D&tabid=7.

Richardson, W. (2012). *Why school? How education must change when learning and information.* Ted Conference, 2012.

Schlechty, P. (2009). *Leading for learning: How to transform schools into learning organizations.* San Francisco, CA: Jossey-Bass.

Senge, P. (1991). *The fifth discipline: The art and practice of the learning organization.* New York: Doubleday, a Division of Random House.

Senge, P., Cambron-McCabe, N., Lucas, T., Smith, B., Dutton, J., & Kleiner, A. (2000). *Schools that learn: A fifth discipline fieldbook for educators, parents, and everyone who cares about education.* New York: Doubleday.

Senge, P., Cambron-McCabe, N., Lucas, T., Smith, B., Dutton, J., & Kleiner, A. (2012). *Schools that learn: A fifth discipline fieldbook for educators, parents, and everyone who cares about education.* New York: Doubleday.

The Holmes Group. (1986). *Tomorrow's teachers: A report of the Holmes Group.* East Lansing, MI: The Holmes Group, Inc.

The Holmes Group. (1990). *Tomorrow's schools of education: A report of the Holmes Group.* East Lansing, MI: The Holmes Group, Inc.

Tyack and Cuban. (1997). *Tinkering toward utopia: a century of public school reform.* Cambridge, MA. Harvard University Press.

United States: National Commission on Excellence in Education. (1983). *A nation at risk: The imperative for educational reform: A report to the nation and the Secretary of Education, United States Department of Education* (Vol. 2). Ann Arbor, MI: University of Michigan Library.

Wagner, T. (2006). *The global achievement gap: Why even our best schools don't teach the new survival skills our children need – And what we can do.* New York: Basic Books.
Waters, R. (2014). *The evolution of teaching: A guidebook to the advancement of teaching, teacher education, and happier careers for early career teachers.* Lanham, MD: Rowman & Littlefield.
Wheatly, M. J. (2006). *Leadership and the new science* (p. 79). San Francisco, CA: Berrett-Koehler Publishers, Inc.

CHAPTER SEVEN

Cook-Sather, A. (2002). Authorizing students' perspectives: Toward trust, dialogue, and change in education. *Educational Researcher, 31*(4), 3–14.
Cook-Sather, A. (2006). The "constant changing of myself:" Revising roles in undergraduate teacher preparation. *The Teacher Educator, 41*(3), 187–206.
Cushman, K. (2010). *Fires in the mind.* San Francisco, CA: Jossey-Bass.
Holcomb, E. (2007). *Students are stakeholders, too!* Thousand Oaks, CA: Corwin Press.
Kelly, F., McCain, T., & Jukes, I. (2009). *Teaching the digital generation: No more cookie-cutter high schools.* Thousand Oaks, CA: Corwin Press.
Mitra, D. L. (2004). The significance of students: Can increasing "student voice" in schools lead to gains in youth development? *Teachers College Record, 106*(4), 651–688.
Mitra, D. L. (2008). *Student voice in school reform: Building youth-adult partnerships that strengthen schools and empower youth.* Albany, NY: State University of New York.
Rudduck, J., & McIntyre, D. (2007). *Improving learning through consulting pupils.* London & New York: Routledge.
Sopovitz, E. H., & Weinbaum, E. H. (2008). *Implementation gap: Understanding reform in high schools.* New York: Teachers College Press.
Waters, R. (2014). *The evolution of teaching: A guidebook to the advancement of teaching, teacher education, and happier careers for early career teachers.* Lanham, MD: Rowman & Littlefield Publishers.
Waters, R. (2016). *Teaching the next generation of teachers: Preparing for the practice of learning communities in secondary school.* Lanham, MD: Rowman & Littlefield Publishers.
Waters, R. (2017). *Teens to teachers leading: Preparing for the practice of learning communities in secondary school.* Lanham, MD: Rowman & Littlefield Publishers.

CHAPTER EIGHT

Deal, T., & Peterson, K. (2016). *Shaping school culture* (3rd ed.). San Francisco, CA: John Wiley & Sons.

Deming, W. E. (1983). *The new economics*. Cambridge, MA: Massachusetts Institute of Technology, Center for Advanced Engineering Study.

Fullan, M., & Heargraves, A. (2012). *Professional capital: Transforming teaching in every school*. New York and London: Teachers College, Columbia University; Toronto, ON: Ontario Principals Council.

Institute of Education Sciences. (2012). *NAEP long term trends*. http://ies.ed.gov/.

Kelly, F., McCain, T., & Jukes, I. (2009). *Teaching the digital generation: No more cookie-cutter high schools*. Thousand Oaks, CA: Corwin Press.

Lalloux, F. (2014). *Reinventing organizations: A guide to creating organizations inspired by the next stage of human consciousness*. Brussels, Belgium: Nelson Parker.

Met Life Foundation. (2012). *Met life survey of the American teacher: Challenges for school leadership*. New York: Met Life, Inc.

Senge, P. (1991). *The fifth discipline: The art and practice of the learning organization*. New York: Doubleday, a Division of Random House.

Senge, P., Cambron-McCabe, N., Lucas, T., Smith, B., Dutton, J., & Kleiner, A. (2000). *Schools that learn: A fifth discipline fieldbook for educators, parents, and everyone who cares about education*. New York: Doubleday.

Senge, P., Cambron-McCabe, N., Lucas, T., Smith, B., Dutton, J., & Kleiner, A. (2012). *Schools that learn: A fifth discipline fieldbook for educators, parents, and everyone who cares about education*. New York: Doubleday.

Wilber, K. (2016). *Integral meditation: Mindfulness as a way to grow up, wake up, and show up in your life*. Boulder, CO: Shambhala Publications, Inc.

Yazzie-Mintz, E. (2007). *Voices of students on engagement: A report on the 2006 high school survey of student engagement*. Bloomington, IN: Center for Evaluation & Education Policy, Indiana University. Retrieved August 27, 2006, from http://ceep.indiana.edu/hssse.

Yazzie-Mintz, E. (2009). *Engaging the voices of students: A report on the 2007 & 2008 high school survey of student engagement*. Bloomington, IN: Center for Evaluation & Education Policy, Indiana University. http://ceep.indiana.edu/hssse.

TINA'S STORY

Fried, R. L. (2001). *The passionate teacher: A practical guide*. Boston: Beacon Press.

Fried, R. L. (2005). *The game of school: Why we all play it, how it hurts kids, and what it will take to change it*. San Francisco: Jossey-Bass.

Wagner, T., & Dintersmith, T. (2015). *Most likely to succeed: Preparing our kids for the innovation era*. New York: Scribner.

CHAPTER NINE

Ames, C. (1992). Classrooms: Goals, structures, and student motivation. *Journal of Educational Psychology, 84*(3), 261–271.

References

Ames, C., & Archer, J. (1988). Achievement goals in the classroom: Students' learning strategies and motivation processes. *Journal of Educational Psychology, 80*(3), 260–267.

Armstrong, T. (2006). *The best schools: How human development research should inform educational practice*. Alexandria, VA: Association for Supervision and Curriculum Development.

Bain, K. (2012). *What the best college students do*. Cambridge, MA: Belknap Press.

Bandura, A. (2006). Adolescent development from an angentic perspective. In F. Pajares & T. Urdan (Eds.), *Self-efficacy beliefs of adolescents* (pp. 1–43). Greenwich, CT: IAP-Information Age Publishing.

Blackwell, L. S., Trzensniewski, K. H., & Dweck, C. S. (2007). Implicit theories of intelligence predict achievement across an adolescent transition: A longitudinal study and an intervention. *Child Development, 78*(1), 246–263.

Blumenfeld, P. C., & Paris, A. H. (2004). School engagement: Potential of the concept, state of the evidence. *Review of Educational Research, 74*(1), 59–109.

Damon, W. (2008). *The path to purpose*. New York: Free Press.

Davis, J. (2015). *Time and teaching*. Boston: National Center on Time and Learning.

Deci, E., Vallerand, R. J., Pelletier, L. G., & Ryan, R. M. (1991). Motivation in education: The self-determination perspective. *Educational Psychologist, 26*(3–4), 325–346.

Deci, E. L., & Ryan, R. M. (2008). Facilitating optimal motivation and psychological well-being across life's domains. *Canadian Psychology, 49*(1), 14–23.

Demerath, P. (2009). *Producing success: The culture of personal advancement in an American school*. Chicago, IL: University of Chicago Press.

Deming, W. E. (1986). *Out of the crisis*. Cambridge, MA: Massachusetts Institute of Technology, Center for Advanced Engineering Study.

Drew, S. (2001). Student perceptions of what helps them learn and develop in higher education. *Teaching in Higher Education, 6*(3), 309–331.

Dweck. C. S., & Leggett, E. L. (1988). A social cognitive approach to motivation and personality. *Psychological Review, 95*(2), 256–273.

Entwistle, N. (1977). Strategies of learning and studying: Recent research findings. *British Journal of Educational Studies, 25*(3), 225–238.

Fransson, A. (1977). Qualitative differences in learning: IV. Effects of intrinsic motivation and extrinsic test anxiety on process and outcome. *British Journal of Educational Psychology, 47*(3), 244–257.

Fried, R. L. (2001). *The passionate teacher: A practical guide*. Boston: Beacon Press.

Fried, R. L. (2005). *The game of school: Why we all play it, how it hurts kids, and what it will take to change it*. San Francisco: Jossey-Bass.

Gamache, P. (2002). University students as creators of personal knowledge: An alternative epistemological view. *Teaching in Higher Education, 7*(3), 277–294.

Garvin, D. (2000). *Learning in action: A guide to putting the learning organization to work*. Boston, MA: Harvard Business School Press.

Gibbs, G., Morgan, A., & Taylor, E. (1982). A review of the research of Ference Maron and the Gotegorg Group: A phenomenological research perspective on learning. *Higher Education, 11*(2), 123–145.

Grant, H., & Dweck, C. S. (2003). Clarifying achievement goals and their impact. *Journal of Personality and Social Psychology, 85*(5), 541–553.

Hattie, J. (2011). *Visible learning for teachers: Maximizing impact on learning*. New York: Routledge, The Taylor Francis Group.

Hong, Y., Dweck, C. S., Chiu, C., Lin, D., & Wan, W. (1999). Implicit theories, attributions, and coping: A meaning system approach. *Journal of Personality and Social Psychology, 77*(3), 588–599.

Humes, E. (2008). *School of dreams: Making the grade at a top American school*. New York: Harcourt.

Johnson, R. E., & Chang, C. (2008). Organizational commitment and its antecedents: Employee self-concept matters. *Journal of Applied Social Psychology, 38*(2), 513–541.

Machiavelli, N. (1940/c. 1517). *The prince and the discourses* (L. Ricci & C. E. Detmold, Trans.). New York: Modern Library.

Martin, F., Hounsell, D., & Entwistle, N. (Eds.). (2005). *The experience of learning: Implications for teaching and studying in higher education* (3rd ed.). Edinburgh: University of Edinburgh, Centre for Teaching, Learning and Assessment at the University of Edinburgh. http: //www.tla.ed.ac.uk/resources/EoL.html.

Marton, F., & Saljo, R. (1976). On qualitative differences in learning: I. Outcomes and process. *British Journal of Educational Psychology, 46*(1), 4–11.

Mueller, C. M., & Dweck, C. S. (1998). Praise for intelligence can undermine children's motivation and performance. *Journal of Personality and Social Psychology, 75*(1), 33–52.

Pope, D. (2001). *"Doing School" How we are creating a generation of stressed out, materialistic, and miseducated students*. New Haven, CT: Yale University Press.

Rawson, M. (2000). Learning to learn: More than a skill set. *Studies in Higher Education, 25*(2), 225–238.

Rossum, E. J., & Schenk, S. M. (1984). The relationship between learning conception, study strategy and learning outcome. *British Journal of Educational Psychology, 54*(1), 73–83.

Ryan, R., & Deci, E. (2000). Self-determination theory and the facilitation of intrinsic motivation, social development, and wellbeing. *American Psychologist, 55*(1), 68–78.

Ryan, R., & Deci, E. (2002). Overview of self-determination theory. In R. R. Ryan & E. L. Deci (Eds.), *Handbook of self-determination theory*. Rochester, NY: The University of Rochester Press.

Ryan, R., & Deci, E. (2006). Self-regulation and the problem of human autonomy: Does psychology need choice, self-determination, and will? *Journal of Personality, 74*(6), 1557–1585.

Ryan, R., & Deci, E. (2008). From ego-depletion to vitality: Theory and findings concerning the facilitation of energy available to the self. *Social and Personality Psychology Compass, 2*(2), 702–717.

Scherer, M. (2008). Perspective/the school scene. *Educational Leadership, 65*(8), 7.

Scott, S., & Dixon, K. (2009). Partners in a learning organization: A student-focused model of professional development. *Educational Forum, 73*(3), 240–255.

Senge, P. (1991). *The fifth discipline: The art and practice of the learning organization*. New York: Doubleday, a Division of Random House.
Senge, P., Cambron-McCabe, N., Lucas, T., Smith, B., Dutton, J., & Kleiner, A. (2000). *Schools that learn: A fifth discipline fieldbook for educators, parents, and everyone who cares about education*. New York: Doubleday, a Division of Random House.
Song, H. J., Kim, H. M., & Kolb, J. (2009). The effect of learning organization culture on the relationship of interpersonal trust and organizational commitment. *Human Resource Development Quarterly*, 20(2), 147–167.
Waters, R. (2012). *Secondary students' transitioning from compliance to intentional learning* (Doctoral Dissertation). UMI ProQuest (Order No: 3504071). Minneapolis, MN: Walden University.
Waters, R. (2014). *The Evolution of Teaching: A guidebook to the advancement of teaching, teacher education, and happier careers for early career teachers*. Lanham, MD: Rowman & Littlefield.
Yazzie-Mintz, E. (2007). *Voices of students on engagement: A report on the 2006 high school survey of student engagement*. Bloomington, IN: Center for Evaluation & Education Policy, Indiana University. Retrieved August 27, 2008, from http://ceep.indiana.edu/hssse.
Yazzie-Mintz, E. (2009). *Engaging the voices of students: A report on the 2007 & 2008 School Survey of Student Engagement*. Bloomington, IN: Center for Evaluation & Education Policy, Indiana University. http://ceep.indiana.edu/hssse.

CHAPTER TEN

Ames, C., & Archer, J. (1988). Achievement goals in the classroom: Students' learning strategies and motivation processes. *Journal of Educational Psychology*, 80(3), 260–267.
Asch, S. E. (1952). *Social psychology*. New York: Prentice Hall.
Ausubel, D. P., & Novak, J. D. (1986). Hanesian. H. (1978). *Educational Psychology: A Cognitive View*, 2.
Blackwell, L. S., Trzensniewski, K. H., & Dweck, C. S. (2007). Implicit theories of intelligence predict achievement across an adolescent transition: A longitudinal study and an intervention. *Child Development*, 78(1), 246–263.
Brown, B. (2013). *Daring greatly: How the courage to be vulnerable transforms the way we live, love, parent, and lead*. New York: Gotham Books.
Capra, F. (1997). *The web of life: A new scientific understanding of living systems*. New York: Anchor/Random House.
Charmer, O. (2009). *Theory U: Leading from the future as it emerges*. San Francisco, CA: Berrett-Kohler Publishers.
Csikszentmihalyi, M. (1990). *Flow: The psychology of optimal experience – Steps toward enhancing the quality of life*. New York: Harper Perennial.
Csikszentmihalyi, M. (1997). *Finding flow: The psychology of engagement with everyday life*. New York: Basic Books.

Damon, W. (2008). *The path to purpose*. New York: Free Press.

Deci, E. L., & Ryan, R. M. (2008). Facilitating optimal motivation and psychological well-being across life's domains. *Canadian Psychology, 49*(1), 14–23.

Dweck, C. S. (2006). *Mind-set: The new psychology of success*. New York: Random House.

Dweck. C. S., & Leggett, E. L. (1988). A social cognitive approach to motivation and personality. *Psychological Review, 95*(2), 256–273.

Entwistle, N. (1977). Strategies of learning and studying: Recent research findings. *British Journal of Educational Studies, 25*(3), 225–238.

Farris-Berg, K., & Dirkswager, E. (2012). *Trusting teachers with school success*. New York: Rowman & Littlefield Education.

Fisher, J. (1999). *Six silent killers: Management's greatest challenge*. Boca Raton, FL: St. Lucie Press.

Fransson, A. (1977). Qualitative differences in learning: IV. Effects of intrinsic motivation and extrinsic test anxiety on process and outcome. *British Journal of Educational Psychology, 47*(3), 244–257.

Fredricks, J. A., Blumenfeld, P. C., & Paris, A. H. (2004). School engagement: Potential of the concept, state of the evidence. *Review of Educational Research, 74*(1), 59–109.

Fried, R. L. (2001). *The passionate teacher: A practical guide*. Boston: Beacon Press.

Fried, R. L. (2005). *The game of school: Why we all play it, how it hurts kids, and what it will take to change it*. San Francisco: Jossey-Bass.

Garvin, D. (2000). *Learning in action: A guide to putting the learning organization to work*. Boston, MA: Harvard Business School Press.

Grant, H., & Dweck, C. S. (2003). Clarifying achievement goals and their impact. *Journal of Personality and Social Psychology, 85*(5), 541–553.

Hatano, G., & Inagaki, K. (1986). Two courses of expertise. In H. Stevenson & J. Azuma (Eds.), *Child development and education in Japan* (pp. 335–355).

Hatano, G., & Oura, Y. (2003). Commentary: Reconceptualizing learning using insight from expertise research. *Educational Researcher, 32*(8), 26–29.

Hattie, J. (2011). *Visible learning for teachers: Maximizing impact on learning*. New York: Routledge, The Taylor Francis Group.

Herbert, T., Dunham, S., & Silver, D. (2008). *High stakes teaching: Practices that improve student learning*. Lanham, MD: Rowman & Littlefield Education.

Maslow, A. (1968). *Toward a psychology of being* (2nd ed.). Princeton, NJ: D. Van Nostrand Co, Inc.

McCarthy, M., & Kuh, G. (2006). Are students ready for college? What student engagement data say. *Phi Delta Kappan, 87*(9), 664–669.

Meece, J. L., Blumenfeld, P. C., & Hoyle, R. H. (1988). Students' goal orientations and cognitive engagement in classroom activities. *Journal of Educational Psychology, 80*, 514–523.

Mueller, C. M., & Dweck, C. S. (1998). Praise for intelligence can undermine children's motivation and performance. *Journal of Personality and Social Psychology, 75*(1), 33–52.

Nicholls, J. G., Cheung, P., Lauer, J., & Patashnick, M. (1989). Individual differences in academic motivation: Perceived ability, goals, beliefs, and values. *Learning and Individual Differences, 1*, 63–84.

Noah, H. J., & Eckstein, M. A. (2001). *Fraud and education: The worm in the apple.* Lanham, MD: Rowman & Littlefield Publishers.

Nolen, S. B., & Haladyna, T. M. (1990). Personal and environmental influences on students' beliefs about effective study strategies. *Contemporary Educational Psychology, 15*, 8–9.

Ryan, R., & Deci, E. (2008). From ego-depletion to vitality: Theory and findings concerning the facilitation of energy available to the self. *Social and Personality Psychology Compass, 2*(2), 702–717.

Schlechty, P. (2002). *Working on the work: An action plan for teachers, principals, and superintendents.* San Francisco, CA: Jossey-Bass.

Schlechty, P. (2009). *Leading for learning: How to transform schools into learning organizations.* San Francisco, CA: Jossey-Bass.

Selligman, M. (2011). *Flourish: A visionary new understanding of happiness and well being.* New York: Free Press, a Division of Simon and Schuster, Inc.

Senge, P. (1991). *The fifth discipline: The art and practice of the learning organization.* New York: Doubleday, a Division of Random House.

Senge, P., Cambron-McCabe, N., Lucas, T., Smith, B., Dutton, J., & Kleiner, A. (2000). *Schools that learn: A fifth discipline fieldbook for educators, parents, and everyone who cares about education.* New York: Doubleday, a Division of Random House.

Senge, P., Scharmer, C. O., Jaworski, J., & Flowers, B. S. (2004). *Presence: Exploring profound change in people, organizations, and society.* New York: Currency Doubleday.

Silva, P. J. (2006). *Exploring the psychology of interest.* New York: Oxford University Press.

Wagner, T. (2012). *Creating innovators: The making of young people who will change the world.* New York: Scribner.

Waters, R. (2012). *Secondary students' transitioning from compliance to intentional learning* (Doctoral Dissertation). UMI ProQuest (Order No: 3504071). Minneapolis, MN: Walden University.

Yazzie-Mintz, E. (2007). *Voices of students on engagement: A report on the 2006 high school survey of student engagement.* Bloomington, IN: Center for Evaluation & Education Policy, Indiana University. Retrieved August 27, 2006, from http://ceep.indiana.edu/hssse.

Yazzie-Mintz, E. (2009). *Engaging the voices of students: A report on the 2007 & 2008 high school survey of student engagement.* Bloomington, IN: Center for Evaluation & Education Policy, Indiana University. http://ceep.indiana.edu/hssse.

Zhao, Y. (2009). *Catching up or leading the way: American education in the age of globalization.* Alexandria, VA: Association for Supervision and Curriculum Development.

Zhao, Y. (2012). *World class learners: Educating creative and entrepreneurial students.* Thousand Oaks, CA: Corwin.

CHAPTER ELEVEN

Davis, J. (2015). *Time and teaching*. Boston: National Center on Time and Learning.
NCATE. (2010). *Transforming teacher education through clinical practice: A national strategy to prepare effective teachers*. Report of the blue ribbon panel on clinical preparation AND partnerships FOR improved student learning. http://www.ncate.org/LinkClick.aspx?fileticket=zzeiB1OoqPk%3D&tabid=7.

CHAPTER TWELVE

Kegan, R., & LaHey, L. L. (2016). *An everyone culture: Becoming a deliberately developmental organization*. Boston, MA: Harvard Business School Publishing.
Marzano, R. J., Warrick, P. B., Cameron, L. R., & DuFour, R. (2014). *Leading a high reliability school (Use data-driven instruction and collaborative teaching strategies to boost academic achievement.)*. Bloomington, IN: Solution Tree.
Senge, P. (1991). *The fifth discipline: The art and practice of the learning organization*. New York: Doubleday, a Division of Random House.
Senge, P., Cambron-McCabe, N., Lucas, T., Smith, B., Dutton, J., & Kleiner, A. (2000). *Schools that learn: A fifth discipline fieldbook for educators, parents, and everyone who cares about education*. New York: Doubleday, a Division of Random House.

CHAPTER THIRTEEN

Kegan, R., & LaHey, L. L. (2016). *An everyone culture: Becoming a deliberately developmental organization*. Boston, MA: Harvard Business School Publishing.

CHAPTER FOURTEEN

American Association of Colleges for Teacher Education. (2015). Clinical practice commission report. www.nysed.gov/common/nysed/files/cpc-aactecpcreport.pdf.
Darling-Hammond, L. (2006). *Powerful teacher education: Lessons from exemplary programs*. San Francisco: Jossey-Bass.
Kegan, R., & LaHey, L. L. (2016). *An everyone culture: Becoming a deliberately developmental organization*. Boston, MA: Harvard Business School Publishing.
National Council on Teacher Quality. (2018). https://en.wikipedia.org/wiki/National_Council_on_Teacher_Quality.

Who Is Rich Waters?

I identify myself, above all, as a career high school teacher of thirty-three years. Now I am a teacher who writes about and advocates for the advancement of teachers and the profession of teaching. My thinking and outlook come primarily from my on-the-ground experience as a teacher. At the same time, I have enriched that experience with attendance at seven colleges and universities. I completed my MA in Kean University and Wesleyan University's National Endowment for the Humanities program called Liberal Studies in which I studied the interrelationship of art, music, and literature. I was a Dodge Fellow at Wesleyan University. I completed my PhD at Walden University in a five-year program doing research in a high school working with and interviewing students who were aspiring to be teachers. My dissertation research over the course of two years inquired into the possibility of affecting students' learning goals through a series of reflective discussions with respect to ownership of learning, authentic learning, and personal learning agendas as opposed to "game of school," strategic learning.

For more than ten years I was a member of the Language Arts Leaders of New Jersey, and I served the New Jersey Department of Education as a member and chairperson of the Union County Professional Development Board. While a teacher, I was an NEA Delegate and president of my local association for five years, settling two contracts. I am a current member of the American Educational Research Association, Phi Beta Kappa, and the Association for Supervision and Curriculum Development. During the latter part of my career I took a strong interest in high school reform working with and for *Princeton Leadership*, an educational consulting firm in Princeton, NJ. As an outcome this, the formation of a partnership with Kean University, and my work with many colleagues, one of New Jersey's first professional development schools was created at Rahway High School in New Jersey. I published several articles in the Kean University School of Education journal, *Connections*, regarding our professional development school, had extensive experience with teacher induction, and went on to become a founding member of the National Association of Professional Development Schools.

More recently, Rowman & Littlefield published my book, *The Evolution of Teaching: A Guidebook to the Advancement of Teaching, Teacher Education, and Happier Careers for Early Career Teachers* (2014). Most recently a pair of books, companion pieces, were published. One intended for the teachers of aspiring teachers in secondary schools is entitled *Teaching the Next Generation of Teachers: Preparing for the Practice of Learning Communities in Secondary School* (Rowman & Littlefield, 2016) and one for students, *Teens to Teachers Leading: Preparing for the Practice of Learning Communities in Secondary School*, was self-published to accommodate color photography. In the summer of 2017, the NAPDS published my article "We Must Face It: PDSs Have Failed to Innovate" in its peer-reviewed journal, *School-University Partnerships*.

All of these publications are derived of research that is conclusive: Teachers who work in professional learning communities produce better student learning outcomes than those who do not. What's more, all of these publications affirm an overlooked part of the teacher preparation and development equation, cultural learning. Recent research shows that cultural learning is, in fact, a much stronger influence on teacher development than all of the rational learning strategies concocted by policy advocates and those who argue for teacher preparation on higher education campuses. All of this research points not to the need for improved teacher preparation in higher education but to evolve a new model school where there is equal focus on student learning and teacher learning and where novice teacher participation would inherently lead to the development of effective teachers.

SHORT FORM

Rich Waters is a veteran high school teacher and PhD whose interest in teacher education led him to assist in the creation and co-coordination of New Jersey's first high school professional development school and later to become a founding member of the National Association of Professional Development Schools. His decades of work and recent research in a high school with aspiring teachers helped him see the need for teacher induction, preparation, and development as more of a function of local schools than higher education.

www.ingramcontent.com/pod-product-compliance
Lightning Source LLC
Chambersburg PA
CBHW021848300426
44115CB00005B/67